Pulling Focus

Intersubjective Experience, Narrative Film, and Ethics

Jane Stadler

continuum

Continuum International Publishing Group
80 Maiden Lane, New York, NY 10038
The Tower Building, 11 York Road, London SE1 7NX

www.continuumbooks.com

© 2008 by Jane Stadler

First published 2008
Paperback edition 2012

Library of Congress Cataloging-in-Publication Data
A catalog record for this book is available from the Library of Congress.

ISBN: PB: 978-1-4411-6302-8

Typeset by Newgen Imaging Systems Pvt Ltd, Chennai, India
Printed and bound in the United States of America

Pulling Focus

Contents

List of Figures

Introduction

Chapter 1

Chapter 2

Chapter 3

Chapter 4

Chapter 5

Chapter 6

Chapter 7

Acknowledgments

I owe an intellectual debt to both Vivian Sobchack and Martha Nussbaum, whose work I so admire. I am particularly indebted to Vivian Sobchack, who gave me the language to express my perception of film and who has been an encouraging and generous reader as well as a great inspiration. My gratitude also extends to Murray Smith, Peta Bowden, William Rothman, Sheila Mason and Mary Frances for insightful, thoughtful feedback on aspects of this research.

I would like to acknowledge the assistance of the Ernest Oppenheimer Memorial Trust for research funding that enabled me to spend a sabbatical working on the manuscript at the University of California, Berkeley. Thanks also to my incredibly efficient publishing team, David Barker, Gabriella Page-Fort, and P. Muralidharan. Finally, I gratefully acknowledge permission to reproduce sections of Chapters 2 and 3, which originally appeared in the following publications:

Stadler, Jane. 2002. 'Intersubjective, Embodied, Evaluative Perception: A Phenomenological Approach to the Ethics of Film' in *Quarterly Review of Film and Video* 19.3: 237–248 www.informaworld.com.

Stadler, Jane. 2002. 'Losing the Plot: Narrative and Identity in *Lost Highway*.' In *Film and Knowledge: Essays on the Integration of Images and Ideas*, ed. Kevin Stoehr, 17–36. Jefferson, New Carolina: McFarland.

Introduction

Figure 1 Eternal Sunshine of the Spotless Mind: *Closing image of Joel and Clementine on Montauk beach.*

The closing image of *Eternal Sunshine of the Spotless Mind* (Gondry, 2004) shows Joel and Clementine running along the frosty Montauk beach, playing together in the snow. The shot repeats itself three times, each time jumping back to exactly where it began, just as the film itself did, suggesting perhaps that the happy couple is destined to repeat the mistakes of their relationship, over and over again. But even if they do, the music signals that it's a destiny they will happily accept. Besides, we have good reason to suspect that they've learned a lot about themselves and each other during the memory-wipe adventure with Lacuna. The lyrics tell us this much, since the song that they sang when they met on that same beach, "You were lost and gone forever, Oh my darling Clementine," has been replaced with a song about "changing your heart" by Beck. The song implies change and growth, progress and love: "I need your loving like the sunshine, 'cause everybody's gotta learn sometime." Then the screen fades to white, the credits roll, the lights come up, and we return to our own lives. But nobody leaves the cinema with a "spotless mind," even if we eventually forget the names of the characters and details of the plot. Even if the story of their relationship doesn't remain clear in our memories, fading as it has done for Joel and Clementine themselves, as audience members we too may be left with a residue of impressions influencing our actions and decisions without our full awareness. Sometimes we leave the cinema with much, much more, deeply marked by the story in which we have been immersed.

The most powerful films have an afterlife, an influence that remains with us when we are affected by the sensory impact of films, captivated by story, character, and conflict, and left wondering about the issues they raise. One of the most compelling aspects of narrative film is the manner in which character engagement invites us to empathize with others and gain insight into their stories and, sometimes, perspective on our own lives and actions. Cinema appeals directly to the senses, locating the spectator within the visual and aural space of the story world and within the subjective experiences of its inhabitants. As such, film works on the emotions, stimulates the imagination, and has the capacity to elicit an affective response in ways distinct from other narrative arts such as literature, theatre, and opera. The technology of filmmaking also records visible and audible traces of the perceptual and representational activity involved in the narration of a story. Film spectatorship involves the audience in these technologically mediated acts of perception and expression, establishing an intersubjective relationship between the audience, the screen characters, and the film.

This study rethinks the significance of embodied experience in both film spectatorship and ethical deliberation, offering a different way of approaching practices that have been conceptualized in terms of abstract paradigms such as psychoanalysis, structuralism, and principle-based moral codes. Through an exploration of identity and identification, the research presented here relates the nature of audience involvement in narrative film to a conception of ethics that emphasizes the complexity and contextuality of human interrelatedness. It analyzes how narrative structure and sensory experience are implicated in ethical understanding, shaping the way moral possibilities, choices, and their potential outcomes are viewed. While the politics of representation clearly has importance in any account of ethics, narrative, and film, this research is primarily concerned with the qualitative nature of perception and with the evaluative practices inherent in spectatorship. By exploring the processes involved in attentive engagement with films, I hope to further understandings of the ways in which narration, emotion, imagination, and embodied perceptions and responses are embedded in the daily practices of ethical life. Ultimately, I also want to suggest that narrative is integral to identity and understanding, and that involvement with film narratives can therefore facilitate a degree of personal insight and social change.

In order to explore how audience members respond to film narratives in ways that have ethical relevance, the ethical dimensions of each of the different elements of engagement with film must be thought through. The chapters that follow show how narrative and narrating are important in ethical life, how emotional responses have a place in rational deliberation, how the imaginative activity involved in watching films enables audiences to envision ethical situations and possibilities, and how character engagement can expand the sphere of moral concern. Each film discussed here contributes to establishing the value of attentive engagement with cinematic narratives by illustrating the interdependent nature of the resources we draw upon in ethical life and in the cinema. Given its emphasis on embodied subjectivity, the primary mode of analysis I will use to describe film spectatorship is experiential phenomenology. A phenomenological approach influenced by the work of Vivian Sobchack provides the means to articulate the semiotic, sensory and affective dimensions of ethical engagement in the cinema, bridging the disciplines of philosophy and film studies.

Many theorists connecting narrative to ethics have focused on literary narratives (notably Martha Nussbaum, whose work on the ethical value of novels is central to the ideas presented here). Since narrative is a discursive form shared by both film and literature (as well as other arts), an exploration of the overlapping, yet distinctive ways in which the narratives of film and literature engage the ethical, emotional, and imaginative intelligence of their audiences has a place in this book. This research not only builds on the body of theory drawing connections between moral philosophy and literary narratives, but also seeks to make a contribution to the philosophical analysis of film by concentrating on ethics.

Each of us have an ethical orientation and a reservoir of resources, values, and attitudes upon which we draw when we reflect and act on moral issues. Following the lead of philosophers such as Alasdair MacIntyre, Martha Nussbaum, and Paul Ricoeur who deal with questions of narrative, I argue that this ethical orientation, and these resources and values are themselves drawn from the stock of stories that inform our understanding of life. As part of the body of stories circulating in our culture, narrative film can be a source of ethical understanding. We reflect on, deliberate about, and discuss ethical situations rationally and lucidly by narrating and interpreting stories. Describing what narration and interpretation involve in the cinema with respect to the ways in which those practices and processes are entwined with ethical agency and understanding is central to the project undertaken here.

In stories events are shaped into a meaningful pattern over time, establishing causal relationships that are both recounted and accounted for as the story unfolds. Narrative then, is a way of making meaning, of forging a relational form of understanding in which concepts, characters, situations, and issues develop and join together as the story unfolds. Narrative can be seen as a unity (the overarching story that holds all of the plot's points and twists meaningfully together), but also as unifying (creating connections that constitute the meaning). Paul Ricoeur emphasizes that narrative is understood as something exceeding the sum or sequence of its parts: "The recounted story is always more than the enumeration, in an order that would be merely serial or successive, to the incidents or events that it organizes into an intelligible whole" (1991e, 21).[1]

Building on the work of Ricoeur, I claim that understanding itself frequently has a narrative structure.[2] Understanding grows in the spaces left in narratives, or in the new ground that metaphoric imagery or analogies open up; it takes root at the points where the viewer is most closely connected to the story, where empathic and imaginative activity assist in generating ideas and insights. Since ethical understanding (which involves understandings of human behavior, aspirations, values, and relationships) inescapably involves narrative and narration on some level, and often overtly takes the form of a story in which we develop an account of motives and mitigating circumstances, actions, events, and their consequences, I've sought it in the structure of narratives. And since it comes to life in the midst of imaginative and emotional connections to stories, I've explored what happens in those moments of intense involvement in stories. One of the ways in which narrative understanding works, according to Ricoeur, is by providing "thought experiments" to the imagination in the form of the lives of fictional characters. It is by following the perils of these characters through the narrative that

> we learn to link together the ethical aspects of human conduct and happiness and misfortune . . . It is due to the familiarity we have with

the types of plot received from our culture that we learn to relate virtues, or rather forms of excellence, with happiness or unhappiness. (Ricoeur 1991e, 23)

In his work on narrative identity, Ricoeur claims that a story is able to grow in a manner much like that of a human being. People and stories both change as they develop, yet the pattern of characteristics, circumstances, and actions in relation to the evolving whole means that each retains a recognizable identity. Due to the hermeneutic principles governing human understanding and the relationship between biography and personal identity, narrative therefore offers a means of understanding and examining our own lives, and a way of connecting to the lives of others. Indeed, puzzling, atypical narrative structures often foreground the significance of narrative to identity and prompt consideration of the limitations of formulaic narratives with falsely reassuring ideological closure.

In order to make sense of either a screen text or the ethical dimensions of a given situation we must have an embodied respone to the information we are making sense of. We see, hear, feel, and in other ways physically form an impression of the subject matter. The physiological experience of sensory data is both a precondition of, and an intrinsic part of the sense-making process. At the same time, one's grasp of what is going on is configured into a narrative comprised of sequences of cause and effect in which the sensory experiences are accounted for in terms of their relationships over time. We don't understand films as disconnected elements of light and sound, as a series of still images projected in rapid succession, or even as discrete events or scenes; instead, we understand them as stories. In a film with a jumbled temporal order (confused by flashbacks and flashforwards), we understand the disjointed plot by working to reconfigure or reorder events to form a narrative, attributing motives and actions to agents, linking consequences to actions, and so on. Though the distinction between the experience of disordered events (points of the plot), and understanding or interpreting in narrative form (reordering events into a story unfolding in linear time) is clearly defined here, it is not always delineated in practice. The point I want to make is that these two elements (sensing and making sense) together constitute the way in which humans, as embodied, storytelling creatures, know the world. Perception and narration are, together, fundamental to human life in terms of both ethical agency and film spectatorship.

Though I argue for the importance of narrative and film in ethics, it is not my intention to suggest that film spectatorship is essential to the acquisition of ethical understanding or that all films enrich ethical life. The development of judgment, strength of character, and practical wisdom, and the possibility of adequately exploring the complex theoretical issues within moral life do not in any way depend on cinema. Clearly, ethical life is not reliant on film or film spectatorship, and when ethical life and film do intersect, some films will be of more value than others (depending on the qualities of the film and its spectators). However, there are elements involved in the practice of spectatorship, and in narrative construction and interpretation, which are essential to viewing a film and also central to ethical agency.

It may seem ironic that one should look to narrative to study ethical life, rather than face the raw experience of life directly. But experience is never raw; it is always mediated through the filters of affective and sensory perception, language, and conception. Furthermore, as Vivian Sobchack's work on phenomenology illustrates, film has the advantage of being able to show us *how* we see, whereas in life we are only able to see *what* we see. It is very difficult to catch sight of the frames, filters, lenses, and viewing angles idiosyncratic to one's own world view, but film makes the fact that we have situated perspectives visibly evident, and it makes the task of addressing and analyzing the effects of these achievable by one degree more. By looking, for instance, at how perception works in film and at how it is expressed, we may realize something previously overlooked about how it works in life, and also see more clearly the relevance of perception to ethics.

The films that I analyze differ considerably in terms of style, thematic and emplotted content, structure, and in terms of the audiences they intend to reach. They all deal with contentious ethical matters, though they have not been chosen on the basis of their subject matter. Though an analysis of the ethical issues and values detailed in the content of each film would be both interesting and productive (more productive, I argue, than a discussion of the same ethical issues based on abstract examples and a schematic analysis of principles and obligations), it is not my sole concern here. This project does more than substitute the extended narratives of film for the brief hypothetical examples most often utilized for philosophical analysis of complex ethical issues.[3]

Cinema has the potential to bring about transformations in perspective, responsiveness, and understanding and as such its influence can be positive or negative, depending on what and whom the audience is invited to identify with, and in the nature of the relationship that develops between the spectator and the screen. Teasing out just how the narration and interpretation of film texts might be connected to ethical life is complicated because it involves accounting for many factors that differ in accordance with context, intentions, and the nature of the individual narrative and its inter- preters. A narrative that activates the imagination of one person may draw an empathic response from another, and for a third it may lend itself to conceptual analysis, aesthetic critique, or to a study of how the industry's technological and economic frameworks operate to produce ideologically inflected narratives. The diversity of responses points to another difficulty within the attempt to ascertain what narration and interpretation entail: there are many levels on which an interpretive response might be located, and there are correspondingly many levels on which the intersection of narrative and ethics might be considered. Form, content, structure, and style all deserve attention, as do issues surrounding the production and reception of stories.

The argument that the expressive form a given work takes ought to be appropriate to the content it is a vehicle for expressing and with which it is intimately entwined is defended by Martha Nussbaum in *Love's Knowledge: Essays on Philosophy and Literature*.[4] Nussbaum's work on narrative and ethics has informed this study and I have taken up many of her ideas about novels in order to extend and apply them to film. Film, though also a nar- rative art, takes a very different form from literature and at times the implications of this difference are significant. Nevertheless, many claims about the importance of narrative to ethics embrace all the different forms that narratives can take, from personal anecdotes and fairytales, through to novels, films, television programs, legends, operas, and theatrical produc- tions. Certainly, each of these types of narrative can raise ethical issues in their content, presenting it in a form that is usually readily accessible and easily understood.

I am not suggesting that a particular film form is conducive to ethical deliberation, whilst others are not. The films I have selected are neither exemplary of all cinema, nor are they to be understood as special cases in the history of cinema (and I do not attempt to locate them as such). My claims about ethical engagement are generally applicable to any films which involve narrative, narration, and narrative interpretation to a significant extent. Because different responses may be elicited when engaging with factual or fictional material and a uniquely charged ethical dynamic comes into play when filmmakers seek to represent the lives of people who are not paid actors, I have not considered documentary films, though there is invariably a narrative component to those too.

I will attempt to avoid making false divisions between the narrative and aesthetic elements of film since the formal and stylistic techniques of cine- matic production gain meaning in relation to the narrative content, and in relation to the way in which the film is taken up by its spectators. There are problems inherent in privileging one element of a film over another. For instance, when the analysis rests on narrative form, attention is necessarily diverted from important concerns within the content of the stories. Perhaps the most difficult part of analyzing any film is deciding which aspects of it to neglect, which scenes not to mention, whether to emphasize the soundscape or the visual style, the characters or the spectators, and so on. Some areas, such as scriptwriting, acting, directing, and marketing, are overlooked altogether in this study. They are beyond the scope of this work, though they are also important, and difficult to separate from the screen text and its reception.

In the first chapter of this book narrative is discussed in general terms since stories can be communicated in a variety of media, but in subsequent chapters the specificity of film will be privileged. It is not possible to make a clear separation between story and style or narrative and narration, but it is useful to consider the broader importance of narrative before making a particular case for audiovisual media and analyzing how cinematic techniques can communicate meaning and inflect a story with nuances relevant to a discussion of ethics. In reading a book that has been adapted for the screen, such as Helen Prejean's novel *Dead Man Walking* (1993) and viewing Tim Robbins' (1995) film by the same name, the differences between conveying information linguistically and imparting it visually become evident. Consideration of the possible ethical implications of differences between seeing and reading, looking and perceiving, telling and representing, opens into the fields of phenomenology and hermeneutics. Here, the ethical importance of perceptual understanding comes into focus, as does the intersubjective relation between seeing and being seen, and the dialectic of narrative and its interpretation. In Chapters 1 and 2 the theoretical complexity of these issues will be teased out and illustrated with reference to *Dead Man Walking* and spectatorial participation in that film. The central importance of embodied understanding that is established here in terms of the spectator's experiential, sensory involvement in the film text will be developed further in the chapter on emotion. Within the story of *Dead Man Walking* itself, Helen Prejean's own commitment to broad social reform and ethical causes, and to caring for particular individuals and trying to see and think and feel her way into different aspects of difficult situations is also important. Prejean's ethical disposition, and her developing understanding of the perspectives and values at stake in the issue of capital punishment are so tightly interconnected with the story of her relationship with the death row inmate Matthew Poncelet and those associated with him, that the study of *Dead Man Walking* opens onto questions regarding the relationship between ethical identity and narrative identity.

Lost Highway (Lynch, 1997), a film in which questions far outnumber answers, problematizes the significance of narrative structure and human identity, particularly in terms of that which is omitted, neglected, or excluded from the narrative, thus revealing how a life differs from a life story. Because the film breaks with the conventions governing narrative, characterization, and even to a certain extent editing, sound, and cinematography, it establishes an equally unconventional relationship with its spectators. Though this chapter follows on directly from a discussion of a phenomenological approach to film involving a semiotic textual analysis and an account of spectatorial engagement, the ethically intriguing questions posed and left unanswered by *Lost Highway* call for a configurative analysis of narrative structure and character structure. Lynch's strange film offers a way of framing the relationship between narrative identity and ethical identity almost by default because it demonstrates the consequences for ethics and identity when narrative structure is dismembered. *Lost Highway* engenders an appreciation of how deeply embedded in ontology and epistemology narrative might be, and how inseparable from ethics these are.

In *The Devaluing of America*, William Bennett claims that "if we believe that good art, good music, and good books will elevate taste and improve the sensibilities of the young—which they certainly do—then we must also believe that bad music, bad art, and bad books will degrade" (quoted in McCrillis 2003, 280). Bennett's words relate to a broader argument about the media's alleged corruption and poisoning of young minds and its responsibility for unraveling the moral fiber of society. Chapter 4 engages with concerns about the ill-effects of narrative cinema and addresses the claim that a medium that has the potential to be a positive part of ethical life can also exert negative influences, particularly on young and impressionable audience members. The films *8 Mile* (Hanson, 2002), *The Iron Giant* (Bird, 1999), *The Lion King* (Allers and Minkoff, 1994), and *Batman Begins* (Nolan, 2005) are analyzed with the intention of assessing the relevance of media effects research findings to the ethical influence of film, using a loose phenomenological methodology to describe the experiential impact of particular scenes and to assess how that might inflect its influence on spectators. Semiotic phenomenology, moral philosophy, and media effects research may seem to be odd if not incompatible companions, and prominent media studies theorists such as David Gauntlett (1998) have detailed many reasons to be suspicious of empirical effects research. However, it seems unwise to discount a large body of research by reputable scholars and, in the belief that humanities have much to learn from natural science and empirical studies even when the aims and methods of the disciplines differ significantly, I have taken the findings of media effects research seriously and attempted to find a way of integrating those insights with my own approach to film and its influence.

In Chapter 5, Rowan Woods' films *The Boys* (1998) and *Little Fish* (2005) invite an exploration of the emotional dynamics involved in responding to films by embracing or resisting identification with their characters, revealing that character engagement does not equate simply with emotional affinity. Understanding how emotion is involved in the perception of ethical salience, and in experiencing the impact of that knowledge on a felt, bodily level, and also understanding how emotions play a part in our connectedness to others is as important as empathic identification with characters that are easy to relate to. In all its various forms, character engagement is at the heart of our involvement with most cinematic narratives and, as Noel Carroll writes, "affect is the glue that holds the audience's attention to the screen" (2006, 217). Often, affect is a conduit for our understanding; sometimes it is an obstacle to it. As Stanley Cavell's rich responses to film suggest, in order to get the most out of a film we must be willing to engage with the characters on a personal level, whether we "identify" with them in a narcissistic sense, or not. If one is not willing to feel for, with, or against a character, questioning their motives and investing something of oneself in their world in the process of exploring the detail of their inner life, "then one will not know, and will not care, what the film is about" (Cavell 1996, 170). Unlike *The Boys*, Woods' later film, *Little Fish* offers a sympathetic central character, though her situation is not one that is easy or pleasant to relate to. In this film the ethical terrain is more complex, and the shifting dynamics between characters and spectators is navigated by a rich and emotively charged soundscape. Hence the phenomenology of sound and its affective dimensions form an important part of the analysis.

My discussion of imagination in relation to *The Piano* (Campion, 1992), a film that works on a highly symbolic level, engages with the complicated relationship between imagery and imagination. Imagination, I will argue in Chapter 6, is involved in much more than image formation or flights of fancy: it plays a productive role in envisioning consequences, motives, and alternatives that is central to inductive reasoning in ethical deliberation. Where analysis of *The Piano* reveals the ways in which imagination can be engaged in ethical understanding, *Eternal Sunshine of the Spotless Mind* goes further. The film mobilizes a rich range of aesthetic strategies to implicate spectators in an experiential journey with a character who is fully engaged in the imaginative process of narrating the ethical landscape of interpersonal relationships, drawing on the elements of memory, imagery, sense perception, affect, and value that previous chapters have established as central to ethical life.

Finally, the points of comparison and contrast between *Nil by Mouth* (Oldman, 1998) and *Once Were Warriors* (Tamahori, 1994) give rise to an analogy between ethical attention and the kind of attention a film devotes to its subjects, and that spectators invest in films. The analogy itself is not to be taken literally. There are many areas where the way in which we attend to human beings bears little resemblance to our engagement with film texts; however, the analogy will prove useful as a point around which to anchor these contrasts and comparisons, thereby progressively clarifying what "attentive engagement" might entail, as it is manifested in ethical, spectatorial, and filmic practices and forms of perception.

The connections between spectators and films are experienced on many levels during time spent absorbed in the vivid, detailed worlds fabricated by the filmmakers. One of the ways in which film narratives are of particular value to ethical understanding (and this also applies in varying degrees to other narrative forms) is the capacity of film to elicit an embodied response from spectators. Films engage the audience physically as well as intellectually in acts of perception, attention, imagining, perspective shifting, and in the experiences of morphic attunement and empathy. A consideration of film spectatorship leads to an appreciation of the location of ethical responses in the actual, concrete perceptions and sensations that inform deliberation and reflection. This conception of the processes of ethical perception, deliberation, and responsiveness is quite different from one in which ethics is located in a set of duties or principles that exist independently, outside of particular individuals and specific situations. As with ethical life, engagement with stories involves the whole person, and with them, a whole range of ethical resources that come into play according to the unique demands of each situation.

Notes

1. In this respect Ricoeur's work differs substantially from the tradition of narratology established by the work of Vladimir Propp (see 1975; 1984). Structural and formal narratologists have, in their quest for a schematic understanding or "science" of narrative, inadequately approximated narrative understanding by identifying its components: specific structures, rules, and generic character functions. Ricoeur demonstrates that narrative and our engagement with it is irreducible to a formula detailing the elements of narrative and their formal relationships because it involves many complex layers of sense and sense making.

2. The "narrative understanding" of which Ricoeur speaks is a creative configuring act distinguished by its emphasis on the connectedness of meaning. Narrative understanding is phronetic or prudential and thus, according to Ricoeur, it relates to "the practical wisdom of moral judgment" (1991b, 22–23). As it does in ethical understanding, the configuring act of narration produces something beyond the sum of its parts; an insight unifying and transcending the attention to detail and observations of context upon which it is based.

3. As Jonathon Ree claims, narrative has a teaching function which extends to philosophical discourse, and considerations of narrative ought to become "central to philosophical form itself, and not just a privileged object of its concern" (1991, 13). Indeed, as Ree points out in *Philosophical Tales* (1987), some of the most renowned philosophical inquiries have been rendered or presented as narratives—a testament, surely, to the power of the discursive form in constructing and conveying meaning.

4. The "form-content" argument is discussed in detail in Chapter 1. The privileged place of Nussbaum's work here is due in part to her interdisciplinarity. In addition to her interest in moral philosophy and literature, and her work on ancient Greek philosophy and Stoic philosophy, her work includes ethical, economic, and legal policy making in the United Nations, based on her field research into the personal and cultural narratives of those whose lives will be directly affected by the implementation of such policies.

1

Ethics in Narrative Form and Content

This chapter uses Tim Robbins' 1995 film *Dead Man Walking* to illustrate connections between narrative and ethics, beginning with an appraisal of the ethical content of narratives, considering the different ways in which stories can be involved in ethical education and practical reason. After considering the role of narrative in structuring understanding and working through different types of storytelling, the relationship between form and content is addressed. Finally, the intersection of the story world with the world of its interpreter is considered briefly, as a precursor of ideas to be developed in later chapters regarding the relationships between audiences and film narratives. The objective is to show, by offering an overview of some of the ways in which the relationship between narrative and ethics has been thought through, how narrative can be a source of ethical understanding and insight.

Dead Man Walking follows sister Helen Prejean's experiences as she responds to a letter from Matthew Poncelet, a convicted killer on death row who persistently denies that he is guilty. As the date of his execution approaches, Helen assists him to appeal his sentence and subsequently agrees to become Matthew's companion in his final days. She attempts to help him come to terms with his fate, make peace with those he has wronged and with those he feels wronged by, and take responsibility for his role in the murders he is accused of perpetrating.

Over the course of the narrative, Helen responds to the often competing ethical claims of those around her as she attempts to develop an understanding of the complex moral, political, personal, and social issues surrounding Matthew's situation. Initially she sets aside personal fears and assumptions about violent criminals and finds the time to read, reflect on, and reply to a letter from Matthew. Helen's efforts to imagine what his life is like on death row lead her to respond with compassion, rather than to make judgments about Matthew's character or conduct. Later, during conversations together when she visits him in prison, she pieces together an understanding of his past, imagining what circumstances and influences might have led him to his present position. Helen's feeling of compassion for Matthew as a lonely, isolated, frightened man with few resources evolves as she discovers more about him. This underlying compassion inflects other emotive responses to aspects of his behavior and to opinions he expresses that she finds repellent.

The narrative of the film reveals a process in which the broad ethical issue of capital punishment is approached by looking at its instantiation in particular circumstances, attending to diverse perspectives, extended contexts, fine details, and the complex relationships between them. Part of Helen's attempt to confront the issue of capital punishment in general entailed looking at (and actively involving herself in) the broad political, judicial, and social context within which it was framed. This was inseparable from her efforts to understand Matthew as a particular human being and as a murderer on death row, which involved reconciling her growing understanding of him with her understandings of those affected by his actions. To this end she listened supportively and with empathy to the stories of Matthew's family, and to the families of the teenagers Matthew was convicted of killing, and she encouraged Matthew to imagine how they might feel.

In the film, Helen responds to the need and the suffering of Matthew and those involved with him with care, support, and generosity, using imagination, empathy, and reasoned thought as ethical resources that enable her to fit Matthew's reprehensible actions into the larger story of his life, and to see his life in relation to the far-reaching issues associated with his death sentence. Helen's ethical approach differs from a more impersonal or impartial approach in which suffering or neediness might be identified in relation to a general ethical issue, prior to steps being taken to rectify the social injustices that give rise to such problems by means such as political lobbying. In the latter case one could act to diminish distress without necessarily experiencing feelings of care, compassion, or personal warmth for those who suffer: indeed one might conceivably feel distaste or even contempt for poor, uneducated criminals and still believe that, in principle, they ought to be treated fairly. However, with a limited appreciation of the extended narratives and concrete personal contexts within which the issue of capital punishment is embedded, to approach ethical life as a rational endeavor governed by impartially applied general principles may be to risk missing what fair treatment and the alleviation of suffering actually mean to those involved. *Dead Man Walking* depicts a conception of moral life in which imagination and empathy are integral to Helen's response as a moral agent involved with particular people in a specific context.

The development of moral fiber and identity is shown in *Dead Man Walking* as being entwined with and influenced by close personal relation-ships, and by the social structures and expectations of the cultural milieu within which ethical agents are situated. In the course of the narrative, both Helen's and Matthew's senses of agency and moral identity alter. For Helen, this alteration is due to the relationship she develops with Matthew and to the people she meets and information she acquires as a result of her con-nection with him. Helen is also altered by the insight she gains from the tales she hears, and by her own search for self-understanding that is both challenged and sustained by these influences. Viewers of the film may also experience inspiration or insight, as we develop understanding of the issues portrayed and the characters involved.

Dead Man Walking contains many different, interconnected stories within its overall narrative. These stories have the dual function of involv-ing spectators in acts of interpretation and engagement and of showing, through the experiences of characters inhabiting the story world, how people learn from stories. The narrative content of *Dead Man Walking* exemplifies some of the ways in which stories function in ethical life through the provision of moral examples, explanations, and role models. The first part of this chapter will examine the ways in which cultural, interpersonal, and personal narratives are central to the ethical lives of the characters within the film. Subsequently, a case will be presented for the value of narrative itself as a form of communication with the potential to further ethical understanding.

Ethics: Care and Virtue

To begin with, an outline of the conception of ethics with which I am work-ing will establish the nature of the insights I am interested in drawing from film narratives. The kind of ethical orientation that Helen demonstrates in the film *Dead Man Walking* provides a good introduction to the concep-tion of ethics that informs this study. Ethical understanding is itself acquired as we experience and reflect on the situations we encounter over the course of a lifetime. As such, it is often incomplete and provisional, and difficult to generalize or abstract from its context. It therefore seems appropriate to approach ethics with careful attention to particular examples (provided here by film texts), and by drawing on the same inner resources and forms of knowledge that we rely on in the daily interactions and deliberations of ethical life.

Carol Gilligan's work in moral psychology suggests that there is a way of conceptualizing ethical issues which entails thinking about and responding to them using a mode of reasoning that "is contextual and narrative rather than formal and abstract" (1982, 19). She refers to this as the ethical orientation of care. Often when the words ethics and morality are mentioned, they are associated with legislative prohibitions or a code or list of principles and obligations.[1] Such an ethical perspective (sometimes referred to as the 'justice perspective,' followin Gilligan) aims to identify moral principles or rules indicating what form of conduct is required or forbidden in a certain situation.

The "justice perspective" or an ethics grounded in universal principles can become problematic because moral principles are necessarily general and abstract and moral dilemmas are invariably specific, concrete, and complicated by individual perspectives and circumstances. Hence, finding a perfect match between the ethical problem and the ethical principle that ought to govern deliberation and action in a given circumstance is notoriously difficult. In looking for the common themes and general rules running through the lives of all ethical agents, it is easy to overlook or diminish the relevance of unique, contingent factors and relationships. In addition, the objective, rational standards that ethical principles appeal to are themselves subject to culturally specific values, biases, and influences.[2] However, this is not to say that approaching ethics based on something other than strict principles necessarily leads to ethical relativism. For instance, in "Non-Relative Virtues" Nussbaum (1993) defends Aristotelian virtue ethics from the charges of both cultural and moral relativism, arguing that it is possible to prioritize ethical particularity and contextuality over a rule-bound, principled approach without relinquishing an ethical ideal of human life that applies transculturally and endures over time.

Although moral principles and rules of conduct have their place, it lies within a richer conception of ethical life that honors and attends to the unique contextual factors and relationships that constitute the irreducible particularity of a given situation. Such an ethical perspective will include valuable norms and guidelines for behavior, but will focus on the interpersonal resources and skills that we put into practice as we engage with and attend to specific ethical issues and unique ethical agents. The simplicity and clarity of guiding ethical principles such as "thou shall not kill" find their force as they frame specific stories and as they cut through the confusing detail of individual circumstances and help to place actual ethical situations in perspective. In *Dead Man Walking*, Helen's actions may be informed by ethical principles relating to rights and the value of human life, but they are enacted in the context of her relationship with Matthew. To avoid getting lost in judgments about his behavior or in her sympathetic alignment with the families of his victims, Helen keeps returning to the idea that killing is wrong, in principle. This conviction grounds her opposition to the death penalty, but it is in her personal relationship with Matthew that Helen's ethical virtue is enacted. Above and beyond her role in opposing capital punishment, many of Helen's words and actions in the narrative are geared toward caring for individuals, trying to understand their pain and helping them to find relief by understanding themselves and others.

The "ethic of care" is one approach to ethics from which my work draws. The "different voice" that Carol Gilligan theorizes not only involves a "contextual mode of judgment and . . . understanding," it emphasizes the centrality of "relationships and interdependence" to ethical life (Gilligan 1982, 22). The ethical orientation of care is a contextually sensitive ethics of responsiveness and attentiveness in which the moral agent is understood as being a "self-in-relation." The importance of this intrinsic interconnectedness with others has far-reaching implications; among them, it displaces the ideals or principles of impartiality and objectivity from the privileged place they occupy in the Kantian tradition of ethical deliberation. Within the care orientation, attention to the specificity of a situation, and the context in which it arises precludes the possibility of applying universal principles such as Kant's categorical imperative.[3]

An ethic of care has some common ground with Aristotelian virtue ethics, particularly in terms of the conception of ethics as an ongoing practice that is inextricably enmeshed with one's character,[4] disposition, or sense of self, and also in terms of the tendency to avoid undue generalization and reliance on inflexible, abstract moral principles in favor of contextual sensitivity and the "priority of the particular." For instance, in *Nicomachean Ethics* (*NE*), Aristotle claims that different methods of acquiring understanding are appropriate for different spheres of knowledge. When he states: "Nor is practical wisdom concerned with universals only—it must also recognize the particulars; for it is practical, and practice is concerned with particulars" (Aristotle 1941b, *NE* 1141b, 14–16), Aristotle's words suggest that ethical deliberation, which requires practical wisdom, entails an appreciation of generality, precision, context, and the proper relation between them.[5] Indeed, Aristotle understands rules and norms to be, ideally, open to revision and progress as new situations arise (see Aristotle 1941d, *Politics* II 1269a, 9–12). It is not my goal to argue for feminist ethics, an ethic of care, or Aristotelian virtue ethics, nor do I attempt to chart and evaluate the points of overlap and divergence between these conceptions of ethics.[6] Aspects of each of these perspectives guide the ways in which I interpret the relationship between ethics and narrative, giving direction to the analyses undertaken and determining what is deemed to be significant in the film texts considered throughout this book.

Narrative and Ethical Education

Although reading, viewing, or listening to narrative fiction is not necessary to develop an ethical orientation, it is, in varying ways, a significant part of ethical education, and it can play a valuable role in projecting what the ethical consequences of particular decisions, experiences, and conceptions of ethical life might be. Furthermore, the practice of engaging with narrative fiction can enhance the ability to narrate imaginary scenarios in one's own mind, again facilitating an exploration of ethical possibilities and consequences. As Carol Witherell proposes in "Narrative and the Moral Realm: Tales of Caring and Justice," ethical education, ethical imagination, and ethical judgment are interlinked by narrative.

> Moral education has profoundly to do with the shaping of persons, that is, with the development of personhood. Our actions become meaningful when we tell about our intentions, or imagine those of others unable to speak. To educate in the moral realm is to enter the world of imagination as well as judgment. What if I had been there? What if I were to experience this dilemma again? What if I were . . . Sethe in Toni Morrison's *Beloved*? Antigone? Elie Wiesel? Such questions are calls for human kinship across the ages and continents—historical and cultural "imaginings." (Witherell 1991, 238)

Witherell claims that through "narrative engagement of the emotions, the imagination, and the intellect" the telling and interpretation of stories is one way of achieving "ever-increasing moral inclusion" by extending the sphere of concern and understanding to embrace the kinds of people, circumstances, and issues we encounter in stories, as well as those encountered within the familiar parameters of everyday life (1991, 238).

Storytelling furthers ethical understanding in the process of articulating the relationships between characters and events. The practice of narration is literally a process of "relating," of accounting for the complexity of ethical situations and the patterns of responsiveness and responsibility within them. As a story unfolds, ethical understanding develops, first when the storyteller constructs the narrative, and later when audiences refigure the narrative content, interpreting it in relation to their own lives. Paul Ricoeur (1992, 141) uses the term "configuration"[7] to refer to the process of selection and composition involved in both the creation and interpretation of narratives. The configuring act has a continually evolving temporal nature in that it involves ongoing adjustment in response to the incorporation of new material. It requires a process of reinterpretation of and reflection on past experiences, and the projection of possibilities into the future to see how the new information will affect the development of the whole narrative.

Fairytales, fables, myths, and religious texts are all narrative means of passing on ideas about how best to live life: they are stories that describe relations with oneself, between people, between individuals and society, and between people and the environment. Each of these relationships has important ethical dimensions that are irreducible to "the moral of the story." Stories can be instructive, suggesting what sorts of behavior are rewarded and punished, and what the type of character and relationships one ought to cultivate in order to be happy or successful (Day 1991). The ethical values and moral understandings of a society are thus dispersed in a variety of widely known written, oral, and visual narratives. By virtue of the multiplicity of possible and plausible interpretations, these stories may function on several levels (literal, archetypal, or symbolic) all conveying information about how best to negotiate the poorly signposted pathways of ethical life. By reflecting on narrative content we may learn, for instance, what motivates the characters of a narrative, and thus where their priorities lie.[8] In addition, through the narrator, we learn what aspects of character and behavior lead the protagonist to be perceived and valued as a hero. In this manner narrative content can convey an understanding of ethical life in distant times and places. As Witherell claims:

> The power of narrative and dialogue for educating is in the opportunities they provide for deepened understanding of others and for bridging morally diverse communities; stories can serve as springboards for ethical action. Narrative invites us to come to know the world and our place in it. Whether narratives of history or of the imagination, stories call us to consider what we know, how we know,

what and whom we care about, and how to be just and caring in
a complex world. (Witherell 1991, 240)

Narrative also contributes to the development of the reader's or listener's
psychological resources and corresponding skills in ethical interaction and
deliberation. A large body of literature concentrates on the importance of
fairy tales and the archetypes in myth, especially in terms of defining the
reader or listener's sense of self and equipping them to negotiate the decisions and challenges of ethical life adeptly.[9]

However instructive the experience of involvement in the narrative
account of an ethical situation might be, it lacks the crucial element of
responsiveness that actual situations require.[10] Despite this, consideration
of other people's moral dilemmas may be helpful in forming and clarifying
one's own commitments, beliefs, and values; reflection and premeditation
on the problems presented in films can thus inform and enhance responsiveness when one is confronted with actual ethical choices.

Narrative and Practical Reason

Narrative plays an important role in ethical education, and in furthering
understanding in a more general sense. In addition to the use of simple
narratives in conveying moral obligations and prohibitions, there has
been considerable interest in the use of complex narratives to teach ethics
to students of medicine and law, and in the importance of narration in
doctor-patient interactions. Education entertainment initiatives have
also woven pedagogical messages about social and ethical values, health,
literacy, and legal and domestic relations into the ongoing storylines
of radio serials and television soap operas (see Singhal et al. 2004). A well-
developed narrative understanding accounts for the unique elements
of each case in a manner more sensitive and responsive to the needs of
the people involved than the traditional list of symptoms and procedures
(in medicine), or case profiles and precedents (in law).[11]

For instance, in medical practice, the accumulation of symptoms or
evidence must be organized into narrative accounts if it is to make sense
because the process of practical reasoning itself is a narrative process.[12] As
Kathryn Hunter claims in "Narrative, Literature and the Clinical Exercise
of Practical Reason," constructing and interpreting narratives is a model
for the development of understanding in both morality and in areas of
practical judgment such as clinical medicine.

Knowledge exercised in the care of patients is, like moral knowing, a matter of narrative, practical reason. Physicians draw on case narratives to store experience and to apply and qualify the general rules of medical science. Literature aids this activity by stimulating moral imagination and by requiring its readers to engage in the retrospective construction of a situated, subjective account of events. (Hunter 1996, 303)

This body of research suggests that we can only fully make sense of ethical situations in the way that we make sense of stories. If narratives are a source of ethical information and also a model for configuring and articulating that information, it follows that constructing and interpreting narratives is a necessary part of the process by which we reach for moral understanding: configuration is the form that practical reason takes. Ricoeur suggests that prior to any act of conscious composition, narrative structure may be prefigured or already present in the projects, practices, conversations, and events that make up human experience: "every narrative configuration has a kind of retroactive reference because life itself is an inchoate narrative; this is what I call the pre-narrative character of life" (1991d, 180). Ricoeur argues for a circular and progressive extension of meaning from this prenarrated level, through the practices of configuration and reflection, to the well-composed narrative text, and back again. At this final level, refiguration, the textual redescription of reality is actualized by an interpreter as she or he "appropriates" the world of the text (see Ricoeur 1991b, 350), incorporating it into his or her own world.

Background Pictures and Narrative Understanding

Philosopher Charles Taylor claims that narrative is important for self-understanding and for our sense of ethical agency:

In order to have an identity, we need an orientation to the good, which means some sense of qualitative discrimination . . . this sense of the good has to be woven into my understanding of my life as an unfolding story. But this is to state another basic condition of making sense of ourselves, that we grasp our lives in a narrative. (Taylor 1989, 47)

Since Taylor attributes such a strong epistemological function to narrative on the level of self-understanding (which I discuss in more detail in the chapter about narrative identity), it is in keeping with the spirit of his work to extend his argument to claim that narrative occupies a similarly pivotal position in the development of ethical understanding more generally.

In *Sources of the Self*, Taylor argues that we function within the horizons of an ontological framework or "background picture," which at once gives definition to and informs our sense of identity and value, and provides necessary resources for ethical life. These horizons enable us to make sense of and locate ourselves in ethical space.[13] When Taylor points to the shared "frameworks" or "background pictures" that articulate and explain fundamental moral reactions or intuitions such as respect for human life, he argues that such frameworks can be seen in terms of an ontological account expressing the implicit assumptions or claims that underpin ethical reactions. Throughout *Sources of the Self*, Taylor refers frequently to well-known theological and historical stories that ground understandings of ethical issues: "the story has tremendous power even for those who have no definite notion of a God or a History . . . even when the theology is lost the story marches on" (Taylor 1989, 96).

In pervasive ways the stories known widely throughout a society (tales such as those we might consider to "inhabit" or "stock" the cultural memory and imagination) form part of the moral identity and ethical life of the people who share them. This sense of the term, "stories" includes fictional narratives, and also extends to journalistic and historical accounts of the progress of social events and of scientific and philosophical understanding. The fictional cultural narratives and the schematic historical narratives that we draw upon, function in several ways. First, they provide the framework against which we contrast and compare the stories in and of our own lives and which, in the process, allow practical ethical insight and self-knowledge to develop. Taylor explains that people understand their lives both *as* stories and *through* stories as we use narrative to try to make sense of our relationship to a concept of "the good": "One way in which people do this is to relate their story to a greater pattern of history, as the realization of good . . . the secret of [the stories'] strength is their capacity to confer meaning and substance on people's lives" (1989, 97). In addition, though Taylor does not make this point explicitly, the "moral ontological accounts" that he refers to are themselves articulated in narrative form. These narratives express and thus bring us into closer contact with what Taylor describes as our "moral source" or our "moral ontology" and so, in this way too, narrative can be seen to underwrite moral understanding.

Having outlined the role of narrative in ethical education, and highlighted some associations between practical reason and narrative understanding,

I will now use *Dead Man Walking* to illustrate the narrative structure of ethical deliberation and understanding.

The Narrative Structure of Ethical Understanding

Several different means of attaining ethical insight through narrative are instantiated in the film *Dead Man Walking*. At least three forms of narrative contributed to Helen's decision to visit Matthew Poncelet in jail and these narratives informed her quest for ethical understanding. The first is the theistic account of what a good Christian ought to do, and this plays in the background of the narrative (just as Taylor suggests these sorts of accounts underlie our moral consciousness). *Dead Man Walking* gestures repeatedly to the ways in which the narratives of the Bible frame Helen's moral intuitions about justice, human rights, and the sanctity of human life.

Dead Man Walking quite deliberately exposes the role that theistic narratives play in expressing deeply held beliefs and values, revealing how these narratives are instrumental in moral deliberation. To give a very obvious example, the film makes it clear that the biblical moral ontology that frames Helen's ethical outlook provides her with a role model for right action. Christ extended his help to destitute beggars, lepers, thieves, and prostitutes, reaching out to those who were socially outcast. Helen draws on the ethical resources of narrative, attempting to emulate a practice of ethical virtue in accordance with the examples from biblical narratives that figure in her moral imagination. She is able to compare examples of Christ's unselfish action to her own situation and look to the model of compassion he offers for guidance. Even for those of us who are not religious, such biblical stories and role models are widely known and have come to figure in popular understandings of right action.

One characteristic of narrative that is brought to light here is that stories can offer examples of ethical action for consideration and evaluation, rather than dictating a code of conduct. In engaging the imagination, narrative thus conceals what might otherwise be perceived (and hence potentially rejected) as a didactic voice. Consider, by contrast with the way Helen sought to emulate the conduct of a role model, her resistance to the directives of the prison chaplain who confronted her with rules and restrictions, rather than providing her with relevant information and allowing her to formulate her own decisions.

The second kind of narrative that influences Helen's decisions throughout the film is the personal account that Matthew gives of his own circumstances. She first responds to his letter describing life in prison and articulating his loneliness. Subsequently she is intrigued and moved by the stories he tells in conversation with her, expressing his understanding of the events on the night of the murder, and of his role on that night. Some of the stories that he tells in order to justify and make sense of his part in the murders are later revealed to be lies. Nevertheless, the goal of helping Matthew accept responsibility for his actions (literally by becoming "accountable" in the process of constructing a narrative relating his motives, influences, feelings, reasons, and actions) constitutes Helen's express motivation for agreeing to be his spiritual counselor over the days preceding his death.

The third form of narrative is Helen's own story, or more accurately, the intersection of her story with those of others. The potential of other people's stories to make us reflect on our own life story is shown by means of Helen's memory narratives. In order for Helen to be able to relate to and feel compassion for Matthew as a particular human being, rather than as one of many victims of a government policy she opposes, Helen draws on stories from her own life experiences. The film narrates a childhood memory involving the young Helen beating an opossum to death in response to peer pressure, and it is this story from Helen's past that enables her to begin to understand how Matthew might have come to commit the crime he was involved in.[14] In this way she moves closer to being able to see things from his perspective, and thus to understand how the situation is *for him*.

The film also enunciates Helen's subjective memories of taking the vows to become a novice. This personal memory narrative, which metonymically evokes the theistic account of moral responsibility to others, motivates Helen to honor her commitment to help society's outcasts. On another level, these narratives within narratives assist the audience in understanding how Helen comes to make the choices she does, potentially offering audience members the opportunity to relate their life stories to hers.

The above examples illustrate that the functions of narrative are diverse and dispersed across a variety of narrative forms, and that narrative is an important way in which we understand human life. Narration can be conceptualized as a fundamental means of interpreting experiences and of giving structure and a communicable form to knowledge. Hunter says of narrative that:

> It is the means by which the meaning of lives and deeds is made known both to the actors themselves and to their community. In this light, moral choice must be seen not as a matter of logic or preference

exercised in the moment, but as a longer process intertwined with history, identity, culture and life-meaning. Like reading itself, the exercise of practical reason is an act of interpretation. (Hunter 1996, 307)

Thus, since individual narratives articulate the development of events as they relate to one another and unfold in time, narrative understanding is closely associated with understandings of the causes and consequences of human behavior. While I am not claiming that we necessarily understand and explain human action through causal structures, I am pointing to the prevalence and importance in ethical thought of narratively configured accounts and suggesting that such accounts are narrated in the process of practical reasoning about ethical actions and motives.

In his thought provoking book *The Company We Keep: An Ethics of Fiction*, Wayne Booth develops the implications of the interaction between narrative art and the narratives of lived human stories, suggesting that the minds we use in judging stories have been constituted (at least in part) by the stories we judge (1988, 40). Booth goes on to say, "we cannot draw a clear line between what we are, in some conception of a 'natural,' unstoried self, and what we have become as we have first enjoyed, then imitated, and then, perhaps, criticized both the stories and our responses to them" (1988, 229). In other words, personal life experiences influence the way the narrative is interpreted, and the narrative then goes on to inform the way in which one reflects on one's life.

We are involved in an ongoing exchange of ideas with the narratives we encounter throughout our lives. MacIntyre has argued that dramatic narrative is the most appropriate form for the understanding of human action, and that this exchange of ideas might be thought of as a dialogue (1977). MacIntyre claims that narratives necessarily include an ethical dimension because they require an evaluative framework (1977, 456). First, the art of structuring material into narrative form necessitates choices being made by an author about how to represent human beings as fictional characters. These decisions carry ethical consequences: even choosing to center the narrative on one character rather than another will have implications regarding whose voice is heard or valued. As elaborated in the chapters to follow, narration and representation necessarily involve acts of discrimination and the selection of some characteristics over others.[15]

However valuable and inclusive, the selective nature of narrative configuration means that stories are also always perspectival and partial, concealing a greater number of voices than they are able to give expression to. For instance, *Dead Man Walking* does not offer an account from the murder victim's perspectives though this could well have provided a powerful beginning to the film. As much as its perspectival character may be a weakness of narrative, it is also a strength in terms of the quest for ethical insight. On the one hand, the gaps, omissions, and silences in the texts may provide openings for listeners and readers to enter the text. We may learn by attending to what remains unexpressed, by piecing together a picture that exposes absences and suggests possible reasons for these other stories remaining unarticulated. In addition, it is futile to seek an omniscient, objective, factual view point, or account of ethical reality, which embraces all the possibilities of moral life. Such a project might not even be desirable since it is often most productive to tackle the larger problems on the intimate and concrete level of individual cases in context (see Nussbaum 1990, 23).

Narration and moral deliberation both involve drawing together the particular and the general, situating specific circumstances within the broader context of a life and a culture and considering abstract, general principles (or guidelines and ideals) against the concrete particulars of human lives. *Dead Man Walking* exemplifies this in a direct way because, in asking both the film characters and viewers to consider whether capital punishment is an appropriate sentence for Matthew Poncelet, it also requires consideration as to whether his particular case might be representative of others. We are led to approach general questions about responsibility, redemption, vengeance, and the sanctity of human life through an analysis of one complex, detailed situation. Spectators might wonder how Matthew is like and unlike others on death row, like and unlike ourselves, at the same time that we are brought to recognize what makes the nature of his situation unique.

There is a further sense in which narrative incorporates an inherently evaluative framework. The act of interpreting a narrative involves another level of ethically significant choices about what is most worthy of attention, and what has least moral relevance of all the things the story relates. Those who interpret a narrative effect a refiguration or reinterpretation of the text in such a way that both the text and the person engaging with it may be altered. For example, Matthew's story in *Dead Man Walking* refigures the issue of capital punishment. Helen was already opposed to it in general principle, though her involvement in Matthew's life story undoubtedly changed the terms in which she understood the death penalty. The detailed knowledge of a particular case offered in *Dead Man Walking* subsequently inflected and influenced the understanding that not only Helen, but also many of the film's spectators had of capital punishment, though this is not to say that spectators necessarily changed their stance on the issue. In other words, *Dead Man Walking* asks its audience to make an evaluation about the justice of capital punishment in the case of Matthew Poncelet, relating general beliefs and values about this matter to the situation in the film. Clearly, the convictions we bring with us into the cinema will inflect our interpretation of the narrative. However, the film also invites us to reflect on our beliefs and perhaps amend them in the light of details revealed in the narrative. Thus, the act of narrating involves an active process of evaluation that may expose and bring us into confrontation with our attitudes and priorities. The nondidactic way in which the issue of capital punishment is framed by Helen's process of reflection means that the film prompts spectators to rethink our own positions without feeling that we have been told what to think, especially as the film gives space to a range of different perspectives.

The ways in which forms of communication position the givers and receivers of information in ethically significant ways has been elaborated by Murray Jardine (1998), not in relation to literary narratives, but in the practical sphere of spoken interactions. As detailed below, Jardine's work articulates the significance of oral/aural narratives and spoken forms of communication, arguing for the special ethical relevance of speech. This work can usefully bring claims relating to the dialogical relationship between cinematic and literary narrative texts and their interpreters into focus.

Oral Narratives

Traditional oral narratives are recognized as an important story form in cultural terms. The Dreamtime stories of the Australian Aborigines, for example, share the functions of myth and spiritual texts mentioned above, and are also involved in the definition of the boundaries of the moral community through ritual, ceremony, and enactment. Oral narratives with similar functions may be present in less formal or traditional guises.[16] All such spoken forms of expression call for different forms of response than those demanded by literary narratives, or by analytic forms of writing. Although the focus here is on the ethical significance of fictional narratives, the category of narrative stretches to include many nonfictional forms that are important in their own right. Spoken, shared stories are formed in the course of discussing personal ethical situations, and those of friends, acquaintances, and public figures. Sometimes such conversations literally entail telling a story, such as the story that Hope's parents tell about her murder and their grief in *Dead Man Walking*. At other times, conversations can only be seen to form a narrative in hindsight, or can best be interpreted as partial or prefigured stories.

In *Speech and Political Practice* (1998) Jardine presents an analysis of the ways that forms of communication structure ways of thinking about or approaching the subject matter in question. Jardine claims that oral-aural forms of communication are characterized by a situatedness, immediacy, and interactiveness that correspond to a participative, concrete way of thinking. Such participative knowledge, he argues, is appropriate for ethical thought because in situating the interlocutors in direct relation to one another, it pulls implicit responsibilities, claims, and loyalties into play, thus potentially providing necessary moral limitations to human action in a contextually sensitive but nonrelativistic manner. Orality, Jardine claims, is situational and largely incompatible with abstraction: it ensures that information is personalized because of the lack of distance between words and their speaker. This discourages thinking in terms of a subject-object dualism where agents are separated from their words and are correspondingly less motivated to honor their word, or to respect and remain responsive to other speakers.[17]

Jardine contrasts the ideal of orality with written communication and the objectivist forms of thought that he believes to be associated with literacy. He argues that objectivist modes of thought are "to an important degree the result of a literate/visualist orientation," and that the epistemological and ethical consequences of this include a tendency toward abstraction, decontextualization, depersonalization, and dualism, resulting in a diminished sense of moral responsibility, a weakened sense of interrelatedness, and limitations to action (Jardine 1998, 87–90). While Jardine's arguments contain significant insights linking dialogue to situation ethics, it is important not to overlook the advantages of written or "visual" communication. Jardine does acknowledge some of the strengths that visual and written forms of communication have. For instance, he concedes that the ability to abstract knowledge from its context and to think impersonally can be enabling in ethical thought (Jardine 1998, 88–89).

Narrative film possesses some of the more positive ethical implications attributed to both literary and verbal forms of communication in that it affords the requisite distance for more objective, generalized conceptual forms of thought in addition to the particular, concrete and immediate claims entailed by verbal communication. It is revealing to look at the conversational exchanges contained within the larger pattern of narration in *Dead Man Walking*. The spoken interactions between Helen Prejean and Matthew Poncelet are articulated not only in dialogue, but also through subtle narrative and filmic techniques that reveal the shifting claims the characters exert upon each other. Since cinematic texts are addressed to a body of spectators, the audience shares in this conversational dynamic and becomes subject to certain ethical claims made by, and within, the text.

For instance, the shot-reverse-shot structure of the dialogue sequence when Matthew finally confesses to his crimes and expresses genuine remorse places the audience first on one side, then on the other of the jail bars that confine him, and the compassion and forgiveness that enable his redemption. His voice falters and his face crumples in tears when Helen says, "You did a terrible thing, Matt. A terrible thing." Her response forces

Figure 2 Dead Man Walking: *Helen helps Matthew accept responsibility for his crime.*

Figure 3 Dead Man Walking: *Matthew breaks down in remorse as he confesses.*

him to accept full responsibility for the atrocity of his crimes in a way that, without the necessity of looking into the eyes of a listener and perceiving their response, a written confession might not have effected. The audibility and visibility of both compassion and remorse give this exchange its ethical force, calling forth a different evaluation of Matthew's character and his actions, distinct from court hearings and media interviews in which the jury and the audience are inclined to convict him on the basis of his unrepentant attitude. Significantly, as the differential focus on the bars of his cell show, Matthew's situation does not change as a result of his confession, but through Helen's eyes, we can see that the truth has set him free.

Ethics and Interpretive Engagement

In words that resonate with the spirit of Jardine's claims about oral communication, Adam Newton, author of *Narrative Ethics*, says: "One faces a text as one might face a person, having to confront the claims raised by that very immediacy, an immediacy of contact, not of meaning" (1997, 11). Newton centers his theory of narrative ethics on the dynamics of the relationship between the text and its interpreters. His work points to the ethical dimensions of narrative as a particular form of expression and communication, rather than concentrating on the moral material contained in individual stories, or alluding to the epistemological, explanatory functions associated with narrative structure more generally. Contrary to Jardine's argument linking written communication with distance, depersonalization, and abstraction, Newton argues that the process of imaginatively interpreting literary fiction engenders relations of an inherently ethical form. Newton focuses on the "intersubjective dynamics of narrative" (1997, 33) in terms of the relations that bind storytellers, characters, and the narrative's interpreters. Like Jardine, Newton is interested in concrete, interpersonal, contextual ethics,[18] but in a significant contrast with Jardine, Newton believes that literature *can* be an avenue to such a mode of ethical thinking.

Although Newton's work presents no challenge to Jardine's claims that oral communication can facilitate ethical understanding, it does suggest that imaginative engagement with others in the richly detailed contexts evoked by literary fiction can usefully supplement actual interpersonal communication. Newton demonstrates that the intersubjective access to others offered by narrative fiction is not equivalent to life encounters (the form of interaction privileged by Jardine), but it has hermeneutical similarities. He argues that the text makes claims on its readers, and at the same time readers invest something of themselves in the narrative: "In each case texts tax readers with ethical duties which increase in direct proportion to the measure with which they are taken up" (Newton 1997, 292).[19] In the act of reading or interpreting narrative texts Newton perceives a model of understanding in which readers have the potential to engage with the text and its characters with a responsive, constructive form of attention that parallels the ideal form in which one might attend to others, or to ethical issues.

Form and Content

In a collection of essays on philosophy and literature that shares some common ground with Newton's work, Nussbaum claims that formal and stylistic choices address and position the text's reader (or audience) in particular ways and entail implicit assumptions about how the text will be received: "Any style makes, itself, a statement: an abstract theoretical style makes, like any other style, a statement about what is important and what is not, about what faculties of the reader are important for knowing and what are not" (Nussbaum 1990, 7).

Since form and style influence and structure ways of thinking about and responding to a subject, some forms of expression may be better equipped to communicate a particular content than others. For example, where poetry implicitly privileges creativity and imagination and requires them of its readers, genre texts often require an accumulated knowledge of popular culture and generic conventions. On the other hand, a formal, academic style of writing makes a statement about the importance of critical reasoning, often implying that the world can be known or understood at a high level of abstraction. The abstract form of expression that moral philosophy so often takes indicates that a restrictive conception of reason is of central importance in ethical life. A more inclusive understanding of what counts as knowledge or "rational deliberation" is appropriate to ethical forms of thought.[20]

Complex, Extended Narratives

Narratives offer an alternative form of expressing and exploring ethics. The very nature of moral concepts and situations means that much of their meaningfulness can be lost in the processes of reduction, simplification, abstraction, and fragmentation typical of analytic thought. As Nussbaum argues, "There is *precision* in the lucid description of a highly complex and indeterminate situation; there is *evasion* and *vagueness* in the simple schematic description of a multi-faceted concrete case" (1993, 236 emphasis in original). In the literary form of the novel (particularly the realist novels around which Nussbaum bases her arguments), one is often able to follow the development of moral character over time, with the benefit of perceiving the details of personal history, contextual factors, and relationships that influence and mould that character. Thus, novels are able to offer detailed moral portraits that, although still selective of certain attributes and details, and neglectful of others, may be more representative of the intricacy of moral life than the glimpses we are given of "character types" in genres like the fairy tale or fable. In literary narratives, the reader is invited to enter another world, a complex story world that may broaden our horizons and provide exposure to different ethical perspectives.

A concern for the lives of others and an ability to imagine what it is like to be in someone else's situation is central to ethics, as Nussbaum makes clear:

> I defend the literary imagination precisely because it seems to me an essential ingredient of an ethical stance that asks us to concern ourselves with the good of other people whose lives are distant from our own . . . an ethics of impartial respect for human dignity will fail to engage real human beings unless they are made capable of entering imaginatively into the lives of distant others and to have emotions related to that participation. (1995, xvi)

It may be comparatively easy to be moved to respond to and relieve the suffering of those we care for, yet it is difficult to even imagine the problems of those we've never met (victims of famine or civil war, for instance)—much less extend our resources and expand our moral sphere to include them. Films, novels, and other forms of narrative fiction, convey, in their mode of address to their imagined audiences, "the sense that there are links of possibility, at least on a very general level, between the characters and the reader. The reader's emotions and imagination are highly active as a result" (Nussbaum 1995, 5).

Narrative film can provide examples to aid in the analysis of ethical issues in a way that is comparable to the role literature plays in Nussbaum's conception of ethical inquiry. Like literary narratives, films have many advantages over what Nussbaum (1990, 19) terms the "hygienically pallid" prose style of abstract examples in conventional ethical discourse and can work as an important complement or corrective to such forms of ethical thought. For instance, beyond inviting spectators to extend their understanding outside their own neighborhood of acquaintances and into the lives of a nun and a convicted murderer, *Dead Man Walking* vividly illustrates the complex, ethically compelling claims that moral agents must deal with when confronted with competing moral demands. At a time when Helen's resources were already devoted to teaching in a poor area, she was also called upon to respond to the neediness and poverty of Matthew and his family. Despite opposition from those who believed she ought to focus her energy on more deserving individuals, Helen generously extends her resources to help Matthew, and then also to comfort his family. Matthew's prison is a long drive from Helen's home and the time she spends with him is time that cannot be spent either with the community in which she works, teaches, and lives, or with those affected by the murder of the two teenagers. Thus the film prompts both characters and spectators to question whether offering comfort, care, and time to a violent, racist criminal at the expense of providing that same service to equally needy but innocent and virtuous people (the poor children in the projects and the distraught families of the dead teenagers) is ethically appropriate.

Dead Man Walking also raises the issue of the personal limitations of care and compassion, and gestures to the need for appropriate sociopolitical structures to compensate for such individual limits. In different ways the film explores the question of the distribution of moral resources amongst those in proximal relationships, or those most needy, or most worthy, or most likely to be responsive. This is most explicit in the scene around Helen's family dinner table where friends and relatives question Helen's ethical priorities, but also when the Percys, Hope's parents, ask Helen, "What about us? Didn't you think we might need you too? Why did you never come to see us?" Helen defends her decision by appealing to the particularity and proximity of Matthew's claim on her attention, saying, "He wrote to me and asked me to come." Helen's failure to care adequately for herself when she stretches her resources too far and collapses is also rendered as problematic as it is shown to inhibit her capacity to function or flourish, much less to help anyone else. In this way the film advocates but also problematizes the expansion of the sphere of moral concern that is, in principle, boundless but is actually subject to the specific constraints of finite moral and practical resources. Helen finds that though we might care *about* everyone (in the general sense of honoring human dignity and the sanctity of human life), we can only ever care *for* a limited number of particular individuals.

In the film, concern about the ethical issues surrounding capital punishment in a more expansive, generalized sense is shown to be dealt with appropriately by means of judicial appeals, political lobbying, and protests.

Because the demands of care and compassion outrun the capabilities of individuals, narrative ethics leans on broader structures of justice and guiding ethical principles in order to counterbalance personal limitations. Once again, the priority of the particular is placed into perspective against the background picture of shared principles and values, and practical constraints.

Another issue that *Dead Man Walking* brings to light (which a more reductive, abstract account of the same issues might neglect) is the dynamic, provisional nature of ethical understanding. The morally relevant elements of any given ethical situation are by no means static, and nor is moral identity: ethical relations change as new developments take place or old ones come to be seen in a different light. The film doesn't exclude the possibility that there may be fixed moral landmarks; things that are always wrong, or always right. Instead it offers a vision of the living terrain of response and responsibility that often moves under one's feet.

The ethical character of Matthew Poncelet's situation changes considerably over the course of the narrative as his sense of moral responsibility develops along with his sense of integrity. As his understanding of what might be valuable or important alters and expands in response to Helen's care and honesty, the ethics of his own situation shift correspondingly. Repentance and accountability come to be seen as significant moral achievements, which somehow alter the nature of the relationship between the criminal and the crime for which he or she is responsible, and for which he or she takes responsibility. The film raises the question of what might be gained from another death.

Matthew and Helen's story illustrates that in addition to reasoned thought, ethical understanding may often require perceptiveness (including the ability to perceive a situation from different perspectives) and attention to the concrete context and detail of the situation. It also calls for an awareness of the relationships, histories, and possibilities of those involved, and the ability to draw on imaginative resources and respond with emotional sensitivity. In a film such as *Dead Man Walking*, the interconnectedness of characters and events that characterizes extended narratives facilitates a kind of practical reason akin to that practiced in ethical life. Yet, at the same time, the audience also has the benefit of being able to step outside of the story world and access a more "objective" perspective. The chapters to follow will further elaborate the ways in which narrative films call upon spectators to practice forms of responsiveness that are integral to ethical understanding, exploring the processes by which film facilitates an intersubjective form of understanding central to practical judgment in ethics.

Notes

1. For example, in his book *The Nature of Rationality*, the influential theorist Robert Nozick describes the rational, principled process of judicial decision making as: "a test of a particular judgment on the assumption that any correct judgment is yielded by some true acceptable general principle, that true particular judgments are consequences of general principles applied to specific situations. Failure to uncover any acceptable general principle that yields some judgment in particular may mean that there is no such acceptable principle, in which case that particular judgment is mistaken and should be abandoned" (1993, 4).

2. For an excellent analysis of the situatedness of knowledge and ways of knowing, see Code (1991).

3. In accordance with the categorical imperative, actions are "right" only if they are guided by rules of conduct that can be universalized to apply to everyone, everywhere, in situations with the same salient ethical characteristics. Proponents of contextual relativism (see Friedman 1987, 191) problematize the criteria for deciding what might qualify as the "same" situation, arguing that every ethical situation is unique and must be considered on its own terms. Though there may be no dispute over the validity of important guiding principles such as "thou shall not kill," differences in judgment abound, regarding when such a principle is appropriate or inoperative, contingent upon many contextually specific factors, as the film *Dead Man Walking* illustrates.

4. Ethical virtue, according to Aristotle's *Nicomachean Ethics*, is "a state of character," (see Aristotle 1941b, *NE* 1106a, 10–15), and something that is both learned, and habituated. "Virtue, then, being of two kinds, intellectual and moral, intellectual virtue in the main owes both its birth and its growth to teaching (for which reason it requires experience and time), while moral virtue comes about as a result of habit, whence also its name *ethike* is one that is formed by a slight variation from the word *ethos* (habit)" (Aristotle 1941b, *NE* 1103a, 14–18).

5. Aristotle elaborates on this theme in Book One of *Nicomachean Ethics* (Aristotle 1941b, 1094b, 11–28 and 1098a, 20).

6. This has been done elsewhere; for example, Alasdair MacIntyre makes connections between virtue ethics and narrative in *After Virtue* (1981) and Marilyn Friedman articulates the relationship between a form of feminist ethical thought and narrative (1987; 1993). See also Larrabee (1993) for a feminist, interdisciplinary approach to an ethic of care.

7. Following Ricoeur, the term "configuration" is used here to refer to the creative process of developing meaning, "the art of composition which mediates between concordance and discordance" (Ricoeur 1992, 141).

8. See MacIntyre (1981), and Simone Weil (1956).

9. Bruno Bettelheim's work in this area is exemplary especially *The Uses of Enchantment* (1975). See also Eliade (1963), Malinowski (1926), Warner (1993; 1994).

10. Stanley Cavell accounts for the fact that cinema spectators engage with fiction film on an ethical level but may "do nothing in the face of tragedy" in the following way:

> In viewing a movie my helplessness is mechanically assured: I am present not at something happening, which I must confirm, but at something that has happened, which I absorb (like a memory). In this, movies resemble novels, a fact mirrored in the sound of narration itself, whose tense is in the past. (1996, 164)

The "past tense" of the production context also applies to documentary films yet, in ways that exceed the scope of this research, documentary has a special ethical relation to the real that may in fact call for direct action from spectators.

11. See, for instance, Arthur Frank's *The Wounded Storyteller: Body, Illness, and Ethics* (1995). See also Hudson Jones (1999), Hunter (1996), and Weisberg and Duffin (1995) on the use of literature to teach medical ethics. In *Poetic Justice: The Literary Imagination and Public Life* (1995), Martha Nussbaum advocates the use of literature as a moral resource for judges. In *Stories Lives Tell* (1991), Carol Witherell and Nel Noddings explore the roles of narrative and dialogue in education and moral life.

12. For instance, Anne Hudson Jones argues for a narrative approach to the resolution of ethical dilemmas in medicine. Hudson Jones claims that rather than distracting from the morally relevant considerations of a case, "the main advantage of a literary work is that it presents ethical issues embedded in a human context made richer and more complex by the complicating emotions, intentions, and relationships of the characters involved" (1996, 267).

13. For a discussion of the concept of background pictures, see *Sources of the Self* (Taylor 1989, 7–8; 27–29).

14. In the novel, Prejean asks herself,

> What's it like to live on Waiting for Death Street? And what's it like to have done something really bad, really evil, something irreparable? I can't bear myself when I hurt someone. I had felt terrible in eighth grade when a group of us during a slumber party called up a fat girl and made fun of her. When I was eight I had had nightmares after I helped torture an opossum some neighborhood boys had cornered. I had wanted to be tough like the guys and I had taken my turn hitting the animal with a stick until the opossum had begun to bleed from the mouth. I dreamed that night of the bloody head. (Prejean 1993, 11)

15. Narratives do not present a neutral perspective: they are projected by a particular narrator to an intended audience for specific purposes, though they may be interpreted in unexpected ways: "Narrative truths are provisional, uncertain, derived from narrators whose standpoints are always situated, particular, and uncertain, but open to comparison and interpretation" (Hunter 1996, 303). As Newton writes, "the mere representation of an other, the translation of human 'background' into fictional form, is fraught with ethical

tensions" (1997, 291), and readers may be complicit with, responsive, or resistant to the ethical dynamics of these textual representations.

16. Consider, for instance, the simple act of telling children stories to convey an understanding or expectation. See also Patricia Meyer Spacks' analysis of the roles of gossip as "fragments of lives transformed into story" (1985, 3).

17. The concrete ethical claim a speaker's personal story makes on listeners was one reason that the stories of those who suffered under apartheid and the confessions of the perpetrators voiced in the South African Truth and Reconciliation Commission had such profound moral and political impact, and was so instrumental in healing the South African community during the transition to democracy.

18. As Newton states:

"Ethics" refers to the radicality and uniqueness of the moral situation itself, a binding claim exercised upon the self by a concrete and singular other whose moral appeal preceded both decision and understanding . . . "Ethics," in this alternative sense, signifies recursive, contingent, and interactive dramas of encounter and recognition, the sort of which prose fiction both crystallizes and recirculates in acts of interpretive engagement. (1997, 12)

19. It is worth qualifying Newton's insight here by acknowledging the diversity of forms and functions associated with narrative. The primary function of some narratives may well be a kind of pleasurable "escapism" from the difficulties and demands of ethical life, and accordingly, such stories may contain characters and situations that do not challenge the reader, listener, or viewer's faculties or draw heavily on their ethical resources.

20. Witherell characterizes narrative as a subjective way of knowing:

Qualitative studies that recognize the primacy of human narratives—their context, interpretation, voice, metaphor, expressive language, and attention to particulars— have emerged as full partners with quantitative studies in the research literature in areas such as cognitive and language development, cross-cultural psychology, psychotherapy, and educational research and evaluation . . . These contributions have expanded our assumptions regarding what counts as knowledge, criteria for truth and adequacy. (Witherell 1991, 237–238)

As the chapter to follow suggests, it is productive to think of narrative understanding as an intersubjective way of knowing, particularly in the case of narrative film.

2

Intersubjective Perception: Phenomenology, Embodiment, and Evaluation

Beginning by building an appreciation of the place of cinematic narratives into the work on narrative and ethics dealt with above, this chapter moves on to address film from a phenomenological perspective. Drawing on existential phenomenology, the ethical implications of cinematic representations are approached by examining how experience, perception, and attention can be described and enacted in films.

Perception, I argue, is itself inherently evaluative and selective in ways that influence the production and reception of representations. Because film texts both reveal, and are open to "evaluative perception," they can serve a double function. First, film makes visible the implicit evaluations inherent in perception, exposing them to the possibility of critical reflection. Second, film also invites spectators to occupy various subject positions or modes of perception, and to have a sense of temporary immersion or participation in someone else's value system and experience.

Building on the analysis in Chapter 1, the film *Dead Man Walking* is used to anchor and illustrate the argument advanced here. As we watch the film and become involved in the relationship that forms between Helen and Matthew, audience members develop insight into the issues, lives, and world views that are expressed in the unfolding narrative. This sense of insight has particular ethical relevance because it carries the experiential weight of being subjectively perceived and impressed upon our senses. As a story form that is felt, rather than just told, film exerts an influence that warrants close attention.

Film narratives can be distinguished from written texts in terms of the nature and degree of embodied involvement that they demand of their audiences, and in the predominantly social nature of their reception, which often entails the sharing of perceptions, perspectives, and interpretations as spectators discuss the film upon leaving the cinema. Christian Metz, whose work is informed by both psychoanalysis and phenomenology, points out that cinema is "*more perceptual*" than other means of expression as it "mobilizes a larger number of the axes of perception" (1977, 43). "That is why," Metz continues, cinema has been described as a "synthesis of all the arts" since it operates across different registers of perception and "contains within itself the signifiers of other arts: it can present pictures to us, make us hear music, it is made of photographs, etc." (1977, 43). The semiotic richness of screen texts entails an embodied engagement and often elicits a visceral response that is linked to the appeal that the medium makes not only to the intellect, emotions, and imagination, but in the way it actively engages the physical senses. The embodied engagement film necessitates is also intersubjective and evaluative, and these characteristics of film spectatorship give cinema an important place in terms of its social and political relevance.

As a visual medium, film bears a high modality. (This can, of course, have both positive and negative consequences, as it includes the potential to be both convincing and deceptive. The negative influences of cinematic texts will be addressed in Chapter 4.) Phrases such as "seeing is believing" and "the perception is the reality" have evolved from a long history of visual metaphors and various conceptions of knowledge as illumination that have prevailed in Western thought at least since the time of Plato. Alasdair MacIntyre claims that at the very core of the Platonic and Augustinian tradition "was a conception of knowledge as analogous to vision: the mind's eye beholds its objects by the light of reason" (1977, 458). Because it is a visual medium with the ability to evoke and represent material in a manner that seems captivatingly realistic (though we understand that it is only a representation), film is a narrative form with qualities of expression and impact that differ from any other. The screenplay or the storyboard for a film, or even the novels, operas, plays, and events on which adaptations are based are not able to articulate human experience with the same precision, impact, or emphasis as the film itself: they make a different statement and they target different audiences, although they follow the same narrative.

Narrative film is a medium in which the stories of human lives and the cultural contexts in which they are situated are inscribed in a way that can foster understanding of people, issues, and circumstances the viewer might not otherwise consider. The practice of film spectatorship necessitates a synthesis of perspectives that approximates the way in which we perceive and seek to make sense of everyday life. The relationship between audience members and the films they engage with is, as I demonstrate below, indicative of the mobility and fluidity of subjectivity, and the permeability of boundaries between subjects and objects theorized within a phenomenological account of perception.

Phenomenology

Phenomenology is a philosophical methodology concerned with the descriptive study of experience. As Maurice Merleau-Ponty puts it, phenomenology "offers an account of space, time and the world as we 'live' them. It tries to give a direct description of experience as it is, without taking account of its psychological origin and the causal explanations which the scientist, the historian or the sociologist may be able to provide" (Merleau-Ponty 2002, vii). The way in which phenomenologists seek to understand experience of the world is by setting aside or bracketing away the assumptions by which human beings recognize and categorize aspects of experience. This process, called a phenomenological reduction, aims to bypass the presuppositions of established ways of understanding things. This includes setting aside science, history, and sociology, as stated above (as well as other epistemological frameworks such as philosophy, religion, psychology, and film theory), in order to describe sense experiences in a way that captures their true essence or nature; the "invariant character" of prereflective experience. Although we cannot ever fully escape our preconceptions, we can at least try to become aware of how they inform our understanding by admitting, examining, and critically accounting for them.

The very act of describing something does necessitate a degree of reflection as the application of labels and explanations coincides with understandings of the significance and salient features of an object, event, or experience. Thus, even on the simple level of describing what something is or how it works or appears, experience is a mediated relation between reflective consciousness and phenomena. For instance, the character of Matthew Poncelet in *Dead Man Walking* is not an objective image of a criminal on death row (or even of Sean Penn acting as such). It is a technologically mediated image of a man seen in a certain light, embedded in a narrative context, shot from a particular angle, and inflected with significance by the emotional responses, experiences, and opinions of film viewers. This phenomenological conception of experience is distinct from the scientific ideal in which data can be impartially observed and objectively recorded. Such insights into the inseparability of perception from the perceiver, of object from subject, of the intentional act (*noesis*) and the act's content (*noema*) are crucial for film theory. Among other things, they help to clarify how subjective and objective shots function in terms of spectatorial identification and pleasure.

Although film cannot offer an objective description of prereflective reality, there is another sense in which film does describe experience: film is a technologically mediated mode of expression that is often akin to the way humans see and hear and feel the world. In what follows I draw primarily on the work of two theorists, taking up the ideas put forward by the existential phenomenologist Maurice Merleau-Ponty in relation to the nature of perception, as well as Vivian Sobchack's development of phenomenological methods for film analysis. My objective is to draw out the ethical implications of the work of these two theorists in relation to narrative film,[1] by putting a version of their phenomenological approaches into practice. This will entail setting aside the received knowledge and assumptions of film theory in order to analyze how films describe experience and to describe how spectators experience film. It will also involve considering the relationship between the viewer and the viewed, and thinking about viewing as an embodied activity.

Phenomenology, especially as it has been taken up by film theorists following Husserl (such as Casebier, 1991) has been criticized for being ahistorical and decontextualized,[2] for assuming an unproblematic norm of genderless experience and consciousness; and for claiming to follow an impossibly presuppositionless method (see Studlar, 1990a). Sometimes theorists undertaking phenomenological analyses also tend to approach film in general terms as a certain kind of object of perceptual experience, rather than attending to the details of particular films. In this way phenomenology has neglected narrative and character engagement. Consequently, the following appraisal of a phenomenological approach to film is undertaken with an awareness that phenomenology needs to be complemented with sensitivity to the importance of content, theme, and context, and the ethical and political positions that the film, its characters, and its audience members occupy.

Cinematic representation is highly selective, irreducibly mediated, and framed by cultural perspectives. The phenomenological method can be employed to consider how film represents reality and positions the viewer, as "the heretofore meaningless (implicit, unnoticed) production techniques become visible and take on meaning" (Studlar 1990a, 84). The different elements of filmic style (including cinematography, editing, lighting, and sound) make a considerable difference to the way in which the content of the frame is interpreted. For instance, if the image itself alters (when the camera zooms or moves with pans, tilts, crane, Steadicam, or tracking shots), this represents a change of the frame of reference of the perceptual or attentive subject (see Sobchack 1990, 25–27). This has ethical significance because, as examples from *Dead Man Walking* will illustrate, changing the frame represents a change in understanding and value, a literal shift in perspective as it alters the spatial and aesthetic relationship between the viewer's body and the viewed image. Such a shift in the viewer's orientation to the image can also be described within a static frame if, for example, the constitution of the image is modified by altering the lighting, sound, or camera lens, using filters or racking focus. As spectators, these stylistic effects impact on how we perceive and experience the images in the cinema screen as meaningful or valuable, irrespective of whether we consciously and critically analyze the cinematic codes and conventions.

A number of film theorists have developed diverse, sophisticated, and subtle ways of utilizing the insights of phenomenology to discuss technological advances in filmmaking, to account for the experiences of spectatorship, and to include factors such as the context of film reception. For instance, in her article "Eye/Mind/Screen," Linda Singer undertakes a phenomenological exploration of the perceptual and behavioral dimensions of cinematic pleasure as they arise from the experience of being in cinematic space (1990, 52). She observes that the experience of viewing a film in a cinema is characterized by a sense of having one's attention directed toward an intense and complex narrative with multisensory appeal. Singer claims that the physical space of the cinema and its decor function to create "a context which loosened ties with a world of habitual reference points and signaled to the patron his/her entrance into another world" (1990, 52). Spectators' attention is directed toward the luminous screen in the dark, quiet cinema; the cinematic space is designed for the purpose of "removing extraneous distractions, thus establishing a clearer set of priorities" (1990, 53). People go to the cinema specifically to see, hear, feel, respond, and attend to the film: spectators' priorities shift from personal concerns to a story concerning others.

Significantly, the outward extension of the self experienced during involvement in cinematic narratives is generally considered to be an enjoyable activity.[3] In the context of narrative film, this enjoyment is not restricted to the pleasure of engaging with and understanding other people's stories, it includes the visual pleasures of voyeurism and scopophilia, such as gazing upon the celestial bodies of film stars enacting romantic and heroic roles. Singer claims that "The phenomenon of cinema as a social institution affirms and supports the pleasure of seeing by providing a context that facilitates the cultivation of those possibilities, legitimating them by acknowledging the need for such a space and making one available" (Singer 1990, 57). As I suggested earlier, it is also significant that film viewing is frequently a social activity (whereas reading a novel is generally not).[4] The practice of sharing interpretations with others can play a valuable part in the process of approaching ethical understanding, which by its very nature entails shared understandings of values.

Another phenomenological film theorist, Harald Stadler, understands film audiences to be involved in an active process of viewing in which the subject generates meaning in conjunction with the film text. In the interpretive relation he describes, subject and object are inseparable. Stadler writes of the interpenetration of the world of the audience and the world of the narrative:

> A mutually constitutive relationship between the viewer's life-world and the reality of the filmic world: non-filmic factors (every-day experience) motivate film reception and make it meaningful; filmic experience, in turn, modifies perception and behavior in the viewer's everyday life. (Stadler 1990, 41)

As Stadler argues, the film text "is seen as a dynamic and dialectical process, an occasion of signification, rather than a stable container of significance" (1990, 41). On this basis, I want to explore the significance of film "as experience" in relation to ethical experience.

The audiovisual mode in which film conveys meaning is in some respects analogous with the experiential and epistemological framework within which we apprehend the world and communicate about it in our everyday life. Sobchack understands film as "*perception turned literally inside out and towards us as expression*" (emphasis added 1992, 12). That is, film renders the process of perception perceptible and enables us to see from another's perspective: the technology of film production and projection enables us to see *how* we see, and to see through someone else's eyes as film describes or expresses experience. In some senses film expresses a "human-like" mode of perceptual consciousness: the camera and microphones can offer a technologically inflected version of what a human body would experience in a certain situation.[5] Without collapsing the distinction between the human body and the film's perceptual technologies, or downplaying the differences between mechanical and organic modes of articulation and sensation, Sobchack suggests that the camera functions as the film's "bodily agency," its optical organ, and the microphone recording diegetic sound is its auditory sensor. By extension, the projector might be understood as the film's expressive organ. We could even say that the edit suite, where the narrative is spliced together, represents the film's conceptual organs, and the score functions as one element of the film's emotional voice.

Each shot in a film expresses the visual and aural perceptions experienced by a sensory body. These expressed experiences may include immediate sensory intake, emotions, memories, dreams, imaginings, or fantasies. Rather than attributing the perceptual agency with which these experiences are associated to a character in the narrative, to the narrator of the story, to the director of the film, or even to a perspective occupied by the "dominant ideology" (though any of these "views" may be represented), Sobchack claims that each shot is properly understood as the film's own view.[6] Each shot is the direct expression of the film's own embodied vision, as its attention shifts focus and perspective. This viewpoint is irreducible to a singular subjectivity because the viewing body, the "film's body," is a composite entity within the collaborative effort[7] that constitutes the film.

Since human beings operate the equipment involved in filmmaking, there is a sense in which the film ends up being an amalgamation of human and machine, a kind of cybernetic organism.[8] In this context, "the film's body" is a descriptive term that includes both the technological instruments that facilitate textual production and reception; perception and expression, and also the intentional and interpretative work of the human beings involved in forming meaning within the project of the film.

Embodiment

Perhaps the most significant contribution of phenomenology to film theory is the emphasis placed on the perceptual engagement of the physical body, rather than on the conscious or subconscious mind, or the sociopolitical body.[9] If we want to describe how human beings experience the world, we must first acknowledge that we know and access the world in and through our bodies.

Empiricist and rationalist epistemology focuses on cognitive understanding, on logic and reason. Often the body is seen as something to be disowned or transcended (because it is full of confusing, undisciplined emotions, and is subject to dreams, memories, hallucinations, and all manner of contingent relationships that allegedly deceive the mind and impede objective knowledge). Where traditional epistemology attempted to overcome subjectivity in order to attain objectivity and access true knowledge, Merleau-Ponty writes that knowledge of the world is always perspectival and has an embodied locus that forms the truth of human experience:

> The perceiving mind is an incarnated mind. I have tried, first of all, to re-establish the roots of the mind in its body and in its world, going against doctrines which treat perception as a simple result of the action of external things on our body as well as against those which insist on the autonomy of consciousness . . . And it is equally clear that one does not account for the facts by superimposing a pure, contemplative consciousness on a thinglike body. (1964, 3–4)

For Merleau-Ponty, the idea of a mind-body dualism, or a transcendental consciousness that generates meaning is *nonsensical* (devoid of meaning in both "senses" of the word—it is both incomprehensible and unavailable to the senses).

When Merleau-Ponty states that our body "is our *point of view on the world*" (1964, 5) in a pervasive and complex way, his words apply with equal veracity to the human body, and to the cyborg filmic body described by Sobchack. The body's functions (including movement, intention, sensory functions, and emotion) contribute to and shape our perception of objects. As spectators we see and hear the film, experiencing it in and through our bodies: we may hold our breath during the suspenseful action sequences, flinch when the villain swings a punch at the hero, jump when a door slams in a horror film, or choke up with tears in sentimental moments. The knowledge or understanding we form of a perceived object cannot be separated from the experience of perception, or from the embodied consciousness doing the perceiving. *Consciousness is incarnate*, as Merleau-Ponty argues so convincingly (1964, 3–4).

We perceive things from a particular perspective, from the position of our own bodies, and therefore a purely objective or omniscient description is an impossibility. The presence of the observer and the acts of observation and description are selective and they influence what we observe and describe. This is true for both the film and its spectators: the observer has a relationship with the observed. The ethical implications of this relationship between the viewer and the viewed, which relate to Merleau-Ponty's claim that perception is inherently intersubjective, embodied, and evaluative, will be traced through the film *Dead Man Walking* as this chapter progresses.

When Merleau-Ponty claims that "perceptual consciousness is the foundational mode of experience" (1964, xviii), he does not mean that all experience can be reduced to perception, but only that perception is a foundation on which other levels of experience rest. There are various modes of consciousness and experience, including a more conceptual consciousness, but the structures of what Merleau-Ponty calls "perceptual consciousness" are fundamental.

Technology

When watching a film our perception is shaped by more than our physical bodies: it is also influenced by cinematic technology[10] and by the position and attitude of the filmic body in relation to the narrative it perceives and articulates. As film spectators our vision is mediated by technology to a significant extent; thus the experience of spectatorship must be described on a fundamental level as a relationship with technology. Stanley Cavell characterizes the material basis of the medium of film as "a succession of automatic world projections," referring to the series of frames moving through the machinery of cinema that express (as well as screen and conceal) aspects of the world (1979, 73). In the cinema, we see the world through the visual agency of the camera: on the movie screen, we are seeing and hearing images that have been recorded and that are being projected. We see the technology (the screen), we see *with* the technology (the camera and the spectator both look at the story world together), and we see *through* the technology (we are largely unaware of the presence of the projector, or of the camera—we see the world through this technology in much the same way that we can see through contact lenses). We also see *in addition to* the technology (we can look away from the screen, or look at one small part of it). We are part of the film, joined in interpretive and immersive embodied relations with it in inseparable symbiosis as we perceive the film as a text, and as we perceive the world through and with the textuality of the cinematic apparatus (see Sobchack 1992, 196–203). So as spectators, we too can be thought of as cyborgs whose perception is technologically enabled and mediated.

The relationship between spectators and the film produces what might be called an intersubjective layering of vision. The visual agencies of a number of viewing subjects are interlinked: the film's body, the characters' bodies, and the spectators' bodies. The technological equipment of filmmaking parallels what Sobchack terms the "incarnate instrumentality" of the human body, directed by the conscious intentions of the filmmakers, hence the expression "intentional technology" in relation to the cinematic apparatus (1992, 165).

The Film's Body

When we think about vision being both embodied and technologically mediated, we begin to realize why Sobchack has said that the film has a body. Sobchack asks, "How might it be legitimate . . . to describe in concrete terms that invisible presence of an other who perceives and expresses perception in the film experience along with, as well as opposed to, the spectator?" (1992, 203). This articulate, intentional, perceiving presence is what she has termed the film's body. The concept of the "film's body" enables us to name the omniscient "other," the viewer who looks at the film's subject when the shots are not an eye-line match related to a particular character's point of view. The film's presence can be like an invisible, mute character inhabiting the screen space, or it can appropriate the perceptual subjectivity of one of the screen characters and take on the role of narrator, but again there will be shots and extradiegetic information that exceed this explanatory framework and that differentiate the film's bodily presence from a human presence. Sobchack's concept of the film's body offers ways of describing perceptual shifts between character positions in film, and accounting for shots that seem to be filmed from no-body's perspective or that "envision" events in ways that human eyes cannot (such as split frames, slow motion, or "bullet time" in Andy and Larry Wachowski's 1999 film *The Matrix* where the viewer moves through space as time momentarily stalls).

The anthropomorphic characterization of the film as having a body is counterintuitive and it fails to describe the experience of viewing a film, thus it at first seems erroneous in phenomenological terms. In particular, conceptualizing and locating a "body" when its instrumental organs are spatiotemporally dispersed, is both challenging and problematic. However, the moment one begins to develop an awareness of the movement of the camera and variations in sound in the film as evidence of the presence and movement of intentionally directed attention, the film's body reveals itself and the accuracy and applicability of Sobchack's terminology becomes evident.[11] As spectators we cannot actually see the film's body, but we can perceive the passage of its attention and intention on the screen. In addition, the concept of the film's body is theoretically productive. In speaking about the film as a body of perceptual experiences and as having embodied perceptual experiences, Sobchack's work offers insight into many of the issues addressed by conventional film theory, especially in terms of realism and spectatorial identification.

In order to illustrate how the film perceives and portrays its subject matter and how spectators experience perceiving the film, I will begin by investigating how perceptual activity is described on film through allusive *mise-en-scene* and shifts in lighting, framing, and focus in the scene where Helen and Matthew first meet in *Dead Man Walking*. In this scene they begin to get to know each other as they navigate their way through a conversation that contains more stumbling blocks than common ground. However, by the end of this first visit to the prison, Helen agrees to try to help Matthew contest his death sentence. Following a rudimentary version of the phenomenological method, I first describe, then thematize, then interpret the text, deciphering how the film itself describes subtle shifts in awareness and response as the two characters converse for the first time.

For the duration of their first meeting that occurs after we have followed Helen's story for the first nine minutes of the film, Helen and Matthew are seated on opposite sides of a sturdy security grill in the Louisiana State Penitentiary. They never appear together in the same frame in this scene, and are initially shot in medium close-up, with the camera alternating between each character's perspectives. Initially the security mesh is more prominent when the camera shoots from Helen's perspective, thereby revealing her more clearly than Matthew, whose character is still unfamiliar to both Helen and the audience. As she looks through the screen at Matthew, the right side of his face is darkened by shadow and partially obscured by the grille. Helen's face is lit softly by a light source motivated by the high window behind Matthew. Because the camera is shooting through the metal screen but not focusing on it, Helen is just slightly out of focus and the geometric pattern of the screen is barely visible over her figure. At this early point in the story the protagonists do not see each other clearly, and neither the spectators nor the film perceive the characters in sharp focus.

The two tentatively question each other about their lives to establish a connection and the film's viewpoint shifts back and forth, following the conversation. When Helen says, "you and I have something in common: we both live with the poor," the subsequent reverse shot depicting Matthew's reaction moves in to show him in close-up, with gentler shadows. At that point the camera's focus is more on his features than on the mesh and we

Figure 4 Dead Man Walking: *A view of Helen, with the security screen barely visible in soft focus.*

Figure 5 Dead Man Walking: *A view of Matthew with the security screen in sharp relief.*

are finally able to see him with the same degree of clarity with which we have become accustomed to viewing Helen.

This equilibrium is maintained until the point in the conversation when they discuss his crime and he says, "I didn't killed nobody. I swear to God I didn't." With those words the lighting and camera angle shift slightly so that the screen catches the light and is thrown into sharp relief, appearing

Figure 6 Dead Man Walking: *Matthew's reaction as Helen says, "Then you and I have something in common. We both live with the poor."*

Figure 7 Dead Man Walking: *Matthew is barely visible through the screen as he denies responsibility for murder.*

almost like a solid wall through which Matthew's face is only just discernible.

This impenetrable visual screen of reflected light is also imposed over Helen in the reverse shot; however, the grille is out of focus, rather than appearing sharp and solid. Helen blinks and the image of her face is intercut with subjective imagery describing what she imagines the crime scene to have looked like: an aerial shot panning from right to left over a dead body—grey flesh in grey light. The screen, which has become a wall between Helen and Matthew, loses prominence again when he begins to talk about his young daughter Allie and shows Helen a picture of his child. It is thrown into sharp relief for a final time (and for the only time, in front of Helen's face) when he sees her hesitate after he asks for her assistance in filing a motion for the appeals court. Then, after she agrees to do her best, their interview is cut short and he passes her the relevant papers through a slot in the grille.

The scene lasts less than five minutes, but it conveys a great deal beyond the content of the dialogue that is exchanged. The film uses the idea (with which the majority viewers are conversant) of the walls or barriers (of prejudice, ignorance, dishonesty, and other forms of difference and distance) that can divide people. The security screen becomes a visual metaphor for this protective and obstructive barrier. The opacity or translucence of the screen varies in response to the degree of resistance or openness each character exhibits in response to the other. The film and the spectators are able to take up positions on either side of the screen, but each character is restricted to her or his own viewing position. Because of this, the audience has the privilege of a sensitive and detailed impression of each character's subjective standpoint in addition to a broader perspective on their interaction, and a sense of the film's own bias (which inclines toward Helen, but also reflects her interest in and involvement with Matthew).

The position of the camera (which prescribes the spectator's viewing position and articulates cinematic space in relation to the sensory bodies of the characters) is very important in this sequence. Cavell writes:

> It is sometimes said, and it is natural to suppose, that the camera is an extension of the eye. Then it ought to follow that if you place the camera at the physical point of view of a character, it will objectively reveal what the character is viewing. But the fact is, if we have been given the idea that the camera is placed so that what we see is what the character sees *as he sees it,* then what is shown to us is not just something seen but a specific mood in which it is seen. (1979, 129)

Cavell is making a valid point about the evaluative, embodied, and contextual nature of perception. However, it is also true that the view we are offered usually only *approximates* a character's point of view unless there is a direct address to camera (when the camera occupies the precise position of the addressee). What we more often see is, of course, the film's own view as it aligns itself closely with a character's visual perspective. Interestingly, we get closest to a true point of view shot (a direct eye-line match, where Matthew is almost looking straight down the barrel into the camera as though meeting Helen's gaze) when the dramatic intensity of the scene is at its highest point.

When Matthew and Helen are awkwardly getting to know one another in the opening moments of the scene, the film's viewing position is always just offset from the characters' own (an indirect eye-line). Yet, between the scene's turning points when the two characters connect ("we both live with the poor") and encounter friction (when Matthew claims his accomplice committed both murders), the film is true to Helen's line of sight. Here the viewer is positioned *as Helen* in screen space and Matthew confronts us, virtually eye to eye, in close proximity. This cinematic strategy works in conjunction with the shifting gradients of light on the wire screen to draw the audience in to share the subjective perceptual experience of the characters. By the end of the scene when the drama is resolved and the tension wanes, the eye-lines also loosen so that Matthew no longer seems to be facing us quite so directly when we are aligned with Helen.

This scene provides an illustration of the capacity of a visual medium to convey layers of information without resorting to explicit verbal cues such as dialogue, interior monologue, or voice-over narration. It also depicts the specific and shifting ethical positions of response and responsibility that arise in a conversational exchange, as discussed in Chapter 1. Indeed, film goes further than a conversation between two parties as the spectators and filmmakers are also implicated in the ethical relations of the dialogue: we too inhabit shifting subject positions and are called upon to make evaluations and offer responses. In its own way, the film traces and expresses the changing ways in which Helen and Matthew perceive each other, conveying a sense that our perception of other human beings is filtered through our own barriers and theirs, and shaped by the mental images, personal resources, and prejudices that inhabit the space between two people. As Matthew and Helen discover that they have something in common (and as spectators also come to realize some of the factors that conspired to bring Matthew to death row), the framing changes from medium-close-up to close-up. This brings the film's body closer to Matthew, and it places him closer to Helen, to the camera, and to the audience. As this technique enables us to perceive him with greater clarity, it also gives the impression that Helen, from whose position Matthew is viewed, experiences a moment of insight into him and his life.

Similarly, in describing Helen's experience when Matthew invokes the name of God to support an outright lie, a novelist would have had to explicitly state something like:

I try to adjust my view of him because it is hard to see through the heavy mesh screen and he tells me to look down sometimes: "This screen can really do a number on your eyes." [. . .] But now I just look at him. I'm not sure how to measure his sincerity. I see the young people getting down on their knees and lying in the cold wet grass. Even if he didn't do the shooting he participated in the kidnappings— not just this couple. There had been others. The silence is heavy. And then he says with anger in his eyes, "I didn't rape [Hope] I never touched her." [. . .] I simply do not know what to make of what he is telling me. I suspend judgment. With the electric chair waiting, with death close like this, who the triggerman was is not the point. Two people are dead, and soon three people will be dead. That for now is the only point. (Prejean 1993, 30 and 39–40)

In the film, Helen does not actually draw away from Matthew in the sense of increasing the physical distance between them when he lies, blasphemes, or expresses bigoted opinions that she finds abhorrent. However, the play of light on the metal grille economically implies the extent to which his words render him temporarily inaccessible to her, and the scant few frames of subjective imagery showing footage of the murder scene evoke a thousand reasons for her to mistrust him. It is evident that Matthew cannot exert the same ethical claim on Helen when he lies to her because his dishonesty acts as a barrier between them, creating a visible imbalance in their relationship on the screen. Film is able to express Helen's experience during these moments economically, depicting what she hears, feels, imagines, sees, and what she looks like as the conversation takes place. As spectators of film, we must attend to all of this information at once, just as we must pay attention to gesture, expression, tone, feelings, and content when we participate in a conversation.

Within the constantly shifting perspectives that find unity on the screen as a narrative lies the film's own viewpoint (though this, in itself, is as unavailable to a singular interpretation as any other). There is a sense in which the film is a participant in the conversations it depicts and also in the larger discourse with the audience. Sobchack refers to the film as a viewing subject, one engaged in perceiving the world through the meaningful, intent gaze of the camera. In Sobchack's innovative conception of cinematic perception, expression, and film spectatorship, *visual behavior* (seeing, looking) is evident in the visibly perceived movement of the camera, and is referred to in the phrase "viewing view." In contrast, Sobchack uses the phrase "viewed view" to indicate the subject the film is looking at: the visible image on screen, that which is visibly produced or expressed by the film's gaze, the *visible behavior*.

The two terms, though distinct, are also conflated in the screen text, implying one another just as the terms subject and object do, since the subject the film is viewing and the object on-screen that we witness it to have viewed are inseparable in the cinema. In the process of recording both visual activity and visible activity, what *is* happening as the filmic cyborg actively participates in looking and what *has* happened (the filmed events) can become confused in the context of moving pictures of vision in motion. Sobchack suggests that:

> The aim of "classical" narrative is to cover the film's perceptual tracks, to disguise the "extra-diegetic" situation of the narrative's narrator, and so to transform an intentional and discursive *activity* (the viewing view) into the intended and produced *object* that is *histoire* (the viewed view). (Sobchack 1992, 227)

This transformation is effected partly by means of the technique of suture utilized within realist conventions of film editing, and most obviously in the shot-reverse-shot convention in which the narrator's position in the text is disguised when a character's subjective point of view is adopted in order to convey elements of experience.

For phenomenologists, realism in the cinema is not a matter of presenting a truthful, factual, or objective picture of the world, but instead, it is a matter of accurately describing the experience of perceiving. Thus, in a point-of-view shot spectators do not "really" see through a particular character's eyes, or hear with their ears (just as we do not "really" infiltrate their interiority during subjective sound and image sequences), but with such techniques, the film does express the perception of that character in a manner that seeks to convey something authentic about their experience at that moment. Of course film can never be totally "realistic" because the instrumental mediation of perception transforms it, reduces it, or amplifies it so the nature of the engagement with the intended perceptual object is subtly different as a result of the mediation and selection process. The attempt to convey the experience of perception cinematically is itself limited and transformed by the instrumental mediation of perception.

Sometimes, in an extreme close-up for instance, we might only be able to see the eyes or mouth of a character framed on the screen. Unless a human being is situated within close range of the object of vision (about ten centimeters), an extreme close-up differs from "real" embodied perceptual experience, but it can reflect real attention. This is the case in the scene when Helen faints in the prison chaplain's office in *Dead Man Walking*. Helen's physical proximity to the priest does not alter, but the camera zooms in to focus on the priest's lips, as though to indicate her effort to focus her concentration on the ugly words issuing forth from his mouth.

Sobchack explains such differences by pointing out that human perception is similar to filmic perception in terms of function and intent, but different in material form (1992, 243). Obviously there are many material differences between human sight and the vision of a camera. For example, human eyes cannot zoom in when our attention approaches something of central importance; still, film typically sees "more or less humanly" as its point of reference is human embodied vision (1992, 182).

Near the middle of *Dead Man Walking* there is a semisubjective sequence in which the film expresses what Helen is experiencing as she drives along, looking out the window; remembering fragments of her past, recalling news bulletins relating to Matthew's crime; thinking about what he has told her about himself, his victims, and the night of the murder. She imagines Matthew and the victims, Hope and Walter, as children. The sequence includes flashes in her imagination of the murder scene, shown from Matthew's perspective in accordance with the details he has confided in her: a retrospective narrative representing an altered state of consciousness and (to the extent that it fails to account accurately for his own responsibility), a lie. Although the scene is a montage of images from a variety of sources, not all of them visibly present in Helen's physical environment (she occupies a moving vehicle in a pastoral landscape and her subjective musings are intercut with shots of the landscape through which she travels), the footage can be described as realistic in phenomenological terms in that it articulates a variety of different forms of perception and expresses ways in which the world is subjectively experienced.[12] This sequence also highlights the point that human experience consists of more than what is directly perceived in the physical world. Helen's attention travels from the physical landscape surrounding her, to her inner world, and from there back and forward in time and space, traversing different perspectives and subject positions as she explores her own past, the present, and the pasts of Matthew, Walter, and Hope to form a more holistic picture of the situation she faces in the present time of the narrative.

Spectatorship

Phenomenology is a methodology that has generated several different understandings of film spectatorship with divergent emphases,[13] but all touch on the idea of spectatorship as a dialogic exchange of meaning,[14] a relationship between the subjects and objects of perception. Sobchack argues that filmic perception is an analog of spectatorial perception; we relate to and engage with the film's mode of vision and with its intentional consciousness as it narrates the story. The above example from *Dead Man Walking* illustrates that although film always expresses its own embodied visual consciousness, within this it also borrows or adopts the perspectives, bodies, and situations of the other subjects who inhabit its vision. That is, it takes on the points of view of the screen characters, enunciating their subjectivity through its own.[15] Hence, although the metaphor of dialogue is a good one, it may be that spectatorial participation in a film is actually more like a polylogue or multivoiced conversation, since we also engage with the characters.

Intersubjectivity

Theorizing film as the visible, audible expression of its own perception, and theorizing spectatorship in terms of sharing and participating in that perceptual activity emphasizes the importance of intersubjectivity to perceptual understanding. That is, understanding arises in and through embodied perceptual experiences and in conjunction or connection with that which is perceived. This is why Sobchack argues that the "address of the eye" instantiated in cinema "enables both the spectator and the film to imaginatively reside in each other—even as they are both discretely embodied and uniquely situated" (1992, 261). In other words, a process of actual (sensory) and imaginative "mutual incorporation" happens in the shifting awareness of self and other that occurs in an exchange of gazes, or when we are able to see something from another's perspective. Phenomenologists understand being a perceiving subject and being a perceived object to be *reversible roles*. This point, the inseparability of perception from the perceiver, of object from subject is crucial for film theory.[16] *Dead Man Walking* often draws attention to the reversibility of seeing and being seen by capturing the play of reflections in glass. This, in conjunction with the shot-reverse-shot convention, provides a visual metaphor for the shared or intersubjective nature of perception and understanding by articulating the transient and multiple subject positions available to an individual through identifying with other people's points of view.

For example, the day before Matthew's execution he asks Helen, "Do you ever get lonely?" wondering whether she misses the opportunity for close personal relationships that he imagined she gave up when she chose the life of a nun over that of a wife and mother. Her answer (which reminds him that she does enjoy intimate relationships, and that if they had taken the form of family life she would most likely be at home with a partner and children rather than conversing with him) reveals more about the nature of shared connections with others due to the way in which the scene is framed and edited. As Matthew asks the question we see him from Helen's perspective, looking at her through a partition of perforated glass that separates them from each other (as a measure of prison security). The film looks over Helen's left shoulder and the edge of her body is just visible in the lower right hand side of the screen, framing the spectator's point of view. In addition to seeing Matthew from Helen's perspective, we can also see Helen herself, both at the side of the frame, as described, and as a reflection in the glass. When Helen answers, the shot is reversed and Matthew's body is visible in the glass and his head can be seen on the edge of the lower left section of the frame. By expressing a vision of Helen and Matthew in which they are held close together in the same frame, despite the fact that they are separated by circumstance and by physical barriers, this sequence illustrates their interconnectedness. (In this respect it also expresses a higher degree of intimacy than in their initial meeting, when they were never shown together in the frame.) The scene also reveals something about the way in which selfhood is constituted, at least in part, by other human

Figure 8 Dead Man Walking: *Reflections in the glass suggest intersubjectivity: Helen can see herself as Matthew sees her, when he looks through the glass at her. The shot shows the viewing subject, Helen, as well as the object of her gaze, Matthew.*

beings' perceptions. In looking at Matthew, the reflection in the glass enables Helen to see herself as he sees her—as a visible object as well as a perceiving subject.[17]

This shot arrangement is repeated during the execution scene, immediately after Helen says to Matthew, "I want the last thing you see in this world to be the face of love. Will you look at me when they do this thing? I'll be the face of love for you." Helen and the others gathered to witness Matthew's execution are in a separate room from him, looking at him through a windowed wall as he is strapped down in preparation for the lethal injection. In visual alignment with Matthew, we see Helen reach out to him and we (the film and the spectators) see his reflection in the glass as he looks back at her and their outstretched hands seem to touch across the intervening space in an intersubjective moment of copresence.

Here, rather than depicting them as isolated individuals, framed separately, the film is expressing the sense in which Helen and Matthew's perception of one another is an intersubjective experience in which they are united in a moment of mutual recognition. It is the nature of their finely attuned perception of one another that enables this intimate connection.

The sharing of experience and understanding is expressed by using reflections to articulate a view of the two characters somehow touching one another, linked by a gaze bridging their actual physical separation. The act of observing is shown along with the observed object. In seeing Helen, Matthew can also see himself as his own act of perception is rendered visible in the glass: the screen between them is a window, a semipermeable barrier, and a mirror.[18] This particular sequence of shots can be understood as an analogy for the way in which film traces and reverses (expresses) the process of perception on the cinema screen and, by extension as a way of understanding the intersubjective nature of perception, lending weight to Merleau-Ponty's idea that "perception takes place precisely in the indistinguishability of perceiving and being perceived, of activity and passivity, and in the reversibility of seeing and being seen" (see Rascaroli 1997, 235).

Film expresses a human mode of perception in which subjectivity and objectivity imply one another, as the above example illustrates. As the camera shifts from a position aligned with Helen's point of view to a vantage point from which she is viewed in the shot-reverse-shot convention, we see that film traces "the constant movement of the cinematographic perception-image from the subjective to the objective and vice versa" (Rascaroli 1997, 235). As I claim in the final chapter, the ability to exercise such a versatile, mobile, and flexible mode of perception so that attention can be focused first on detail, then expanded to include a broader, more general perspective is important to ethical understanding.

As spectators sitting in the dark, looking toward the bright screen, we slip through the fluid space between subjectivity and objectivity, feeling sometimes within, and sometimes outside the narrative world. The film moves between "subjective" and "objective" shots (as it alternates between its own perceptual subjectivity and the utilization of subjective sound and imagery to enunciate the subjectivity of its characters). In engaging us in the dialogic nature of spectatorship and the reversibility of subjectivity and objectivity, the cinema instantiates a deeply felt, human requirement for intersubjectivity, a need to be understood ourselves and to be able to see things from another's point of view. The reciprocal transition between self and other, subject and object is central to the way human beings access meaning, experience the world, and understand ourselves. Filmic techniques such as the shot-reverse-shot convention replicate or represent patterns of perceiving and engaging with others that are central to ethical forms of perceiving and engaging (the reversibility of perception, intersubjectivity, entwining distance, and involvement). This is also so for ethical understanding as Susan Babbitt points out: "Whereas rational deliberation does require attention to details, it is often necessary to take, or at least to move toward, a "distanced" theoretical perspective to be able to see which particular details are relevant and for what purpose" (1996, 201). In film this "distance" is not "opposed to involvement" (Babbitt 1996, 204).

As spectators we experience an intersubjective involvement in film which operates on a number of levels, as illustrated in the execution scene described above. As a human component of the filmic cyborg, we engage with the film's subjective perception of the situation as it articulates its own point of view in an evaluative, selective manner. At the same time the film is describing the sterile, cold environment of the death chamber with stark lighting and allusive *mise-en-scene*. The film is also voicing emotion or mood with the mournful musical sound track. In this sequence the film is borrowing the bodies of its characters to articulate or express their optical point of view, rendering this information available to spectators so that we literally have our sensory experience aligned with that of Helen and Matthew momentarily. But, once again, the characters in the room are experiencing more than just what they see: they are all also imagining or seeing the murder in their mind's eyes, and remembering the murder victims, feeling their presence in the room. These experiences are expressed as interstitial flashes of the murder scene, and as the faces of Hope and

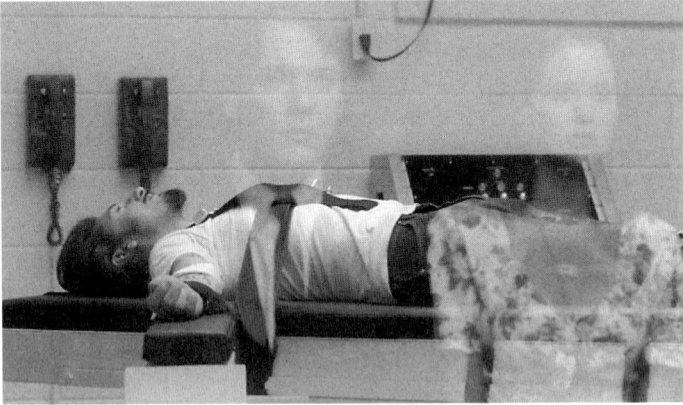

Figure 9 Dead Man Walking: *Walter and Hope's presence is superimposed over Matthew's death, expressing levels of experience beyond visual perception.*

Walter superimposed over the image of Matthew's death. The transition between shots exclusive to the film's subjective vantage point (such as the bird's eye views of both the execution and the murder scene), and those also associated with the viewing positions and subjective perceptions of the characters makes us, as spectators, perceive an overall picture of the situation, comprised of varying perspectives.

****

A phenomenological approach to film offers a way of describing the inherently selective, evaluative nature of perception and the actual process of shifting perspectives that is revealed as we (film, characters, and spectators) develop a narrative understanding of a situation. Sobchack has claimed that camera movement and optical movement in a film can indicate changes in perspective, attention, or frame of reference, or objects swelling or diminishing in importance in relation to the viewing subject (1990, 25–27). As the examples from *Dead Man Walking* have demonstrated, tracing this movement of attention can lead to an ethical or political analysis of the way in which a film takes up its subject matter and exposes it to the audience's equally evaluative gaze. As spectators, we know what the film and the screen characters value or "see as important" when shots aligned with their point of view zoom in, pull focus, or track in close. The long takes and the long scenes can be understood as moments of sustained concentration or focused attention, hence the relationship between perception and evaluation is exposed by film as it expresses perception in intentional and qualitative ways.[19]

The inherently *evaluative* nature of perception is made visible by the film's expressive acts that reveal the unseen judgments of seeing, and articulate the unnoticed selectivity of hearing, making these perceptual activities visible and audible and subject to analysis. As practiced here, a phenomenological approach entails describing how the film describes and narrates reality. This can include describing how the film's body inhabits space, experiences time, how it focuses attention, what moods and judgments it expresses aurally and visually, what and who it ignores. We might also describe the use of a nondiegetic world music score juxtaposed with the quintessentially American sound of Bruce Springsteen as a metalinguistic evocation to the universality of the issues the film confronts, and the narrative structure and editing in terms of moments of insight and foresight, oversight, and hindsight. As film spectators or analysts, the phenomenological approach to film involves thinking of acts of perception as evaluative acts, and thinking of the film as articulating its own viewpoint as it expresses perception.

Merleau-Ponty's phenomenological point that perception is *embodied* is also of significance because it suggests that "ethical insight" is a felt experience, rather than something that can be grasped on a purely conceptual level. Indeed, as Merleau-Ponty claims, all knowledge of the world is accessed and shaped by the instrumental capacities of our physical bodies. Ethical deliberation, therefore, calls upon more faculties and resources than rational thought alone: it necessitates embodied actions and responses including sensory perception, emotive and imaginative experiences, and practices of attention in which the ethical agent's mind and body are a functional unity. Spectatorial involvement in the cyborg filmic body is a technologically mediated form of experience which is important because, as it entails both sensory engagement of the physical body and intersubjective engagement with other perceiving bodies, it has the capacity to evoke a keenly felt sense of shared understanding.

When Merleau-Ponty claims that "our subjectivity is an intersubjectivity" (cited in Rascaroli 1997, 243) his words relate to the kind of connectedness to others which is both embodied and illustrated by film. Film enables us simultaneously to see, to see how we see (as the film makes visible the process and practice of perception), and to see through the eyes of other viewing subjects. In film spectatorship, the interconnectedness of subjectivity is experienced on a number of levels as we participate in the perceptual activity of the filmic cyborg, as we borrow the perspectives of the film characters whose subjectivity is enunciated by the film, and (often) as we construct shared interpretations of the narrative with other spectators when discussing the film.

This intersubjective quality of cinematic experience offers insight into multiple perspectives in a way that raises awareness of the situatedness of all action within the field of specific interests and intentions, and within a broader sociocultural context. The sense of actively feeling the way through other people's stories, and into their perspectives and their lived experience, differs significantly from a cognitive interpretation and analysis of the salient ethical rules or principles operative in a given context. With important qualifications relating to the content and context of that which is perceived in particular films by individual audience members, the medium of film potentially offers richer insights than those provided by the abstract hypothetical examples which are often the basis for the analysis of complex ethical issues. Indeed, the cyborg experience of film spectatorship effects a transformation and synthesis of perspectives that is capable of inflecting and refashioning perceptions of self and other. Film can be involved in the development of ethical understanding as it extends the individual's range of experience, understanding, and empathy into contexts that she or he might not otherwise occupy, revealing how the concrete conditions of human lives shape moral character, decisions, and possibilities.

The intersubjective bonds of engagement and attention that link a story's interpreters to its characters are, according to Adam Newton, ethical relations. Following Newton, ethics is a constitutive force in the process of narration because it is involved in the acts of selection, discrimination, and composition during the author's creative work, and in the interpretation of stories by audiences. Of course film does not necessarily express a *positive* or politically correct vision—it can also express inhumane, racist, sexist, and homophobic modes of perception—hence narrative content and cinematic style can have adverse effects on audience members. The chapters to follow elaborate on the different levels and processes through which forms of ethical evaluation are involved in our engagement with film narratives, and the ways in which narrative structures personal identity, experience, and interpretations of ethical life.

Notes

1. While this research concentrates on narrative film, it also has relevance to other forms of screen media such as animation, video art, computer games, narrative television,

and documentary film. Teasing out the differences and similarities between the modes of spectatorship, conventions of signification, and forms of narration entailed in these different screen media is beyond the scope of this work, but some of these concerns have been taken up by other theorists. For instance, Sobchack discusses a range of "concretely visible ethical gazes" in an excellent article on documentary entitled "Inscribing Ethical Space" (1984), revised and updated in *Carnal Thoughts* (2004). Laura Marks uses phenomenology to account for the sensory impact of experimental film and video art in *The Skin of the Film* (2000) and *Touch* (2002).

2. In "Aural Objects" Christian Metz draws attention to the fact that phenomenology is not only "a certain kind of relation with the world," but also a culturally specific product of that relation (1992, 315).

3. Making a related point, Nussbaum claims that works of narrative fiction "which promote identification and emotional reaction cut through self-protective stratagems, requiring us to see and to respond to many things that may be difficult to confront—and they make this process palatable by giving us pleasure in the very act of confrontation" (1995, 6).

4. Book club members will be aware of the difference between reading as a solitary pursuit and sharing impressions and interpretations of a narrative together with a group of interested people.

5. Of course, some films such as art films and experimental cinema using what David Bordwell and Kristen Thompson (2004) term abstract and associational form or parametric narration have no intention of approximating normal or naturalized facets of human perception or experience. For instance, Godard often deliberately creates a disjunction between signifier and signified by running the sound track out of sync with the visual images so that what we hear has little to do with what we see. Other films aspire to a form of visual poetry articulating a feeling or atmosphere, rather than narrating a sequence of identifiable sights and sounds. However, such films still express humanly recognizable forms of perceptual experience.

6. That all shots are point of view shots in a film (1992, 22) is part of what Sobchack seeks to articulate with the phrase "viewing view," a term discussed in more detail in the section of this chapter titled "The Expression of Perception."

7. Though phenomenology acknowledges the importance of the director's intentions in creating a film, in comparison with *auteur* theory it offers a very different way of understanding the director's input. Filmmaking is a collaborative process in which film is more than the sum of its parts: camera, lighting, edit suite, projector, technical crew, actors, audience and so forth. Each one of those parts is necessary to film, but only in a dynamic, functional unity do they constitute sufficient conditions for the existence of a film (see Sobchack 1992, 169). In a phenomenological analysis, by contrast, the director is not privileged: she or he is just one part of the human component of the film. For this reason, I use the term "filmmakers" to refer to the combined intentionality of the screenwriters, cast, and crew.

8. Cybernetics involves the replication or replacement of human functions with mechanical or electrical systems.

9. Sobchack has explored this theme explicitly in an article entitled "Is Any Body Home? Embodied Imagination and Visible Evictions" (1999), reprinted in *Carnal Thoughts* (2004, 179–204).

10. The ideological implications of the relationship between cinematographic technology and the viewing subject have been explored by Jean-Louis Baudry in work that draws on philosophy, psychoanalysis and phenomenology (1986; 1992). The idea of spectatorship as a relationship with technology, as well as with fantasy, is also evident in the writing of Christian Metz (1992). Conceptualizing a film as anthropomorphic, or filmmakers as cyborg beings dates back to the earliest years of cinema. The Soviet filmmaker Dziga Vertov saw the movie camera as a "mechanical eye" that fused with the cinematographer's own vision to reveal and transform the world viewed on the screen by cinema spectators. His most famous film *Man with a Movie Camera* (1929) reveals decisions that were made about selecting and editing footage in order to make the film audience aware of how filmmaking technologies manipulate, intervene in, and construct the "realities" they screen.

11. For instance, *Dead Man Walking* expresses a very sensitive, nuanced, perceptive form of attention, primarily through sophisticated and subtle cinematographic techniques, though also by means of editing and *mise-en-scene*. Other films, such as *Lost Highway* utilize the soundscape extensively to articulate the intentional presence of the film's body. In *Once Were Warriors* the film's body is present as an unobtrusive witness, whose only intervention in the narrative seems to be the selection of subject matter, and in *Nil by Mouth* we are aware of the film as an interested, involved "interviewer."

12. Film can describe the atmosphere or feeling of being in a certain place using the elements of *mise-en-scene* and it can "intend" texture, temperature, and scent, though we do not actually feel or smell the screen (see Sobchack 1992, 185). Think of *The Cook, The Thief, His Wife and Her Lover* (Greenaway, 1989) in which the stench of the alley, the heat of the kitchen, and the atmosphere of the different rooms are conveyed through color, light, and costume. It is not realistic for everything to change color when one walks through a doorway, but Greenaway's film effectively expresses the way different spaces and atmospheres are perceived and experienced by characters in the story world.

13. See, for example, Casebier (1991), Singer (1990), Stadler (1990), and Studlar (1990a).

14. For instance, Harald Stadler argues, "Reality constitutes us as much as we constitute it. The human existence is a dialogue with the world" (1990, 40).

15. "For the most part, however, even as a film occasionally borrows upon the bodies and situations of the other subjects who inhabit its vision (as, in fact, we humans do also), a film inscribes its perception as the natural and easy result of an ambiguous and embodied visual consciousness" (Sobchack 1992, 246).

16. According to Merleau-Ponty,

The phenomenological world is not pure being, but the sense which is revealed where the paths of my various experiences intersect, and also where my own and other people's intersect and engage with each other like gears. It is thus inseparable from subjectivity and intersubjectivity, which find their unity when I either take up my past experiences in those of the present or other people's in my own life. (Merleau-Ponty 2002, xxii)

Here Merleau-Ponty uses the term "being" in reference to Heidegger's existential phenomenology, arguing that our perception of the world makes sense in terms of personal
experiences (including memories, behavior, acts of consciousness) and intersubjective
engagements with others. Interestingly, he believes that the "objective" world and the "subject" who experiences it meet in the process of sensory perception such that there is "no
distance between me and it" (Merleau-Ponty 2002, 3). For instance, perception leaves
no distance between music that I hear and the ears that I hear it with, or between the "objective" aspects of a person that I see or feel and the "subjective" process of experiencing
those sensations: "I might be said to have sense experience precisely to the extent that
I coincide with the sensed" (Merleau-Ponty 2002, 3). Subjectivity and objectivity may
indeed coincide in the sensory encounter, but this notion of "coinciding" with objects that
we sense is disturbing if one considers its implications for smelling a fart or living in an ugly
and polluted environment, or overdosing on films directed by Quentin Tarantino or Todd
Solondz.

17. In Chapter 12 of *Carnal Thoughts*, "The Passion of the Material: Toward a Phenomenology of Interobjectivity," Vivian Sobchack discusses the "co-constitutive experience
we have of ourselves and others as material objects" (2004, 296). She argues that the
origin of ethical responsibility "lies in the subjective realization of our own objectivity"
(2004, 310) and details the ways in which we sometimes experience ourselves as objects
and momentarily stand removed from our own subjectivity, feeling what it is like to be
perceived or treated as an object. In Sobchack's terms, a film character might then be understood as a "*subjective object* whose intentionality and alterity can be sensed from *without*"
(2004, 290).

18. In a sense, the viewer's position is also inscribed in the intersubjective dynamics of
perception. Though the spectator is never visibly present on the cinema screen, in the
experience of viewing a film the spectator is vicariously present within the story world in
the image or gaze of a character with whom we identify. In an analysis of spectatorial identification in the cinema Metz makes the psychoanalytic distinction between primary
identification (in which we recognize ourselves or our own image, as we do during the formation of the ego in the "mirror phase" of psychological development) and secondary
identification (in which we identify with others perceived to be similar to ourselves, such as
screen characters). According to Metz's "Identification, Mirror" in *Psychoanalysis and the
Cinema: The Imaginary Signifier*, we also experience identification with the camera as a
transcendental subject (1977, 42–52).

19. The evaluative nature of perception is not only related to ethical value, but also to
aesthetic value, practical value, ideological value, and so forth.

3

Losing the Plot:
Narrative Structure and Ethical Identity

This chapter questions the role of narration in understanding ourselves and our interactions with others. Like its sister *Mulholland Drive* (2001), the film *Lost Highway* (David Lynch, 1997) raises questions of personal identity, responsibility, and accountability. Its convoluted storyline and unconventional characterization furnish a space within which the concepts of narrative, ethics, and identity are intertwined and unraveled. Narration is an important way in which people structure knowledge and it plays a significant role in self-understanding and understandings of interpersonal relations.[1] *Lost Highway* exposes the ruptures that form in the absence of an intelligible narrative structure.

Narrative, in so far as it involves the synthesis or interweaving of disparate elements, has a dialectical structure. Following Paul Ricoeur, I characterize identity in terms of the synthesis of past actions with future possibilities, and as a dialectic relation between individuation from, and identification with others. I argue that the structural characteristics of narrative lead to a form of understanding that is unified, yet also elliptical in nature. As this narrative mode of understanding is central to both self-understanding and ethical understanding, it follows that narrative also structures ethical identity.

Narratives typically have a three part structure: a beginning, a middle, and an end that form a meaningful unit in which changing relationships between various characters, events, and elements are described. This structure is central to rendering life meaningful in a number of related ways: it is instrumental in the configuration[2] of knowledge; it is a precondition for considering, performing, and accounting for intentional, goal-oriented

66

actions, and it is fundamental to conceptions of personal and ethical identity. After detouring through narrative theory in order to develop these ideas, I will elaborate on their significance through an analysis of *Lost Highway*.

Lost Highway's reception by spectators is reliant on the process of narration and, although the film lacks a conventional narrative structure overall, it includes scenes and sequences that are intelligible as stories. Each of these scenes has elements that link it to other scenes, though there are never sufficient links to draw the entire film together into a unified story. Even if audience members interpret the entire film as episodic glimpses into the lives of doppelgangers living in parallel worlds, or as the psychotic delusions of a disturbed mind, we remain uncertain whose story it is, what they did to whom, when, and why. It is as though the film itself is paranoid, and intent on restricting the disclosure of information in order to protect its secrets. Throughout the film, characters and spectators are introduced to a set of peculiarly related people and events that intersect at intervals, but do not connect to form a coherent causal chain or overall pattern. Despite this, spectators never cease to seek narrative motivation and resolution. This chapter investigates the different ways in which identity is problematized in *Lost Highway*, tracing the repercussions of the various dislocations of psychological and physiological continuity present in the film.

We encounter Robert Blake's nameless character, a ghoulish man with a video camera, a ghastly laugh, supernatural powers, and make up reminiscent of German Expressionist horror films. We are also presented with a cool central character called Fred Madison (played by Bill Pullman)—a man who may or may not be as crazy as his name suggests, who is uncertain whether he killed his wife, Renee, and whose focal position in the plot is later inexplicably usurped by another man, Pete, (played by Balthazar Getty) whose life and memories overlap incompletely with Fred's. The events on the night of Fred's transformation and on the morning of Renee's murder remain swathed in mystery.

As spectators we are left floundering in the protagonists' own confusion and in the labyrinthine body of the film text itself. Even when characters move from one room to the next they travel through darkness: their destination and course of passage are concealed by indeterminate moments in black screen space that compel us to strain our eyes in futile attempts to perceive the undisclosed mysteries of the film's internal cavity. By scrutinizing the way *Lost Highway* and the characters within it have been constructed, and the ways in which spectators work toward interpreting the film, I hope to show more clearly the place narration has in everyday life. The development of narrative meaning is, as I have suggested, an ethical activity that relates to ontological and epistemological issues. Unlike the chapters that take a phenomenological approach to film, the emphasis of the following analysis of *Lost Highway* rests on narrative structure and character function, rather than on cinematic style, sensory impact, or spectatorial identification.

Life, Narrative, and Intelligibility

Beginning, then, with *Lost Highway's* incomprehensibility as a complete story featuring a consistent cast of protagonists, the very denial of narrative cohesion makes it evident that narrative is instrumental in our efforts to make sense of the world: it is a mode of explanation that assists interpretation by providing temporal order, describing interconnections, and rendering complex causal relationships intelligible. Classical Hollywood narration relies on a fairly stable, formulaic structure supported by a set of familiar screen conventions as articulated by David Bordwell, Kristen Thompson, and Janet Staiger in *The Classical Hollywood Cinema* (1985). Typically, narratives follow a three-act structure in which the plot is kick-started by a catalyst that disrupts the initial equilibrium of the story world, creating an enigma or narrative question that fuels audience interest and generates goals for the protagonist. The middle of the story follows a causal chain in which individual characters play clearly defined roles motivated to solve the enigma and attain or thwart the principal protagonist's goals and desires. Conflict between the protagonist and the antagonist drives the plot forward, whatever form the forces obstructing the hero might take. The tension between these opposing forces reaches a crisis point in the third act and is resolved in the climax, providing a reassuring answer to the questions posed in the narrative. All stories are narrated and understood relative to the perspectives and values of those who construct and engage with them, but in classical Hollywood narration the conventions of continuity editing, unobtrusive cinematography, and realist sound design frequently elide the narrator's perspective and present it as an objective and ideologically neutral viewpoint on a story that unfolds naturally in space and time. One aspect of attempting to make sense of *Lost Highway* involves the ways in which audience members relate it to their own experiences of space, time, causality, human relationships, and conflict. In this way, the meaning of the story comes to life within a social and ethical space as well as within a spatiotemporal context.

The second sense in which narrative is involved in ascribing meaning to human existence occurs on a prefigurative level: before purposeful actions even take place there is a sense in which they are, to a certain extent, narratively structured. Intentional actions are motivated and teleological, and they are situated within a temporal frame that corresponds to narrative form. In the words of Brian Fay:

> As teleological, actions necessarily look toward the future, at some possible state of affairs that the act is supposed to bring about. As motivated by reasons, actions necessarily look backward to the past, to one's situation and how one got there. The moment of acting is precisely the coming together of the agent's sense of his or her past history, present situation and future possibilities. But note that this temporal dimension has a narrative structure: a beginning (the past), a middle (the present), and an end (the future). (Fay 1996, 191–192)

By this Fay means that a narrative structure of understanding is necessary as a condition for the possibility of intentional action, and that narrative is the form from which such action originates. We think forward in time to predict the outcomes of our actions, to organize our actions into an integrated sequence oriented toward short and long term goals, just as the plot of a story unfolds in a particular order with one thing following on from and relating to another, as it moves toward dramatic resolution.

Not only does intentional action rest on narrative structure, but narrative structure also provides the means for understanding and accounting for human action. If ethics relies on the capacity to have intentions, to make choices, and to take responsibility for them, then narration is intrinsic to deliberation and accountability. Later I will take up these notions of ethical responsibility and accountability in relation to the characters Fred and Pete in order to demonstrate that it is through narrative construction and interpretation that we are able to grasp and articulate causal sequences unfolding over time.

Turning now to the third aspect of narrative's importance in the ascription of meaning to human life, personal identity can be conceptualized in terms of a life story. In his influential book *After Virtue*, Alasdair MacIntyre develops the idea of a life story in which narrative identity is characterized by its embeddedness, contextual particularity, and its inherently relational, holistic nature (1981, 203–207). According to MacIntyre, each element of a life or of a narrative is made sense of in terms of the entire story, with each part relating to and connecting with others. Furthermore, the roles and relationships that define an individual's circumstances give form to a unique social identity around which particular moral responsibilities and claims are located:

> The story of my life is always embedded in the story of those communities from which I derive my identity . . . the self has to find its moral identity in and through its membership in communities such as those of the family, the neighborhood, the city and the tribe. (MacIntyre 1981, 205)

Thus moral identity is in large part the story of our connections with others,[3] but this presupposes (as a necessary condition) an internal interrelatedness: the narrative unity of personal identity.

Narrative is crucial to theorizing personal identity because it is uniquely able to articulate the complex interrelatedness of our identities with others and accommodate the changes that a person experiences over the span of her or his life, retaining a sense that these differences are integrated aspects of the same self. Even if severe trauma, extreme change, psychosis, or injury were to cause a radical disjunction to the extent that a person would describe their experience in terms of leading a double life, or having a plural or fragmented persona, the understanding of a life as belonging to someone is associated with its narratibility (the narrative must have a narrator). The necessity of "narratability" in this sense is made evident by the uncertainty that film spectators feel and the difficulty encountered in relating to characters in *Lost Highway*.

As stated previously, narrative form is distinguished by the capacity to link together disparate strands, unifying them within one interrelated whole. Terms like scene, chapter, and episode (which may often be applied to points of rupture or discontinuity in a person's life as in "creating a scene," "ending a chapter," or "having an episode") are reliant on the concept of ongoing narrative development and are made intelligible by it. For this reason the hypothetical examples used by philosophers such as Locke, Hume, and Parfit[4] in their attempts to explore personal identity in terms of memory, psychological continuity, and bodily identity are inconclusive. While they divide human lives unnaturally into parts, they do not acknowledge that the parts themselves are fragments of narratives, and that a narrative that is capable of unifying all of the parts is required to give an adequate account of personal identity. MacIntyre claims that theorists wrestling with the problem of personal identity "have failed to see that a background has been omitted, the lack of which makes the problem insoluble.

That background is provided by the concept of a story and of that kind of unity of character which a story requires" (1981, 202). Narrative, in this sense, can be seen to provide the background picture, schema, or framework that encapsulates identity, establishing the horizons that frame a whole life and also frame significant but smaller sections within it. Again, in *Lost Highway* we lose focus on the framework of space, time, character, and value in which identity and narrative are normally bound.

The idea that we understand ourselves as we narrate our own life stories, rather than understanding ourselves in terms of a set of qualities or characteristics, or as subjects affected by discreet events and relationships is associated with the Aristotelian notion of character virtue.[5] Virtue ethics can be understood to be narratively structured in that virtue is a character trait or disposition to the good that is embedded in relationships and behavior spread over an entire life. In other words, ethical virtue is comprehensible only as part of a narrative pattern. Hence, lack of narrative coherence within a life story undermines the intelligibility of virtue and responsibility; it erodes the very possibility of moral identity. The insight that a given virtue becomes an integral part of the self, incorporated into moral identity when practiced over time, helps to illuminate the ethical implications of Ricoeur's theory of narrative identity.

Personal Identity and Narrative Identity

Ricoeur suggests that identity and narrative can be understood as sharing a dialectical structure in which the synthesis of the thesis and antithesis develops over time (1991f). According to Ricoeur, narrative provides the structure within which the dialectic of individuality or selfhood (*ipse*, Latin; *ipsete*, French) and identicality or sameness (*idem*, Latin; *mimete*, French) produce personal identity. Individual differences and selfsameness are two connected aspects of personal identity.[6] These two senses in which personal identity is understood (as something identifiably distinct or different from all others, and as something identical to itself, an unchanging essence) are central to Ricoeur's theory of narrative identity and they will provide points of entry for the discussion of personal identity in *Lost Highway*.

The distinction between these two aspects of identity is interesting in relation to spectatorial identification with screen characters. Recognizing aspects of oneself in another is what Ricoeur terms "acquired identification," a process that involves incorporating difference or otherness into an individual so that the self becomes a composite entity (Ricoeur 1992, 121).

This is best explained by Diana Fuss, who writes: "Identification is the detour through the other that defines a self . . . [It] is, from the beginning, a question of *relation*, of self to other, subject to object, inside to outside" (1995, 2–3). Thus it is through "identifications with values, norms, ideals, models and heroes" that self-understanding is deepened (Ricoeur 1992, 121). In film, spectators remain different from characters in the story even while recognizing commonality with them.[7] In this sense, the act of identification with others shows that personal identity has a plurality within its own narrative unity as it is intersubjectively formed and recognized through shared narratives.

Lost Highway disrupts narrative conventions so completely that both viewers and characters are left with a pervasive sense of disorientation. As a consequence of being frustrated in attempts to construct a story from the plot of the film, we come to realize how crucial narrative is in explaining and understanding ourselves and others, as well as accounting for unfolding relationships and events. In the end, audience members are uncertain who the characters in *Lost Highway* are, and remain unclear about how they stand in relation to each other because their stories cannot be understood. It is difficult for spectators to relate to the film's characters because the dialectic of selfhood and sameness is not organized in terms of recognizable individuals with narrative identities. We speak about a person "not being themselves" if they are showing signs of lunacy (here *idem* or the component of constancy and sameness in identity is undermined), and we are equally unsettled if we are unable to distinguish between two selves that ought to be unique, as when we are confronted with identical twins or clones. (In the latter case *ipse*, that aspect of identity comprising the selfhood of an individual or the individuality of a self, is challenged.) *Lost Highway* meddles with both of these identity relations.

David Lynch is well known as a director who disrupts the conventions, norms, and expectations of Hollywood cinema. The opening sequence of *Lost Highway* in which we first encounter Fred Madison immediately destabilizes the viewer. We hear a low, ominous drone as we see Fred's profile in close-up, looking off-screen to the right, enshrouded in shadow and barely discernible in the umber glow of his cigarette.

Then he is lost in darkness momentarily. The next shot brings us even closer, but we can see even less clearly. The final shot in the sequence reveals Fred's face in better light; as he draws on his cigarette once again and at last we feel that we know who we are looking at—but we are disoriented. During the interval of darkness, one of the many moments of black screen time throughout the film, it seems that either we (in association with the

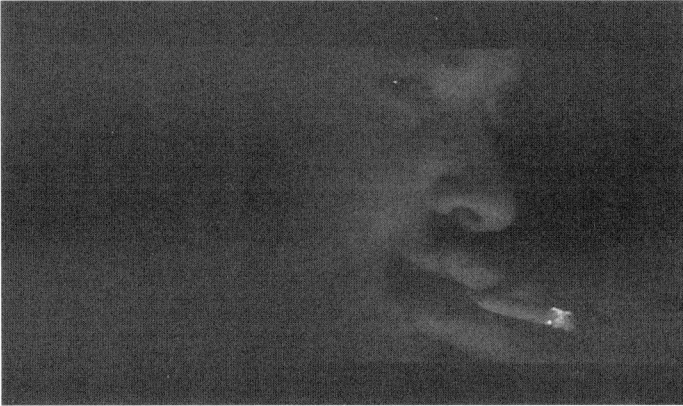

Figure 10 Lost Highway: *Opening shot of Fred Madison, facing right.*

Figure 11 Lost Highway: *Sequential shot of Fred Madison, facing left.*

camera) or Fred have shifted position: Fred now seems to be facing in the opposite direction, looking off-screen to the left.[8]

During the last of the three close-up shots introducing Fred Madison to us, we hear the doorbell of his house buzz and witness him listening as his own voice speaks through the intercom, saying flatly, "Dick Laurant is dead." (At that point the film audience does not recognize Fred's voice as we have yet to hear him speak; the significance of the moment is understood retrospectively.) The shot directly preceding the sequence detailed above is of the broken yellow line down the middle of a desert highway passing under the headlights of a car speeding through the darkness. The highway and Laurant's obituary are repeated in reverse order at the end of the film, but Fred is no longer in the same position that he occupied in the beginning. When, along with Fred, we revisit the point where we hear the words, "Dick Laurant is dead," we relate to the information differently though we still only dimly understand its significance.

Indeed, time in the film is not strictly linear and Dick may not be dead when those words are first uttered: Fred has yet to meet him. The film distorts narrative time and defies our understanding of physical space and the journeys bodies undertake within it. This short sequence of shots sets the tone for the film: if ever for a moment it seems to emerge from its own darkness and mystery, everything is sure to have shifted and changed when the lights were out. In the end no one knows which direction they're facing: characters and spectators alike have strayed from the narrative path into unchartable terrain, just as the title suggests.

The storyline of *Lost Highway* bites its own tail, it has no clear starting point, and no ending, though there are identifiable, self-contained stories within it, such as the tale Alice tells about meeting a sleazy character called Andy. Again, there are causes and effects attributable to recognizable characters (for instance, a man named Mr Eddy is definitely responsible for running a certain impudent tailgater off the road). Yet in the context of the entire film, even these simple assertions are brought into question because of the inconsistency of the characters' identities. Perhaps it was Renee who met Andy, and Dick Laurant who was the agent of the tailgater's doom? In such cases, and especially with regard to Pete and Fred's actions, we cannot attribute responsibility to the characters for their deeds because, so often in the film, the motivating factors happen to someone else. As Fay reminds us, "The experiences of agency are inescapably narratival in form and . . . our acts are acts only in so far as we see them as embodying some narrative" (1996, 197). Consequently, the possibility of mistaken identity or of an identity that has no coherent narrative form draws notions of agency and responsibility into question.

In *Lost Highway* the psychological continuity ordinarily maintained throughout a life history is problematized because, in conjunction with the loss of bodily continuity, the Fred/Pete character also confronts lapses in the ability to remember, and instances where he remembers moments of someone else's life (that lived by his doppelganger). Clearly, *Lost Highway* draws the connection between narrative and identity into question, unsettling notions of what it is to have a recognizable human identity.

Personal identity is reliant on psychological factors such as memory narratives, but it also has physiological and emotional dimensions (and these are interrelated). Personal identity is relative to bodily identity, and to the ways in which bodies extend themselves through, claim, inhabit, and manipulate space; to the way each person has a distinctive way of walking and speaking, to one's sense of home and place, to objects and styles that express preferences, and hold significance for individuals. Even people who go by different names or who reinvent themselves in different contexts tend to carry with them constellations of physical habit patterns and object relations that identify them and which they identify with. In this sense what people do and the roles that they play have a bearing on their identity. Most importantly, personal identity and ethical identity are both consti-tuted by relationships and emotional attachments or loyalties to significant people, places, values, ideals, and so forth.[9]

There are three primary levels on which identity is disrupted for the characters in *Lost Highway*. In consequence, on a fourth level the possibili-ties for spectatorial identification are also restricted, particularly with respect to the improbabilities of the mysterious ghoulish character. Begin-ning with the simplest case, Mr Eddy, the power-monger, porn-king, and perpetrator of road-rage, is identified by the police as none other than the notorious Dick Laurant. It appears that this unsavory character (played by Robert Loggia) is one and the same person; he is just known by two differ-ent names, presumably to conceal his illicit ventures. In this instance the confusion over the character's identity is negligible once we know that an alias is involved. It is only the temporal schema of the film that remains confusing, as the time of Dick Laurant's death is difficult to determine in relation to other plot elements.

Dick Laurant and Mr Eddy are identical both numerically and qualita-tively. They look the same, they act the same, their life story unfolds as one uninterrupted narrative: they are recognizable as the same person. This is in itself problematic only in terms of identifying an individual. As Ricoeur says, "a single name among the list of available names, permanently desig-nates a single individual in opposition to all others of the same class . . . The same individual is designated by the same name" (1992, 29) unless, of course, one wishes to be known to others as two separate identities or to deny one's identity by designating oneself as another. Names represent a significant site of connection with others. Dick Laurant *is* Mr Eddy: one man who lies about his name. His moral identity is unstable because his personal identity is based on deception. Though he could, of course, choose to express different selves or different aspects of his personality at different times, particularly in relation to his two names and the people who know him by each, the fragmentation or distortion of his identity is limited by the fact that he has only one body and can be in only one place at one time.

Patricia Arquette's characters, Renee and Alice, present a somewhat more puzzling scenario. Though we never really get to know either woman well, they both seem to have the same personality (distinguished by variable fashion sense) and they certainly play the same role: that of a sugary seductress with a shady past who every man suspects is sleeping with someone else. They look almost identical, though Alice could be younger and her golden locks contrast with Renee's brunette tresses. To further confuse the issue, at one point Pete opens a door in Andy's house and looks through time and space to room 26 in the Lost Highway Hotel to see a third woman, a racy red head with Renee and Alice's features.

It is tempting to think of Renee and Alice as being the same person not only because of the strong physical resemblance, but because of the ways in which they relate to men, and men relate to them. Significantly, the way Renee and Alice define themselves in relation to men is identical and remains constant over the film. Throughout the film they sustain relationships with the same (or closely connected) men, though these relationships are riddled with deception and ellipses. Their relationships remain on the level of instrumental interactions, and the repetition of these interactions becomes a source of identity.

There is a sense in which Renee and Alice are not intimately connected with their partners at all. The pattern of intense erotic desire seasoned with an aura of impending betrayal is of greater significance to Alice and Renee than the identities of their partners. This is also what makes each of them seem most inhuman: men are substitutable entities for Alice and Renee rather than emotionally valued, unique people. In this respect the aspect of personal identity that is of central importance to ethical identity is revealed to be that of emotional affiliation: the relationships we form with others. Thus, to fail to care about and relate to people as unique individuals is to live somehow in ethical disconnection.

One criterion for identifying an individual from others of the same type is that "individuals belong to a single spatio-temporal schema" localized around one body (Ricoeur 1992, 32). Alice and Renee are different things (*idem*), though they appear to be the same self (*ipse*); they are not numerically identical as we discover when we see the two women standing side by side in the same photograph at Andy's house. When Pete sees this he asks Alice, "Is this you? Are they both you?" Without hesitation she claims the image of the blonde as her own. Interestingly, the possibility of a twin sister is not mentioned. When we see the same picture at a later point in the film only Renee is present: Alice has vanished. Indeed, toward the end of the film the identities of these women begin to merge, in terms of both what and who they are. Renee leaves Lost Highway Hotel wearing Alice's slinky silver shift and Alice exchanges her signature silver nail polish for Renee's favored blueblack hue so their physical differences are reduced to hair color alone. The women also end up sleeping with each other's partners and they share memories of the same past, at least to the extent of the story they both tell about meeting Andy at Moke's and hearing about a job. When Fred asks the ghoul where Alice has gone, after she disappears in the desert, he receives the aggressive reply: "Alice who? Her name is Renee. If she told you her name is Alice, she's lying. And your name? What the fuck is your name?"

Figure 12 Lost Highway: *A photograph of Renee and Alice, side by side, with Mr Eddy/Dick Laurant, and Andy.*

The identity of Pete and Fred is most problematic of all. Fred is an enigma in his own right because he is able to be in two places simultaneously: outside speaking into the intercom and inside listening to his own voice. Fred and Pete both experience a contorted temporality due to memory lapses, and precognitive glimpses of Alice and Renee. The men differ in age, aptitude, and appearance, and they seem to have completely different histories up to the point where Fred disappears from his cell on death row and Pete wakes up in his place. Subsequently they share some of the same memories. They also share confusion over the severe headaches and flashes of blue light that terminate in a primal scream occurring on the night the transformation takes place and their identities inexplicably converge. They both experience a recurring nightmare about the house in the desert imploding (this inward explosion backward in time results in chaos and fragmentation that could function as a metaphor describing the events occurring in the film as a whole). Fred's saxophone solo playing on the radio is familiar to Pete, and Alice, who looks so much like Fred's (dead?) wife becomes Pete's lover within hours of their first smoldering gaze into one another's eyes. When Fred returns to the film, he takes Pete's place, naked in the glare of a red sports car's headlights out in the midnight desert. He immediately begins searching for Alice, with whom Pete has just made love, though he couldn't possibly know of her existence unless he is able to remember Pete's experiences.

To the extent that there is a narrative in *Lost Highway*, Fred and Pete live the same story and perform the same character function. They both play the role of a confused protagonist, captivated by a beautiful woman with a mysterious past, a woman of whom they are deeply suspicious. However, because they have self-contained lives with predominantly different memory narratives, they cannot be said to be the same person. The narrative paths of these two men never cross; one takes up where the other left off but they cannot be held accountable for each other's actions, nor can either character really be said to make rational, responsible choices because they are unable to remember significant segments of their own actions or that of their doppelganger with any clarity.

Both personal identity and ethical identity are reliant on memory narratives, relationships, roles, and enduring values—but these factors are themselves dependent on a consistency of body and personality ensured by being both self identical and distinguishable from others. Without narrative, and therefore without the possibilities for responsibility and accountability afforded by narratively structured understanding, the characters in Lynch's film lack ethical agency. In a world of discontinuous identity and relationships, the moral terrain slips away. Ethics is only relevant in an extended temporal context where actions have consequences, and where selves relate to others. Keeping a promise, being altruistic, or maintaining a social contract become irrelevant when identity and time are ruptured and memory narratives are obliterated.

Finally, the ghoulish character's identity and the problems he poses for spectatorial identification must be considered. According to Ricoeur, the most fundamental features of the individual are "that it is a type that is neither repeatable nor divisible without alteration" (1992, 28). Where Renee's personality, body, and experiences seem to be *repeated* in Alice, and Fred and

Pete's life seems to be *divided* between the two men, the ghoulish man breaks all the requirements of identity: he is neither the same as himself nor different from others. He is able to be in two different places at the same time and he is associated with the troubled conscience, dreams, and memories of several characters. For instance, Fred awakens from a dream to see the ghoulish character's face superimposed on the face of his wife, Renee. In *Lost Highway* it seems that the characters are so unstable and hybridized that the audience is alienated from their schizoid reality and can barely identify with them.

Figure 13 Lost Highway: *The Mystery Man's face, superimposed over Renee's features in Fred's dream.*

Acquiring identification with any of the screen characters is particularly difficult because there is no possibility of intersubjectivity. Intersubjectivity and identification are in part reliant on an overlap of identity arising from shared characteristics or experiences, cultural values, and narratives. In *Lost Highway* the characters intersect but they can hardly be said to share or relate, and I have already claimed that they do not have ethical agency because they can't be accountable or responsible, and it is impracticable for them to sustain a value system over time. It is impossible for characters to explore and map out potential courses of action in *Lost Highway* just as it is impossible to offer a coherent account of a character's actions. For these reasons it is also difficult to find an ethical orientation within the terrain of the film. No possibility exists for locating the self, or for evaluating the actions of others in a manner that extends meaningfully through a life. At best one can make limited or episodic evaluations, bounded by a scene that relates in inconsistent and partial ways to other elements in the film.

In unsettling temporal, spatial, and associated causal relations, these elements are revealed to be the fundamental functional units of narrative, identity, and ethics. Without some semblance of stability in these categories, selves can neither exist nor interrelate in ways that are familiar, meaningful, reflective, or projective. As Ricoeur points out, with reference to Derek Parfit's book *Reasons and Persons*: "How can we ask about what matters if we do not care to whom it may matter?" (1992, 137). In other words, matters of value and therefore morality are reliant on selves-in-relation.

Abject Horror and Unnarratability

In order to examine further, how selfhood has been problematized in *Lost Highway,* I will turn now to considerations of genre, another arena in which a familiar set of assumptions are important in constituting meaning. A number of factors make it difficult for spectators to construct a story from the events depicted in *Lost Highway*. One of these is the way in which the film disrupts generic expectations formed on the basis of familiarity with many narratives of the same type. As spectators of film, we draw upon a backdrop of stories and stock characters that populate our culturally informed understanding of life. However, expectations formed on this basis are not as effective in guiding our interpretation of the plot of *Lost Highway,* as they would be in a more conventional narrative.

For example, in most cinematic narratives, the construction of the scene where Alice and Pete meet would make one of two endings inevitable. In glorious Hollywood style devoid of any subtlety, the scene is established as a romantic interlude. When the eyes of Alice and Pete first meet their gaze is captured in slow motion and soft focus, with celestial backlighting. The diegetic sound drops out and the lyrics of Lou Reed's "This Magic Moment" communicate the chemistry that will draw the two characters together. Background knowledge of film language, cultural archetypes, and generic plots leads to a tendency to interpret plot points in *Lost Highway* as if they were leading us toward an ending where the redemptive power of romantic love will save Alice and Pete from the machinations of the malevolent Mr Eddy. Alternatively, the obvious stylistic parallels with *film noir* that characterize *Lost Highway* suggest that Alice, cast as the *femme fatale*, will double-cross Pete and probably Mr Eddy too, to achieve her own devious ends. The denouement of this film, however, is not quite so straightforward. Our expectations of a preexisting narrative structure are thwarted.

The disturbing power *Lost Highway* has is drawn, at least in part, from its command and manipulation of conventions and expectations based in narrative genres that are geared to unsettle norms and debase identities. *Lost Highway* is far from a generic text; however, it does make forays into the territory of road movies, *film noir*, action flicks, and the *cinefantastic*.[10] Though ultimately unclassifiable, it is interesting to consider *Lost Highway* in relation to the broad cinematic genre of the fantastic, especially in terms of its adoption of the codes and conventions of horror. Horror is stylistically portrayed through the use of excessive shadow and foreboding nondiegetic sound to describe and amplify the fear experienced by characters and spectators caught together within the architecture of doom. Fred and Renee's house is *unheimlich* (uncanny[11]) in that it is furnished with austere decor, darkness, silence, and an undercurrent of fear articulated by an ominous nondiegetic drone. The rooms have no clear spatial relationship to one another, and it is impossible to tell how long it takes to move from one part of the house to another. Horror also capitalizes on the corruption of normality and in *Lost Highway* the secure touchstones of home, self, and lover become the terrible places inhabited by fearful creatures, the place of "the other." Their own lives, minds, bodies, and homes become the monsters that characters can no longer trust and must struggle to escape.

Horror films are, in some important ways, locations in which identity is under threat or in crisis, and morality is violated. Problematizing identity is horrifying because it results in a disruption of responsibility and accountability, thereby destabilizing or undermining ethics and opening up the possibility for the perpetration of atrocity. In the world of horror the nuances of ethical life are lost in the immediacy of fear and the struggle for survival: preservation of the physical body becomes paramount and time is collapsed into the fearful present. Continuity of memory, of bodily identity and integrity, and the stability of time and space are essential for both the construction and maintenance of a coherently human ethical identity and the construction of a conventional narrative with intelligible chains of causality.[12] The disruption of these norms is essentially horrifying because it is dehumanizing. This is why radical metamorphoses, transitional states, horrifying places, and spatiotemporal distortion are generic features of horror: clustered together, these things are a terrifying corruption of human identity. Insanity and possession make one no longer the same as one's self, whereas cloning, replication, body doubles, imposters, shape-changers, and twins make an individual indistinguishable from others. Thus both elements of the dialectic of personal identity, *idem* and *ipse*, are disrupted in *Lost Highway,* as they are in horror.

The links between horror, slasher films, and pornography are taken up within the text of *Lost Highway* itself as siblings within a family of perversion.

The powerful, successful, businesslike figure of Mr Eddy/Dick Laurant draws freshfaced women like Alice and Renee into the seedy underworld of parties, porn, and snuff films where figures such as Andy and Marilyn Manson preside. On another level *Lost Highway* is like a horror film in that it lacks narrative resolution. It is important for horror that the fear continues to lurk in our minds and cannot be completely disposed of or contained by reasoned explanations, nor can it be isolated from the security of everyday life. This is why horror films are so prone to the syndrome of sequels and, similarly, why the inconclusive final scenes of *Lost Highway* leave unresolved mysteries lingering with the audience.

Despite these similarities, *Lost Highway* does deviate from the horror genre in crucial ways. There is no single character that personifies evil and inspires fear—these traits are dispersed among the characters, though concentrated most powerfully in the figure of the ghoulish mystery man. At the same time, the audience does not experience a strong visceral response to the text: *Lost Highway* disturbs us but does not terrify or horrify its viewers. It tends to activate an intellectual struggle for meaning, rather than an affective response such as that evoked in cinema spectators by abject horror. Julia Kristeva's account of the abject describes it as being ambiguously of and not-of the self; that which is at once incorporated in one's body and rejected from it.[13] Abjection includes things like vomit, pus, blood, mucous, and excrement, though one might well argue that it extends to include the texture of delusions, dreams, and nightmares originating somewhere beyond the conscious mind. In all of these instances we are forced to integrate something that seems to be simultaneously alien yet intimately related to ourselves with our conception of selfhood.

On another level, the hint of madness, the possibility that we are constantly asked to entertain and then dismiss at intervals throughout the film that the entire narrative may exist in the paranoid mindscape of Fred Madison, contributes to the alienation of the viewer. *Lost Highway's* force is located in its ambiguity, which is precisely the site at which the elements of the uncanny, the horrific, and the fantastic become operative. It does not function as a horror film, because rather than provoking a gut reaction to the abject (by instilling fear and depicting decapitation, blood, and gore etc.) it makes personal identity itself a site of abjection (both self and not-self), thus inhibiting the possibilities for identification with screen characters.

Lost Highway draws to the surface the ways in which narrative understanding provides a foundation for identity, and for orienting oneself in relation to others. By disrupting fundamental categories like time and space; the continuity of consciousness (and, within these, corporeal indivisibility), *Lost Highway* denaturalizes narrative as a structural schema that details webs of relation and causation, and by default it highlights the reliance of any conception of ethical agency on a narrative understanding of identity in and over time. When time, space, and continuity of identity are not only brought into question, but radically distorted and rendered discontinuous (i.e., when their narrative structure is dismembered), there remains no possibility for locating the self in ethical space. While this foregrounds the tenuousness and fragility of ethical systems, it simultaneously impresses on us the necessity of narrative coherence, spatiotemporal continuity, and emotional interconnectedness in locating identity and structuring an ethical character, or in informing moral deliberation. The sense of projection and retrospection, of prefiguration, configuration, and refiguration integral to narrative is essential to ethical consciousness, to understanding causation and responsibility, and to projecting and exploring value-laden possibilities.

Narrative Realism, Narrative Constructivism, and Narrativism

Outside of film theory, there are a number of ways of conceptualizing narrative structure with respect to human lives and it is interesting to consider these in relation to *Lost Highway*. The three main theories of narrative can be described as narrative realism, narrative constructivism, and narrativism (Fay 1996). Though these perspectives differ in emphasis, they all express the central importance of narrative to human life.

MacIntyre, whose ideas about life stories are discussed above, might be described as a narrative realist. He writes:

> Human life has a determinate form, the form of a certain kind of story. It is not just that poems and sagas narrate what happens to men and women, but that in their narrative form poems and sagas capture a form that was *already present* in the lives which they relate. (emphasis added MacIntyre 1981, 117)

MacIntyre also claims that ethical understanding is narratively structured.[14] Understanding an action as being virtuous or immoral entails understanding its place in an "enacted story." MacIntyre states that storytellers do not impose a narrative order on events; they report the narrative that is already inherent in the events:

> It is because we all live out narratives in our lives and because we understand our own lives in terms of the narratives that we live out that the form of narrative is appropriate for understanding the actions of others. Stories are lived before they are told—except in the case of fiction. (MacIntyre 1981, 197)

Here "understanding the actions of others" entails an implicitly qualitative form of knowledge because the nature of narrative understanding is, as I have claimed above, an appreciation of value relationships (by virtue of this, narrative understanding is an ethical form of understanding). Narratives provide the links and associations between actors and their intentions, their actions, and the impact of those actions.

Contrary to the narrative realist position, I will argue that the events within a life must be understood as a story in order to properly constitute a narrative. MacIntyre's argument that action, conversation, and all meaningful human projects are narratively structured and situated in temporal and social contexts presupposes a world in which things relate to each other and to themselves in intelligible ways. *Lost Highway* fabricates a world in which stories do not just happen. Things happen without apparent reason, and the audience struggles (often in vain) to construct a story because the causal sequence is repeatedly disrupted and obscured. The viewer's understanding of *Lost Highway* is retarded by the difficulties encountered in placing the events depicted into any coherent order and relating them to the larger narratives and "background stories"[15] about roles and relationships that are part of our cultural identity, and with which we are already familiar.

The intriguing thing about narrative realism is not what it says about the structure of life and events (evolution, life cycles, social patterns, and so on), but what it implies about the kind of minds we have, and thus the particular form our ability to engage with and make sense of life can and does take. Rather than saying "human life has a determinate form, the form of a certain kind of story" (MacIntyre 1981, 117), it may be more relevant to say that human beings have a psychological predilection for narration. We are endowed with long memories, with the capacity to make causal connections, to attribute responsibility, to formulate intentions and hypotheses about future possibilities, and we are social creatures involved in relationships, roles, and responsibilities. Narrative patterns are fundamental to our attempts to render our lives intelligible.

Narrative constructivism[16] takes the position that, as MacIntyre himself acknowledges, human beings are storytelling creatures (1981, 201). Without making a claim about narrative structure being *inherent* in events and in life itself, constructivists claim that humans are disposed to interpret things in terms of stories, imposing narrative structure on the world whether it is already there or not. In this view, stories are more accurately characterized as processes, not things. The narrating of the story *is* the story and the text is inseparable from the creative acts of configuration and interpretation that constitute it. Any narrative which, according to realists, might lurk within events, preexisting the telling of the tale, is best understood as a latent or prefigurative structure that comes to life in the process of narration itself. Though potentially narratable, these latent stories cannot yet properly be described as narratives because it is the act of structuring and interpreting that is important, rather than the structure itself (as any good mystery story illustrates). Narrative constructivism suggests that life is only formed into stories in these acts of composition, retrospection, and projection.

The debate between narrative realists and constructivists becomes even more complex when one considers that there is never one true way to tell or interpret a story. Even in a narrative film, the plot is always contested and the meaning is polysemic—continually retold and reworked as spectators engage with it. The same structure or material can generate many quite different stories, and this draws the significance of narrative realist claims into question. What does it mean to say that the stories are embedded in the substance of life before they are told, if we must manipulate that substance to such an extent in our efforts to extract from it a narrative understanding? And what if, after ignoring a great deal and fabricating or forgetting still more, we find not one story but a multitude of differing stories? Although the existence of an underlying structure does not rule out the possibility of multiple perspectives on that structure, it seems that somewhere within the multiplicity of possible configurations, the location of the story shifts, situating itself within the narrating consciousness instead of the narrated material.

The complexity of causal relationships contributing to any one event is so great that it forever outstrips human comprehension: we are incapable of grasping unlimited perspectives and infinitely regressive, connected causal factors at once. However, since it is not the actions and events that are multiple and variable, but the explanatory stories spun around them, it seems more appropriate to attribute both the status of narrative itself and the composition of stories to the creative engagement of narrating minds with the material the narrative is drawn from.

Narrativism[17] brings together some of the insights of narrative realism and narrative constructivism without taking a firm position about whether stories precede their own telling because they inhere in the structure of life, embedded in human time and action. From a narrativist perspective, stories may be both lived *and* told:

> Stories are lived because human activity is inherently narratival in character and form: in acting we "knit the past and the future together." But stories are also told in that with hindsight we can appreciate narrative patterns which we could not appreciate at the time of acting. We tell stories in acting and we continue to tell stories afterward about the actions we have performed. (Fay 1996, 197)

On a fundamental level, narrative structures our motives for acting and it is also used to decode and make sense of those same actions and their ramifications.

The act of relating or "telling" a story can imply ethical accountability through self-justification and clarification: storytelling functions to inform and convince irrespective of whether the audience is oneself or another person. Narrative, then, is integral to (meaningfully) enacting and understanding human lives, to thinking about what we ought to do and to considering the consequences of what we have done in the past. It is a primary way of structuring significance and engaging with life in terms of value and meaning. It seems to be much more important that narrative is one of the central ways in which we make sense of life, than whether stories exist in the structure of our lives prior to the act of configuration, recounting or interpreting them.

Narrative Structure

It is partly because of the differences between lived lives and the stories we tell about them that narrative is able to fill its unique interpretive and explanatory role within human understanding. When we look closely at the structure of stories, we notice that the plot itself excludes a plethora of details that aren't considered to have relevant ramifications.[18] Think, for instance, of the moments of black screen time that punctuate *Lost High-way*, signifying among other things, the "uneventful" passage of time or the presence of a dark secret. Narrating involves an ongoing process of evaluating and selecting which details are important, and choosing which to leave out. When we try to recount a story and communicate a sense of its meaning, a great deal of the emplotted content is omitted, but at the same time, much that the plot allowed to remain implicit is included and becomes central to our understanding of its meaning. The meaning we arrive at is often inventive and metaphorical, extending beyond the details presented in the plot.

Narratives are characterized by ellipses.[19] In order to constitute a narrative, an account must skim over or omit events and details that follow trajectories belonging to other stories; otherwise it lacks the integrity of a unitary identity itself. It becomes unmanageably interwoven with other things, and lost in the endless complexity of overlapping causal relationships. The account then becomes a description rather than a narration, or it loses its distinctness (as a dialectical, synthetic structure) from a list, or from a replica of life.[20]

It is no coincidence that both life and stories are so often described in terms of material, fabric, texture, and tapestries.[21] In *Lost Highway*, the constructed nature of the story is more obvious than in most cinematic texts because the interludes of darkness signaling certain edits. The unintelligible rifts between scenes also draw attention to the fact that images, moments, and scenes are cut and spliced together. The transitions between shots, scenes, or chapters are spaces occupied by material that was, for whatever reason, not chosen to feature in the story. Through challenging the conventions of narrative, *Lost Highway* reveals the threads that usually run invisibly through all narratives, suturing points of relevance together and concealing the fact that a great deal of material is cut out and much more is imagined to patch over the tears and holes.

Every narrative (whether linear and coherent, or unfolding as a stream of consciousness) is riddled with lacunae, punctuated with moments of time that are not considered eventful or momentous enough to be recorded, and whose significance in the causal chain goes unrecognized. The choices to leave things out or to make a transition to another scene are as much a part of the structuring endeavor as the choices to include certain elements, and to sustain focus. While narration entails the choice of points of significance, connecting sometimes disjointed elements of life and identity across time to form a life story, the ellipses inherent in narrative structure also reflect such intermittency and lapses of attention.

This chapter began with an image of the holistic nature of narrative and an appreciation of the explanatory capacity of a structure able to draw together disparate elements in such a way that they form an interrelated unity over time. Although storytelling has often been likened to the art of creating an intricate tapestry in which different threads are woven together to form one fabric—one picture, the process of thinking through some of the questions raised within *Lost Highway* has disclosed the resemblance this narrative fabric might bear to lace, rather than to the neatly worked and tightly woven design of a tapestry. To state the obvious: without its holes, lace is no longer lace, a fabric defined by vacant space. The same principle applies to the elliptical structure of narrative: if an account included each detail and described every causal connection it would be a reproduction of reality rather than a story.[22]

Because *Lost Highway* overtly signifies the points of rupture in the text, it points to some interesting possibilities about the ways in which our lives and identities might be structured and understood. *Lost Highway* could be described as embodying a rhizomatic form. It features all the principles that Gilles Deleuze and Felix Guattari associate with rhizomes in their exploration of postmodernity, identity, and meaning in *A Thousand Plateaus* (1987). *Lost Highway* follows the principles of "connection and heterogeneity" of rhizomes in that any point of its story can, like a rhizome, be connected to any other: "it has neither beginning nor end, but always a middle (milieu) from which it grows and which it overspills" (Deleuze and Guattari 1987, 36). In Lynch's film the end and the beginning of the narrative are indistinguishable from the middle: the text can be taken up at any point and its boundary points seem arbitrarily defined by the limits of screen time (actual time spent in the cinema). Each point or element connects to other points in the film, but not in a way that contributes to building one unifying theme or pattern of meaning. In this sense *Lost Highway* shares the quality of "multiplicity" with rhizomes; both are characterized by the presence of multiple entryways and irreducibility to a single structure or interpretation (Deleuze and Guattari 1987, 35).

Again, like rhizomes, *Lost Highway* exhibits points of "asignifying rupture." The text contains many points at which the lines of meaning are discontinuous: the life of one character we have been following is abandoned and we are asked to take up with another. Other sites of rupture include transitions between different codes, conventions, and styles. The film leaps from gloom to brilliance, from cheesy Hollywood clichés to art house idiosyncrasies, and from horror to road movie to *film noir* in ways that Deleuze and Guattari would describe as deterritorialization and reterritorialization (1987, 23). Like the relationship of visual similitude between the wasp and the orchid that Deleuze and Guattari use as an example, *Lost Highway* "captures the codes" of mainstream film, and the art film transforms itself into a Hollywood drama, which in turn becomes aestheticized and politicized as it is drawn back into the territory of the *auteur*. For instance, *Lost Highway* bears the stamp of Hollywood during the car chases and in the scene when Pete meets Alice, while at the same time Lynch distorts Hollywood conventions for his own strange, sometimes satirical purposes.

Partly because of these qualities of form and content, *Lost Highway* is not a film in which spectators are able to trace meaning along a well lit pathway charted by the intentions of the filmmakers. In accordance with the principles of "cartography and decalcomania" any meaning in a rhizomatic text must be mapped, not traced. The meaning is performed or constructed, rather than extracted. This is because maps produce something new; they do not mimic or reproduce an original since the very notion of a point of origin is alien to the nature of rhizomes. Finally, like a rhizome, *Lost Highway* has no ultimate meaning or deep structure, it is "not amenable to any structural or generative model" (Deleuze and Guattari 1987, 34).

In different ways Lynch, Deleuze, and Guattari all shift the focus of attention to reveal less immediately visible aspects of the ways in which we humans make sense of ourselves and our lives. Their "postmodern" approaches expose the inherent incompleteness of the meanings we make by drawing attention to the elements that don't connect with our sense-making structures. It would, however, be erroneous to assume that because Lynch, Deleuze, and Guattari have each touched on something that rings true in the ways in which they describe the disjuncture of meaning and identity, that the explorations of rhizomes or of the psychogenic fugue that occurs in *Lost Highway* have accurately characterized human identity.[23] Instead, what they describe is a limit case. What is interesting is the increasing prevalence and popularity of puzzle-plots involving elliptical, metaleptic, and multiform narrative structures in contemporary cinema. In "The Effect of Multiform Narrative on Subjectivity," Alison McMahan claims that multiform narratives involve several loosely interwoven linear storylines in which "each separate strand still follows the classic rules of causal transformation" (1999, 148). Janet Murray uses the term multiform narrative to refer to a story that offers various ontological[24] possibilities by presenting "a single situation or plotline in multiple versions, versions that would be mutually exclusive in our ordinary experience" (1997, 30). Experimental narrative forms have been present since the earliest days of cinema, but films featuring an ensemble cast and fragmented, interwoven storylines now feature quite regularly even in mainstream cinema and dominate storytelling in other screen media like television and digital games. More complex and convoluted story structures are also leaking out of the *cinefantastic* and into other genres, perhaps due to the ever-increasing complexity of technological, social, and economic interconnectedness and crosscurrents of cultural value systems experienced in the era of globaliza-tion and to the associated instability of subjectivity that finds expression in multiform narrative (see McMahan, 1999). Arguing that multiform narra-tive is gathering momentum because living in the contemporary mediascape means being aware of multiple intersecting stories and "alternative possible selves," Murray writes:

> Print and motion picture stories are pushing past linear formats not out of mere playfulness but in an effort to give expression to the characteristically twentieth-century perception of life as composed of parallel possibilities. Multiform narrative attempts to give simultane-ous form to these possibilities, to allow us to hold in our minds at the same time multiple contradictory alternatives. (Murray 1997, 38)

Amidst these multiple and sometimes contradictory alternative value systems and interpretations of lived events, the "shared" values and stories that inform ethical life are constructed and selected, rather than absolute. They are structures of inclusion and exclusion, and as a consequence they are provisional and must be subject to progressive questioning, clarifica-tion, and development. However, if we encountered others with the radical unpredictability of a rhizomatic life form, there would be no possibility for even a provisional understanding of shared values and consistency of character, or for the predictions about the future upon which ethical thought depends. The unification and interrelation of complex and diverse elements and themes that is typical of narrative is also typical of narrative identity. Beyond the prefigurative level, narration requires the cultivation of deliberative, interpretive, creative, and responsive skills that are invalu-able in ethical understanding. It is the extent to which a narrative, or the interpretation of a narrative, is reductive or coherent that renders a given story more or less helpful in making sense of life.

There are structural similarities between narrative understanding and ethical understanding. Narrating, like ethics, is about selecting and relating salient points. The choices involved in narration and the decisions about what qualifies as "salient" reveal values and carry consequences. Ethical identity must entail a greater degree of stability than rhizomes exhibit, in order to make possible the process of moral deliberation and the enduring (though not fixed or final) values and relationships that are so much a part of ethics itself. As I have said in different ways throughout the analysis of *Lost Highway*, the capacity for narration is necessary if human beings are to understand themselves and their world in terms of right and wrong, or care and virtue.

Arguing against a postmodern conception of selfhood in favor of a narrative approach to making sense of social life and ethical agents, Elisabeth Porter claims that "the narrative approach is vastly different from the emphasis on fracture and discontinuity prominent in postmodernist positions" (1991, 21). However, the narrative conception of identity that the above analysis of *Lost Highway* gives rise to indicates that this may not entirely be the case. Our lives do contain fragmentation, discrimination, and ellipsis as part of both personal and ethical identity, but these are integrated within a narrative whole. To embrace an unnarratable conception of identity would be to emphasize the elliptical, fragmented aspects of life at the expense of the equally important "cover story" that draws the points together to create a meaningful pattern.

Ricoeur says: "stories give unity—not of substance, but of narrative wholeness" (1991c, 437). I have claimed that narrative wholeness is far from "whole," it is "holey," selective, and partial, yet it is also a unifying structure that is centrally important to understanding. Narratives require empty spaces, spaces to be filled by the imagination and to enable points of relevance to be connected across time without the intrusion of details that lack a close relationship with the whole story. Similarly, ethical deliberation requires value-judgments regarding which aspects of a situation are most worthy of consideration and attention. While we tend to habitually disregard the negative spaces in the narratives that inform our understandings of life, ethics, and identity as we focus on the threads that hold it all together, in ethics, issues of inclusion (the choice of what is valuable and relevant), exclusion (blind spots and nonsalient details), and relationship (the connections that bind us to one another and the conceptual links that enable us to make sense of our situations) are of equivalent importance. Ethical deliberation, like narration, therefore requires both scissors and thread; it includes acts of discrimination and elimination, as well as unification and relation.

Ethical identity *is* narrative identity in at least two important senses. First, identity is reliant on a dialectical synthesis relating self to others, and aspects of oneself to the developing whole. Without the unity of narrative wholeness that this dialectic produces over a lifetime, the possibility for giving an account of action attributing ethical responsibility to an agent is radically diminished. The practice of relating a story and the possibility for recounting a personal history are crucial to the placement and articulation of responsibility. Second, ethical values are inscribed in a life by means of narratives linking those values to the contextual specificity of the lives and relationships in which they are embedded: the formal structure of narrative reflects the interrelatedness of the human beings who practice narration. Though one can never truly know the whole of any story or understand every side of it, since one perspective is always related to another, narrative is nevertheless crucial to developing ethical understanding. Narrative form, with its dual nature of holism and ellipsis, is a form that is necessary to and closely resembles central aspects of personal identity and ethical deliberation; hence, narrative film can be expected to exert a degree of ethical influence. The chapter to follow considers research into disturbing content and the potential negative influence of narrative, drawing on phenomenological techniques to analyze whether particular ways of filming violent, sexual, or prejudicial content might be likely to have a negative impact on viewers.

Notes

1. Claims about narrative's importance in no way exclude or diminish the significance of reason, care, attention, or other ways by which we come to know and value the world and orient ourselves within it.

2. For Ricoeur, narration is present on different levels of experience and consciousness. Narrative is *prefigured* in the structure of time and intentional action, and the ability to narrate is inseparable from the ability to carry out any meaningful project. *Configuration* refers to the creative process of structuring understanding in the form of a story. Although configuration operates in both the construction and interpretation of narratives (see Ricoeur 1991e, 26), *refiguration* or reconfiguration refers to changes in meaning and understanding effected at the intersection between the text and the world of its interpreter.

3. In a section of *The Human Condition* titled "The Web of Relationships and the Enacted Stories" Hannah Arendt indicates that personal identity, conceived of as the story of a life enacted and embodied by an individual, is largely understood in terms of connections with others over time. In an account of the "boundlessness of human interrelatedness," she writes, "This unchangeable identity of the person, though disclosing itself intangibly in act and speech, becomes tangible only in the story of the actor's and speaker's life" (Arendt 1958, 193).

4. Many philosophers of personal identity employ abbreviated narratives to sketch hypothetical body transplants and brain transfers, but their examples rarely engage with the concrete details of living a life; hence, they miss the valuable insights that might be found within the extended stories of novels and films. For example, in *An Essay Concerning Human Understanding* (1961, volume 1, book 2, Chapter 27) Locke employs the hypothetical

example of a cobbler swapping bodies with a prince in order to illustrate that bodily identity is logically distinct from personal identity, and to argue that personal identity is constituted by psychological continuity, especially experiential memory. For further examples of this nature, see Hume's "Of Personal Identity" in *A Treatise of Human Nature* (1939a, volume 1, section 6, part 4) and Parfit's *Reasons and Persons* (1984).

5. See *Nicomachean Ethics* (Aristotle 1941b, 1143b, 25).

6. This problematic of personal identity has its origins in Locke's essay "Of Identity and Diversity" (1961, 274–293), and in Hume's struggle with the evolving nature of self-identity and the necessity of identifiability and selfsameness in one person changing over time (see "Of Scepticism With Regard to the Senses" 1939b, 182–210).

7. The complicated processes of spectatorial identification and engagement with fictional characters are taken up in detail in Chapter 5.

8. Some theorists interpret this sequence of images as Fred looking at himself in the mirror, a visible doubling of identity that prefigures what is to come, and yet no mirror is visible (see "Cognitive Theories of Narration: *Lost Highway*," in Elsaesser and Buckland 2002, 168–194).

9. See Elisabeth Porter, *Women and Moral Identity* (1991). Porter emphasizes the contribution to identity made by our relation to the political matrix in terms of the range and availability of roles, the ways in which others respond to us, and the sociocultural structures that interpellate us within a given stock of identity narratives.

10. James Donald points out that the fantastic can be present as an element in a variety of genres, including horror, fantasy, and science fiction. The fantastic surfaces in "films which show worlds . . . that depart from the rules of everyday reality, often using cinema's spectacular capacity for illusion and trickery to conjure up before our eyes weird creatures and strange happenings in impossible narratives" (1989, 10). As an effect, "the fantastic is created by a narrative strategy that constantly undermines any certainty about what is going on" (1989, 13).

11. See Sigmund Freud, "The Uncanny" (1985).

12. Donald explores Todorov's (1973) work on the fantastic in his paper, "What's at Stake in Vampire Films?" Donald says "the fantastic, in short, plays upon the insecurity of the boundaries between the 'I' and the 'not-I,' between the real and the unreal" and he locates "the fragility of the limit between matter and mind, the multiplication of the personality; collapse of the limit between subject and object; and lastly, the transformation of time and space" as fantastic themes of the self which are central to the horror genre (1989, 237). All of these themes are taken up in different ways in *Lost Highway*.

13. See Julia Kristeva (1982) *Powers of Horror: An Essay on Abjection*. See also Barbara Creed's fascinating discussion of abjection in *The Monstrous Feminine* (1993).

14. See also Peter Kemp, "Towards a Narrative Ethics" (1989) and "Ethics and Narrativity" (1995).

15. Charles Taylor's (1989) analysis of the "background stories" that structure and inform understandings of self and society is discussed in Chapter 1. The small scenes and sequences of everyday life are often understood in relation to the larger narratives within which they are enmeshed in an ongoing process of developing comprehension. This corresponds to our interpretation of minor sections within a film narrative.

16. A sophisticated narrative constructivist position has been attributed to Paul Ricoeur (see Fay 1996, 198) whose concept of prefiguration leaves room for the existence of a narrative structure that may be intrinsic to intentional action, but is seldom consciously acknowledged. Ricoeur associates prefiguration with the particular ways in which humans experience and understand time, rather than with the practice of narration or with a structure essential to time, or to human life. As he tends to emphasize the acts of construction or configuration involved in narrating stories and the refigurative or transfigurative effect they can have on understanding, his work is linked with the constructivist position. White (1991) and Mink (1970, 557–558) are also constructivists, as is Arendt who writes: "Even though stories are the inevitable results of action, it is not the actor but the storyteller who perceives and 'makes' the story" (Arendt 1958, 192).

17. David Carr takes a narrativist position in *Time, Narrative and History* when he says, "Narratives are told in being lived and lived in being told" (1986, 61); see also Carr's discussion "Ricoeur on Narrative" (1991, 160–187), and Theodore Sarbin's *Narrative Psychology* (1986).

18. David Bordwell distinguishes between narrative and narration, pointing out that a film's story is never actually present in material form; it is only represented (narrated) by stylistic and technical means, and extrapolated or construed imaginatively (1985, 49). Bordwell adopts the Russian Formalists' distinction between *fabula* (story: the chronological causal order of events and their consequences which audiences create through narrative assumptions and inferences) and *syuzhet* (plot: the patterning or order of presentation of events as they actually unfold in the text).

19. I want to retain two senses of the word "ellipsis": the oblique circular form of an ellipse and the omission or suppression of elements, resulting in a perforated text in which gaps serve the purpose of ambiguity or economy. *Lost Highway* itself is elliptical in both respects, in terms of its circularity and its omissions. In many ways, all stories are like this because narration entails linking the beginning to the ending (where the connection between the beginning, the ending, and the middle parts of the plot necessitates a form of circularity) and drawing together nonadjacent points across the intervening space and time. Puzzle-plot films like *Lost Highway* are often also characterized by parallel or interwoven narrative strands, or by metalepsis. According to Debra Malina in *Breaking the Frame: Metalepsis and the Construction of the Subject* (2002), metalepsis is a disruptive narrative strategy involving the transgression of boundaries between mutually exclusive narrative levels or zones such as interiority/exteriority, past/present/future or parallel dimensions.

20. As Aristotle writes, narrative requires a formal unity that life may lack: "The story, as an imitation of action, must represent one action, a complete whole, with its several incidents so closely connected that the transposal or withdrawal of any one of them will disjoin and dislocate the whole. For that which makes no perceptible difference by its presence or absence is no real part of the whole" (Aristotle 1941c, *Poetics* 1451a, 30–35).

21. The following passage by Carol Witherell is a typical example. Stories "attach us to others, to our history, and to ourselves by providing a tapestry rich with the threads of time, place, character, and even advice on what we might do with our lives. The story fabric offers

us images, myths and metaphors that are morally resonant and contribute both to our knowing and our being known" (Witherell 1991, 293).

22. Although, as Ricoeur points out, even the rich and complex detail of actual life fails to encompass all possible events: "it may be said that every event, by the fact that it has been realized, has usurped the place of impeded possibilities" (1991d, 187). Fictional narratives elaborate some of these possibilities.

23. In an interview from *Lynch on Lynch* (edited by Chris Rodley 1997), David Lynch describes *Lost Highway* and Fred Madison's experience and, indeed, the form of the film, in terms of an amnesic mental disturbance caused by extreme trauma and known as a psychogenic fugue. The person suffering from a psychogenic fugue forgets his or her past identity and creates a completely new identity that originates in their mind. A fugue is also a musical term. According to Lynch, a fugue "goes from one thing, segues to another, and then I think it comes back again. And so it *is Lost Highway* . . . it gets pretty crazy with two themes churning, finding a way to separate and then coming back again" (Lynch and Rodley 1997, 239).

24. Ontological metalepsis involves "a transgression of levels that causes contradiction" such that one level of narrative reality "invades" another and derails the metaphysical basis by which we usually understand existence (Ryan 2004, 451). David Cronenberg's *eXistenZ* (1999), a film about a virtual reality video game, its designer, and its players is a very clear example of this as the real world and the game world bleed into each other in seemingly impossible ways, so that the actual spectator is unable to distinguish the status of reality in the closing sequence. This is similar to our inability to distinguish what elements of the closing sequence of *Lost Highway* might be confined to Fred Madison's mind. Metalepsis is not just restricted to narrative and the other arts: as Ryan points out, it also occurs in logic, mathematics, language, and science (Ryan 2004, 445). Ryan argues that by disturbing narrative logic or disrupting the orderly framework of mathematical or scientific enquiry, metalepsis tests the limits of human understanding by raising questions about the reliability these modes of knowledge, but it does not invalidate them (see Ryan 2004, 448). Similarly, I argue that the time loop paradox and layers of narrative disjuncture in films like *Lost Highway* and *Eternal Sunshine of the Spotless Mind* problematize but do not invalidate the presumptions of causality and accountability that underpin narrative ethics. Matthew Campora's fine Doctoral thesis on multiform narrative and metalepsis is an extended study of puzzle plot film narratives. His research, which explores the ontological ramifications of such narratives, introduced me to the work of Ryan (2004) and McMahan (1999).

4

Under the Influence:
Vice, Violence, and Villainy

Debates about media ethics and the negative influence of screen texts are frequently staged in terms of representation (often in the context of *mis*-representation, stereotyping, and identity politics), or in terms of the perception that screen texts are responsible for unraveling the moral fiber of society. This chapter is interested in the ethical impact of screen content related to the classifiable elements that regulatory bodies consider when formulating consumer guidelines and film ratings. It engages with the anxiety that if screen texts can be a positive influence on the lives and values of audience members, they can also exert negative influences, particularly on young and impressionable viewers. The films *8 Mile* (Curtis Hanson, 2002), *The Iron Giant* (Brad Bird, 1999), *The Lion King* (Roger Allers and Rob Minkoff, 1994), and *Batman Begins* (Christopher Nolan, 2005) are analyzed with the intention of evaluating media effects research findings and assessing their relevance to the ethical impact of film. These texts cover a range of ratings and content restrictions from the contentious R rating of *8 Mile*, through fairly typical examples of PG-13 rated violence in *Batman Begins*, and a PG rating for fantasy action and mild language in *The Iron Giant*, to the hugely popular and seemingly unproblematic G-rated family favorite, *The Lion King*.

This research seeks to understand the negative influence screen media might have on audiences, focusing on the ethical issues pertaining to screen violence.[1] It concentrates on the influence on young audience members because that is where the epicenter of the moral panic about "media effects" is located. Since the ethical impact of media violence cannot be adequately understood using the cause-effect model of the media effects research paradigm, this chapter explores the ways in which narrative and phenomenological analysis can contribute to assessing how viewers make sense of the ethical dimensions of screen violence, and how such depictions of violence might influence ethical sensibilities. The focus in this chapter is therefore necessarily on content-specific instances rather than diffuse general effects, working from the assumption that generalizations about the "effects" of violent content must be grounded in a considered analysis of the context, meaning, style, and narrative consequences of violent scenes. Textual cues in screen media influence but do not define the responses and experiences of audience members. Because the text is the only constant in the production and circulation of meaning across varying contexts and demographics, I take a text-based approach that reviews but does not undertake ethnographic or quantitative audience studies, whilst acknowledging the significance of many variables in the viewing environment and amongst audiences that augment the polysemic nature of texts.

There are wide ranging concerns about how audiences engage with violent or disturbing filmic content that may be deemed "immoral" or otherwise harmful by the standards of regulatory bodies and the communities they seek to represent and protect. An important impact of screen media on young audience members is that screen violence is often disturbing or frightening enough to cause direct, immediate effects like agitation and nightmares in case-specific instances (see Cantor 1994, 1996, 2001), or cumulative, long-term effects ranging through desensitization, timidity, and paranoia to aggressiveness (see Gerbner 2006, 49). Some lobby groups and researchers have even argued that screen violence is a form of "electronic child abuse" that inflicts trauma and encourages or even causes viewer aggression and involvement in violent crime (see Buckingham 2006, 279). While such claims about screen violence causing criminal and aggressive behavior foreground real concerns about media ethics, they also deflect attention from the many prosocial[2] effects of screen media and from "more significant contributory causes of violent crime" such as social inequity and the accessibility of firearms (Buckingham 2006, 280). David Buckingham observes that even "negative" responses to media violence (such as fear and anger) can have "positive" consequences including self-protective behavior and enhanced critical media literacy that enable audience members to "understand and deal with real life anxieties and concerns in the comparatively 'safe' arena of fiction" (2006, 280–284). Gerbner also argues that representations of violence are not necessarily undesirable as screen narratives can represent cautionary tales of the tragic consequences of violence (2006, 46).

The idea that children are vulnerable to and must be shielded from morally corrupting texts dates back to Victorian England, if not further (Mintcheva 2006, 167). Anxieties about the influence of the media have escalated as contemporary culture has become increasingly media saturated. Most claims and concerns about the negative influence of screen media focus on the impact on young audiences as adult critics rarely consider *themselves* to be at risk of negative influences (Gauntlett 1998). Only adult viewers who are already psychologically disturbed or mentally deficient are commonly thought to be influenced by negative film content. This rests on the assumption that young audience members lack sufficiently developed ethical frameworks, critical faculties, or adequate life experience to distinguish between fact and fiction, to negotiate or resist the messages communicated in a film, or to foresee the consequences of imitating filmic content (Weaver and Carter 2006, 6). The influence of films aimed at the youth market[3] is considered in light of developmental phases and age-specific responses to screen media, with attention to the effects of screen violence in different narrative contexts.

Semiotic phenomenology can be used to question how audiences might experience and interpret media violence, given that the ethical responses of viewers to violence is influenced by its style, form, content, and narrative context as well as degrees of character identification and other variables. Using a phenomenological approach, I investigate how audience responses can vary in relation to the textual features that signal the distinction between fantasy and reality in particular stories. I suggest that film spectatorship provides a model for ethical attention and that certain films impress themselves on individual spectators in ways that can reframe perception and offer or obscure ethical insight. Empirical media effects research is, by contrast, centrally concerned with calculating and predicting the impact of screen media and is based on the premise that the medium in general or individual films in particular can directly alter the way spectators think, feel, or act in the real world. In order to address concerns about the ethical responsibilities of filmmakers, regulatory bodies, and the carers of young viewers, the assumptions and perspectives that inform claims about film's negative influence are outlined below.

Media Effects Research: Overview, Generalizations, and Limitations

The debate about the detrimental effects of screen media[4] on young people hinges on the rights and responsibilities of parents to make informed decisions about what is best for their children, versus the rights and responsibilities of the media industry and regulatory bodies to protect audiences, whilst maintaining freedom of expression. In a review of research conducted throughout the 1990s into the impact of the media on young people, Susan Villani concludes, "The primary effects of media exposure are increased violent and aggressive behavior, increased high-risk behaviors, including alcohol and tobacco use" (2001, 392). With few exceptions (see Milavsky et al. 1982) most media effects researchers concur with the findings Villani reports regarding the link between screen violence and aggression (see for example, Bushman and Anderson 2001; Bushman and Huesmann 2001).

Although these findings present a cause for alarm, the media is just one of a huge number of factors affecting socialization and behavior and it is difficult to isolate its causal role. Media effects research can be reductive, oversimplifying the range of variables and modifying the context of reception (see Gauntlett 1998). Furthermore, the response of a viewer to disturbing content in a film will vary, depending on the age and gender, culture and class of that person; their media consumption habits and media literacy, narrative comprehension, and the degree of desensitization; their family, community, and educational background and preexisting beliefs and experiences. Viewer responses are also affected by who they watch the film with and whether they discuss the content; whether they identify with "positive" or "negative" characters in the film; whether the film seems realistic; and whether it is viewed at home, in a laboratory, or at the cinema. Comparing the findings of researchers focusing on different aspects of this complex picture is like evaluating the relative merits of smoked salmon and chocolate mousse.

The matter is further complicated by differences in the methodologies employed by media effects researchers, and the fact that different types of effects ranging from direct, short-term impacts to cumulative attitudinal shifts have been studied. It is difficult for regulatory bodies to prevent harm to viewers when they can only make recommendations based on the likelihood of short-term, content-specific, direct effects. The incidence of disturbing content in one particular film may be infrequent, but its contribution to the long-term effects of viewing may have a greater significance that case-specific text-based analyses miss.

The lack of consistency or consensus amongst media effects researchers has led many researchers working in the literary and cultural studies tradition of film theory to dismiss such research as flawed (see for example, Gauntlett 1998; and Heins 2006). However, the benefit of media effects experiments, longitudinal cultivation studies, and content analyses is that they enable researchers to identify patterns running through large numbers of texts and viewer responses, sometimes over long periods of time. In spite of the difficulties outlined above, this chapter attempts to offer an overview of recent research, and to report significant findings in order to frame the textual analyses that follow. There can be a productive interface between different research disciplines by bringing together text-based research and audience-based research. The combined insights of film theory and effects research can help to direct enquiry, focus research in neglected areas, and highlight variables that have not been adequately accounted for in media effects research or film analysis to date.

In an article entitled "Cultivation Revisited," Jonathan Cohen and Gabriel Weimann regard film and television as "an important source of socialization and everyday information," and focus on the influence of screen media on viewers' attitudes and beliefs, rather than on behavior (2000, 99). According to cultivation theory, sustained exposure to the "stylized, stereotyped, and repetitive images" portrayed in mainstream screen media can cause reality to be perceived very differently from what it might otherwise be (Cohen and Weimann 2000, 99). Cultivation theory has been used to support the argument that viewing screen media, particularly television, "cultivates a sense of personal risk in the real world" and shapes perceptions about how hostile the world is (Bushman and Huesmann 2001, 237). It also suggests that heavy viewers tend to become desensitized and believe that violence is justified:

> Aggressive marketing of violent material to children and teens is evident in all forms of media and is at least partially to blame for a desensitized population. For example, by the time the average American child reaches the age of 18, they have witnessed 16,000 simulated murders and 200,000 acts of violence . . . children constantly exposed to carnage become desensitized and begin to accept violence as a normal part of life to be imitated. (Richardson and Scott 2002, 178)

However, Cohen and Weimann caution against reductive assumptions about the media's ability to cultivate certain attitudes, reminding us that different texts and genres offer different images of the world and different meanings associated with violence contained therein (2000, 102–103). Different theorists have suggested the cumulative impact of screen violence may have effects as varied as "mean world syndrome" (Gerbner 2006, 49), "compassion fatigue" (Moeller 1999; Sontag 2003; and Tester 2001) or to "the fostering of a collective global compassion" that challenges audience members to "include strangers in their moral conscience" (Hoijer 2006, 347). Such research clearly has ethical relevance, but the challenge is to determine how stakeholders might utilize the disparate findings to make sense of the ethical implications of violent content in film narratives and hence to understand how viewers make sense of ethical life as it is represented in and extends from such narratives.

One of the explanatory frameworks that has credence in the literature regarding the effects of the media on young audiences is social cognitive theory, which details how people learn by observing social models and forming cognitive scripts (Bandura, 1994; 2006). According to Bandura, children learn how to behave not just through personal experience, but also by observing role models and remembering the "script" that was performed so that they can play the part themselves if they encounter a similar situation. A script is like a narrative that offers ways of behaving or dealing with particular circumstances, and it can be derived from witnessing real or fictional interactions. Research indicates that "scripts for behavior are also constructed early in development, and it is likely that continued exposure to media violence influences the development of aggressive scripts" (Dubow and Miller 1996, 136). The script is most likely to be reinforced if the situation an individual faces is very similar to the one seen on screen; if the scenario is very realistic; if the child identifies with the role model, and if the role model receives positive reinforcements or is perceived as having desirable characteristics such as being attractive, wealthy, or powerful (Bushman and Huesmann 2001, 236–237; Geen 1994).

Research on observational learning pertains to viewer identification in the Eminem biopic, *8 Mile*. Given *8 Mile's* imperfect reflection of biographical facts, it is significant that the opening image of the film is a distorted view of Eminem's face, seen through his own eyes in the cracked glass of a mirror. For this defining moment, which serves to locate the audience in the story world, we *are* Eminem. We are placed in a position to see him as he sees himself in the initial direct point of view shot, and the subjective sequence that follows.

In this bleak, beautifully shot film, Eminem is set up as a positive role model and a magnet for audience sympathies. Not only is he the attractive central character who is granted the best lines, repeated point-of-view shots, and intimate close-ups, but he is established as well-intentioned, hardworking, and talented: a diamond in the rough. With a subdued color palette and a grungy, realist aesthetic reliant on Steadicam footage to convey a sense of immediacy and authenticity, *8 Mile* depicts Eminem's struggle

Figure 14 8 Mile: *Eminem, his reflection, and the cracked mirror in the opening sequence of* 8 Mile.

to come to terms with his dysfunctional family, his working class ("trailer trash") status, and his unfaithful, dishonest girlfriends. With the help of his good-natured friend, an African American rapper called Future (Mekhi Phifer), Eminem's character even overcomes reverse racism, making a name for himself as a white rap artist in what is represented as a dangerous black subculture. As the following script spoof highlights, Eminem can literally do no wrong in the film:

8 MILE: THE ABRIDGED SCRIPT

By Rod Hilton

FADE IN:

EXT. DETROIT

EVERYBODY wrongs EMINEM. EMINEM wrongs NOBODY.

EMINEM

All I want is to be a rapper.

People continue wronging EMINEM. Eventually, he realizes the people who wronged him the fewest number of times are his TRUE FRIENDS. He RAPS.

END[5]

The film's endorsement of Eminem's ethos and actions is amplified by his status as a real life rap star. Despite the fact that the story is only semibiographical and glosses over his more sinister characteristics (his reputation for homophobia and misogyny), Eminem's celebrity appeal is likely to heighten the impact of the actions of the character he plays, Jimmy "Rabbit" Smith Jr. Indeed, celebrity is a factor that should be considered when evaluating the influence that the actions of a screen character might have on the behavior and attitudes of young audience members. Brown and Fraser write that "Celebrities often become role models and are emulated by large numbers of people who identify with them across sociocultural, political and economic boundaries" (2004, 100–101). Eminem's role in the film as an idealized version of himself affects the film's relation to the real, thereby modifying its relevance to and impact on viewers.

In addition to considering physical violence against screen characters, researchers and regulatory bodies often take the following manifestations of violence or aggression into account: verbal violence, psychological violence, and expressions of aggression and prejudice relating to race, ethnicity, gender, or religion. The overall message or theme of the film and the destruction of property can also be taken into account when assessing the degree and impact of screen violence.

Verbal Violence: Offence and Harm

In an article addressing the use of crude language in screen media, Barbara Kaye and Barry Sapolsky observe that despite the lack of evidence regarding the effects of profanity in film and television, "legislators, watchdog groups, and other concerned viewers claim that rampant use of foul language on the airwaves is contributing to the decline in moral and social values" (2004, 563). In cinematic texts, "foul" language most often takes the form of verbal violence or prejudice and can therefore be understood in relation to those categories, or can be considered offensive and vulgar rather than harmful or ethically problematic. In the interests of representing "authentic" rap culture, the vocabularies of characters in *8 Mile* frequently include words like "motherfucker" and "nigger." The high incidence of such words was sufficient to attract not only a content advisory warning about "offensive language," but also an age-restricted classification even though the overall theme of the film offers a prosocial, antiviolence message.

The film *8 Mile* specifically promotes the use of words and music to express feelings of rage and disenfranchisement as an alternative to physical aggression. A contextual consideration that should moderate judgments about the effects of "offensive language" in the film is that only African American characters refer to themselves or others as "niggas." In *8 Mile* as in much of rap culture the term isn't necessarily linked to negative stereotypes or deployed as a form of verbal abuse. Use of the term nigger can be inflected by "class-consciousness, inner-city life, poverty, and violence. 'Nigga' is a synonym not only for oppressed but also for the strong, streetwise men that fight to overcome oppression," according to Armstrong (2004, 345). The "offensive language" in *8 Mile* is in keeping with rap's status as a countercultural mode of expression and a means for self empowerment, "allowing Black urban youth previously systematically silenced, to name the injustices of poverty and their subjugation" (Richardson and Scott 2002, 189).

Kaye and Sapolsky point out that of the elements that ratings boards consider, offensive language is among the most likely to be imitated because "it is easier to imitate verbal aggression than physical violence" (Kaye and Sapolsky 2004, 558). Furthermore, the authors claim that "Repeated exposure to coarse language, especially when reacted to positively, can lead to negative social consequences such as imitation and desensitization" (Kaye and Sapolsky 2004, 558). Certainly, in *8 Mile* Eminem is rewarded for utilizing expletives and insults in rap lyrics, but it remains unclear from the research reviewed why the use of profanity is automatically considered to be a "negative social consequence." Such claims would have weight if applied to hate speech, which is a form of speech that has clear ethical ramifications. However, in relation to profanity, which most often functions like an exclamation mark in film dialogue, it is hard to treat the "harm" vulgar language may cause as seriously as other aspects of film content. Kaye and Sapolsky make the point that "scientific evidence supporting anti-social outcomes from exposure to offensive language" is lacking and that "future research is needed to examine whether exposure to such language warrants protection" (2004, 563). Such research must take contextual narrative factors into account and should heed the intended purpose of legal restrictions on free speech, designed to protect citizens from harm, rather than offence.

Prejudice, Stereotyping, and Intergroup Hostility

When evaluating the ethical impact of screen violence it is worth considering who the victims and perpetrators are, and who benefits from the production, representation, and circulation of media violence. According to Weaver and Carter, "What is needed is a more nuanced and politically aware understanding of the complex ways in which the growing 'normalcy,' 'banality,' and 'everydayness' of media violence influences our relationships with each other in the world" (2006, 13). For similar reasons, research on the media and multicultural awareness suggests that including content information about prejudice is important when classifying disturbing or potentially harmful material (Berry and Asamen 2001). While deciding whether a film contains prejudice that might be harmful, a ratings board may need to assess representations of sexuality, gender, race, age, disability, and intergroup hostility. Intergroup hostility is a serious issue whether those represented are recognizably human or not, since films like *The Lion King* and *Star Wars: The Phantom Menace* code nonhuman characters with the traits of minority groups (see Brooker 2001). While the media can foster cross-cultural understanding, respect, and tolerance, the prevalence of negative images of different sociocultural groups in films and other media texts "may undermine trust and empathy across racial or ethnic barriers" (see Berry and Asamen 2001, 365). This tendency is due to a variety of factors including the association of marginalized groups with negative values and antisocial behavior, the presupposition of fundamental differences from the dominant group, insufficient individuation, and the failure to represent sufficient close cross-cultural relationships between screen characters (Berry and Asamen 2001, 365). Gerbner's extensive content analysis finds that women play only one-third of the characters on television, and that young people, old people, and minorities are underrepresented compared to their numbers in the actual population (2006, 47). According to Gerbner's research, the lack of accurate, balanced, or proportional representation in screen media can give rise to stereotyped assumptions about heroes, villains, and victims, sparking negative perceptions and attitudes in viewers. This skewed cast of characters "sets the stage for stories of conflict, violence, and the projection of white male prime-of-life power. Most of those who are underrepresented are also those who, when portrayed, suffer the worst fate" (Gerbner 2006, 47). Such research suggests that screen media construct and reinforce political and ethical positions and judgments, but content analysis can only speculate about how people attribute meaning to depictions of violence or victimization, much less to underrepresentation. A more nuanced understanding of how viewers respond to violent expressions of prejudice requires attention to particular narratives, representational strategies, and viewing behaviors. Berry and Asamen argue that inaccurate representations of marginalized groups "can become a part of the individual's schema about others and can serve as the basis for faulty beliefs about others, prejudiced thinking, and subtle and not so subtle stereotypes" (2001, 371). Depictions of prejudice may also cause alienation and resentment where viewers feel that in order to be proud of their identity they must reject the values and norms of the dominant group, which can lead to antisocial behavior and divisiveness (see Huntemann and Morgan 2001, 317). The propensity for young viewers who do not have well-developed ethical skills to form behavioral scripts based on media role models suggests that prejudice should be taken particularly seriously in films viewed by children under the age of seven.

With regard to the issue of prejudice, the representation of women and homosexuals in *8 Mile* must be read intertextually with Eminem's broader oeuvre, not just the rap lyrics heard in the sound track and diegetic music of the film itself. In the process of film classification, Eminem's lyrics and his personal attitude to homosexuals and women cannot be taken into consideration. It could, however, be argued that such factors are inseparable from the impact of a film that purports to represent the artist's life and is likely to be viewed by audience members who are familiar with his albums and interviews.[6] In the film itself, Eminem's character Rabbit stands up for gay and female characters (neither of which are given significant character development, however). Two scenes in particular show him genially swapping shifts with a gay coworker and rapping with a black female worker while on lunch break at the steel factory. In the latter, a male steel worker disparages the female rapper for complaining about employment conditions and uses rap to verbally attack their gay colleague, Paul, saying to him:

> When you travel you probably pack panties in your suitcase/
> Made out of lace from Victoria's Secret/
> If ten men came in a cup/
> You'd probably drink it.

At this point Rabbit raps "OK folks/Enough with the gay jokes" and takes up the freestyle battle, silencing their aggressive opponent by calling him a homo and a faggot and suggesting that he carries HIV. Grundmann argues that:

> His coming to the aid of his female and gay co-workers is a transparent attempt to soften Eminem's well-known image as a misogynist

and homophobe. To make matters worse, what was intended as damage control turns into its opposite, as the script flaunts Rabbit's conviction that the only suitable putdown for a homophobe is to one up him by accusing him of being HIV positive. (2003, 34)

Significantly, given the research problematizing stereotyping and under-development of members of oppressed groups in screen texts, the way the lunch break scene is filmed literally marginalizes Paul and denies him any subjectivity. He doesn't speak up for himself and he is not given any point-of-view shots; instead he is shown standing at the edge of the frame partially obscured by other characters. This may reinforce any negative influence that the representation of homophobia might have.

In contrast with Rabbit's use of rap to defend women and gay men in *8 Mile*, Eminem's rap lyrics have been accused of demeaning women and advocating violence against women and homosexuals (Armstrong 2004, 341). Discussing Eminem's homophobic lyrics in an article entitled "Eminem: Pied Piper of Hate," Robin Tyler writes:

Many of the eight-to-eighteen-year-old males who buy Eminem's records do see him as a hero and do take his message to heart. The majority will never commit a violent crime. But the homophobia and misogyny hammered into their psyche will stay with them the rest of their lives. (Tyler 2001, 14)

Tyler's assertions appear in an opinion-based article, but even if such claims about the effects of Eminem's lyrics were substantiated it would be difficult to draw conclusions about the related influence of *8 Mile* on viewers. None-theless, the views expressed in the work cited above do serve to illustrate the complex, intertextual nature of media effects and the fact that each film is embedded in a network of social influences that mediates interpre-tations and moderates effects. To classify films and to assess any harmful material that they might contain is to accept that filmic communication is inextricable from the social power dynamics it depicts, comments on, and contributes to.

Property Destruction and Illegal or Harmful Activities

Another form of violence that ratings bodies take into account is the destruction of property, including illegal acts such as vandalism. Films that fail to present the consequences of dangerous or criminal activities are a concern, especially for younger children whose life experiences may not immediately enable them to foresee the effects of emulating the behavior shown on the screen. Destructive and illegal activities are depicted in *8 Mile*, but not in a way that necessarily endorses or glorifies them. For instance, a scene in which Rabbit and his crew shoot paint guns at a police car makes them appear childish and foolish, despite the fact that the gun looks real. As they flee the scene, Rabbit's old junker of a car suddenly cuts out and they are nearly arrested. Like guilty schoolboys, they crouch down to avoid being seen, and then fumble to restart the car. After the police speed past without apprehending them, they erupt in a chorus of "You were scared! No, *you* were scared!" Although the perpetrators do get away with this petty destructive act, this scene hardly associates lawbreaking with a tough, streetwise gangster image that viewers will seek to emulate.

Another scene in which the protagonists torch an abandoned home is depicted as dangerously risky. Rabbit himself is nearly caught in the blaze and his fear is communicated in the shaky hand-held footage of his escape from the burning building, a vertiginous point of view shot as he jumps from the upper storey, and the intensity of the orange flames leaping against the grimy grey *mise-en-scene* that characterizes the rest of the film. It is open to debate whether watching a major celebrity engage in vandalism will encourage mimesis even in a narrative context in which such actions are represented as being unadvisable. It is probable that, just as identification with screen villains and negative characters is discouraged through the punishment and negative consequences meted out in the narrative resolution, the depiction of unwanted outcomes for illegal and irresponsible behavior is likely to discourage mimesis for most viewers.

Screen Violence and Viewer Aggression

In her account of research into the impact of the media on young people, Susan Villani concludes that screen violence contributes to harmful effects on viewers including aggression, desensitization, and fear, although not all violence contributes to these effects in the same way. She outlines a number of factors that raise the likelihood that a particular image of violence will generate one of the three main effects identified above:

> The predicted impact of contextual factors based on social science research rated attractive perpetrator, presence of weapons, and humor as associated with learning aggression; graphic violence and realistic

violence associated with generating fear; and humor and graphic violence associated with predicting desensitization. (Villani 2001, 395)

Recent research into media violence has also been exhaustively reviewed by Brad Bushman and Craig Anderson, who report that "repeated exposure to violent media, for example, a couple of hours a day for 15 years, causes a serious increase in the likelihood of a person becoming a habitually aggressive person and occasionally a violent offender" (2001, 481–482). The strong correlation (not to be mistaken for a causal relation) between media violence and aggressive behavior holds for all social classes, especially demographics where violence is more prevalent in the community and where there is heavier viewing of televised violence (Bushman and Huesmann 2001, 242).

The developmental level of young viewers is a crucial variable in the media effects equation. Young children who do not fully understand much of what they see are more likely to be affected by obvious textual features like spectacular instances of screen violence with impressive special effects. Unlike more sophisticated viewers, they may miss important cues about motives and consequences that modify the overall message, and may simply imitate the action that they see (Van Evra 1990, 83; see also Geen 1994). In other words, narrative comprehension and understanding of complex motivation and causation is related to developmental factors, which affect responses to stories.

Children under the age of six or seven are most susceptible to screen violence, and are most likely to mimic it as this is the stage at which they are developing their behavioral scripts and are less conscious of the fantasy/reality distinction, or the complexity of narrative context, motives, and justifications for violence (Bushman and Huesmann 2001, 241). Up until around eight years of age children tend to mimic both realistic and unrealistic depictions of violence if the perpetrator's actions are rewarded or go unpunished since they interpret narratives based on appearance and other superficial features (see Funk et al. 1999, 291). An extensive content analysis undertaken by Yokota and Thompson revealed a troubling ethical dimension to the depiction of violence in children's films in that "a striking behavioral message implied by many of the G-rated animated films that the good guys triumph over the bad through the use of physical force" (2000, 2720). Preschool children have limited narrative comprehension and short attention spans so they may miss the relevance of behavioral rewards and punishments administered in the narrative resolution. In addition, young children have yet to develop a stable sense of identity or ethics, so they are capable of very fluid identifications in the cinema and may relate to either the antagonist or the protagonist, depending on who has the upper hand, who is rewarded, and who seems most attractive or interesting (see Funk et al. 1999, 291). Some research predicts that:

> Televised violence may enforce this early-stage moral reasoning because it portrays justified violence that is perpetrated by heroes with little, if any, negative consequence. By glorifying violence in this way, empathy for the victim, and therefore perspective taking by the children, may be discouraged. (Krcmar and Valkenburg 1999, 622)

Even when viewing does not lead to aggressive behavior, repeated exposure to violent media may foster tolerance of violence, desensitization, or the belief that violence is an acceptable conflict resolution strategy (Van Evra 1990, 97). Given the serious ethical implications of these findings, the restriction of exposure to media violence for children under school-age seems advisable.

For teenagers, the violence that is present in film texts is linked to perceptions and experiences of violence in their daily lives and in popular culture more generally, as the discussion of rap in *8 Mile* has illustrated. Richardson and Scott (2002) claim that in the United States, young audience members spend on average over 38 hours per week engaging with entertainment media. In this media-saturated context, "Given the hours of exposure to real and fictitious characters engaging in violent escapades and antisocial behavior, youth come to believe violence is not only 'normal' but also admirable" (Richardson and Scott 2002, 177). *8 Mile* buys into the stereotypical depiction of violent masculinity in the hood while simultaneously attempting to promote an antiviolence message. For example, Rabbit himself aggressively attacks Wink and his mother's boyfriend but later realizes the error of his ways and refuses to fight back when Wink and the Free World gang viciously beat and kick him, threatening him with a gun. In another scene, Eminem's friend "Cheddar Bob (Evan Jones) attempts to break up a fist fight by pulling out a real gun but literally shoots himself in the foot" as his mates yell "Man, put that shit away, before you fuckin' kill somebody!" (Grundmann 2003, 35). The consequences of this misadventure with a firearm are illustrated with gruesome images of bloodshed and panic.

The relationship between verbal aggression and violence is evident in the way the first rap battle in *8 Mile* is filmed. During this scene the mouth

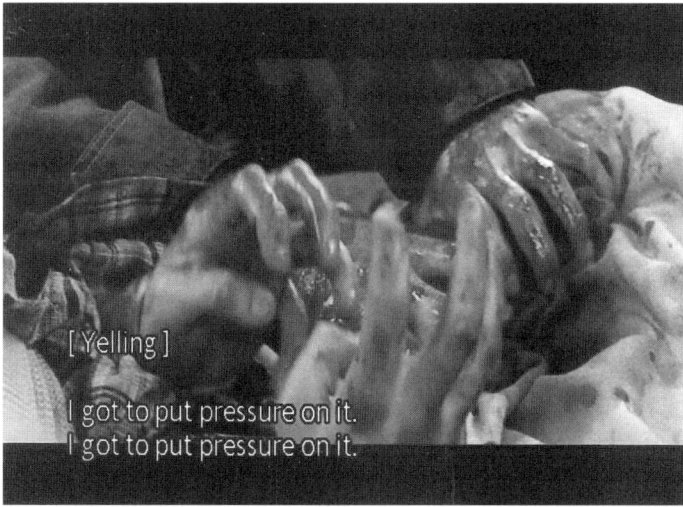

Figure 15 8 Mile: *The gory consequences of violence are shown when Cheddar Bob accidentally shoots himself.*

and eyes of Papa Doc, the reigning rap champion, are framed in intimidating extreme close-up. The amber gleam of his iris and the vitriolic spittle spraying from his lips are described in confronting detail for the viewer as he assaults his opponent with the words: "I'll slaughter you/Make your mom wish that her fat ass aborted you." The menacing staging of the scene is accentuated via the use of unstable, hand-held camera and rapid whip-pans shifting from one competitor to the other as though the body of the viewing subject is surging with adrenaline. When Eminem's character goes into battle with Papa Doc's henchman Li'l Tic in the subsequent round, we see repeated shots of the hostile, jeering black crowd from Rabbit's point of view. The unease that Rabbit evidently feels as an inexperienced white artist in an all-black environment is made palpable when the rules of continuity editing are disregarded and the axis of action is violated, alternately filming the battle from behind the competitors and from the crowd's perspective. This literally communicates a feeling of jumpiness and situates the viewer inside Rabbit's experience, in the midst of the action. Rabbit is taunted with racial slurs like "wigger" (white Negro) and "honky." Rabbit "chokes" with stage fright and is unable to retaliate against the stream of insults and threats targeting his status as a racial outsider in the rap scene, and in black subculture. He is literally silenced by the barbs of what could, in a different context, amount to hate speech. The visceral impact of this scene intensifies the aggression and fear it represents, perhaps more so than scenes of physical violence in *8 Mile*.[7]

To summarize the research findings so far, in the words of Richardson and Scott:

> One of the reasons for concern about the relationship between expo-
> sure to violence and violent activity are features of identity development
> and social expectations in children. It is believed that children shape
> their identities, values, and behaviors by drawing clues from their
> environments. Role models, for purposes of this article, are persons
> held in high esteem by children who possess characteristics, skills, or
> attributes worthy of emulation. Inordinate exposure to fictional
> and real images in television, video games, music videos, sports, and
> movies provide an endless array of role model choices and perhaps
> more importantly, cultural messages about acceptable practices and
> behavior. (Richardson and Scott 2002, 179)

A narrative like *8 Mile*, while not addressing children, will almost certainly be viewed by them. For the young adults who form the target audience, the film's overall prosocial message is likely to be both clear and influential, but for school children the nuances of the film's ethical import may be lost.

Perceived Realism, Relevance, and Modality

Classification boards are unlikely to recommend restricting films from younger audiences when "fantasy violence" (unrealistic or animated vio-lence, especially with nonhuman cartoon characters) is present in a screen text (Funk et al. 1999, 294). This section draws on the research findings about violence and fear and applies them to two films, *The Iron Giant* and *The Lion King* in order to explore assumptions about realism as a factor that influences the impact of films on children.

"'Modality' concerns the reality attributed to a message" (Hodge and Tripp 1986, 104). It is a judgment about degrees of certainty and realism. When applied to screen media, texts featuring actual child actors will have a higher modality or a more definite relation to the real than animations with talking animals, mythical creatures, or giant robots from outer space. Anything that signals the relation between the message and reality can be termed a "modality marker" (Hodge and Tripp 1986, 105) and can either strengthen or weaken the text's relation to the real, thus modifying its effect on the viewer's beliefs, attitudes, feelings, responses, and behaviors.

While modality does not create an emotional response, "it determines the valency and force of that response, and hence contributes decisively to whatever effects may come from watching television" (Hodge and Tripp 1986, 115–116; see also Tulloch 2000). Dialogue, the sound track of a film and nonverbal and paralingual cues like body language, tone of voice, and special effects can also influence the modality of a scene (Hodge and Tripp 1986, 106). Hodge and Tripp also point out that modal judgments draw on experience and prior understanding or knowledge of reality so, for instance, if a child does not know whether unicorns exist, the presence of a unicorn in a text will neither raise nor lower the modality, nor lessen the effect of the message on the child as it would for someone who is certain that unicorns are not real.

While Hodge and Tripp emphasize the ability of children to make sophisticated distinctions between fantasy and reality, they do acknowledge that "this capacity takes time to develop, so there will be a period when children can be expected to make different modality judgments from adults, and be affected differently by the same content" (1986, 103). Children under eight are more likely than older children to confuse appearance and reality in film media, and so are more likely to be affected strongly by both cartoon violence that seems unrealistic to adults and by more realistic violence (see Van Evra 1990, 86). Since young children make up the biggest audience for cartoons, and since cartoons contain more violent acts per hour than prime time adult television (Van Evra 1990), this finding is significant.

Drawing together the research reviewed thus far, the film *The Iron Giant*, based on the book *The Iron Man* by British Poet Laureate Ted Hughes, is an interesting case to consider in detail since the narrative communicates an explicit antiviolence message, and it does confront the consequences of violence. Although the narrative content grapples with the very real threat of nuclear destruction during the cold war, the broader modality markers signify that the film has a weak relationship to reality since it is an animated text. Even very young children will be able to tell the film is "not real," and according to the research above, this should minimize the impact of the violence and lessen the possibility that it will cause either aggression or fear. Around the world *The Iron Giant* has been given different classifications, ranging from "suitable for all ages," to recommendations of "parental guidance."

After the giant robot has mysteriously arrived from the night sky and has been discovered and befriended by a boy called Hogarth, the iron giant and the boy are playing a war game in which the giant pretends to be

"Superman" and the boy pretends to be a bad guy with a gun. Unbe-knownst to the audience or any of the characters at that point in the narrative, the iron giant is a military robot programmed to shoot back if he has a gun pointed at him. His eyes turn red, we are immersed in a dehu-manizing point-of-view shot through the cross hairs of the iron giant's computerized gaze and he responds without conscious volition, shooting a laser at Hogarth suddenly, with dramatic, loud sound effects. Fortunately, Hogarth's bohemian friend Dean intervenes just in time and shouts at the giant, telling him it's not a game, accusing him of almost killing the boy, and ordering him to go away. Hogarth, who can obviously identify with the experience of being yelled at for doing something wrong by mistake, pleads: "It was an accident; he's our friend." Dean responds, "He's not our friend, he's a weapon . . . It was a defense mechanism. He reacted to the gun."

Like Hogarth, young viewers are encouraged to identify with the child-like giant who runs away after being reprimanded, ashamed of himself, wanting to be good but not knowing how. This scene represents a familiar scenario in which kids play rough when imitating fantasy figures like superheroes: inevitably someone gets hurt, and someone gets into trouble. The film is both critiquing and (as is likely in the case of viewers under school age) unwittingly contributing to the process by which children learn to play out the violent action hero behavioral script provided by cultural images of heroism.

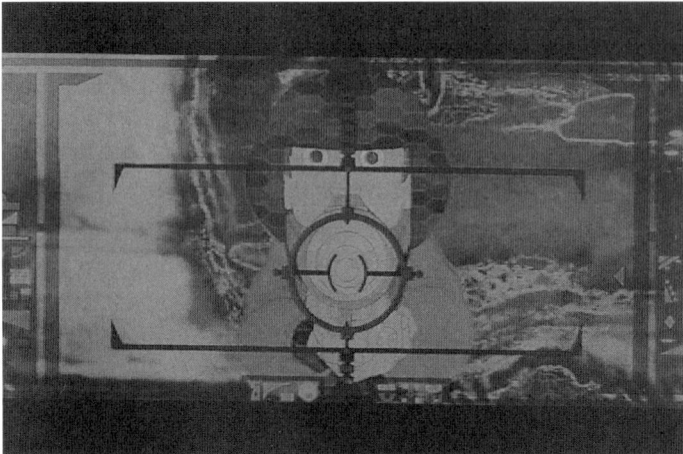

Figure 16 Iron Giant: *A robotic, computerized point of view shot, with Hogarth in the laser's sights, when the giant fires at Hogarth as an automatic defense mechanism.*

Attentive engagement with screen characters, and responsiveness to the aspects of their stories that have relevance to the story of the viewer's own life can lead viewers to cancel out their dominant modality system (to "willingly suspend disbelief"). Ethical deliberation and the process of cinematic identification both involve narrative comprehension and the ability to put oneself in another's position, and these higher level responses are only well developed in older children.[8] It is plausible that the strength of character identification and involvement in the story world can result in a more intense response than "fantasy" material would ordinarily warrant, even when viewers are old enough to make sophisticated distinctions between what is real and what is not. Van Evra's research shows that the "length of the content (e.g., movies over brief shows) with more character development may have greater impact" and that "violence was more disturbing when characters came to life enough to evoke empathy in viewers" (Van Evra 1990, 87). Discriminations and judgments about what is real are an important part of how we respond to narratives, but something with a low modality can still have a powerful influence on behavior and attitudes if there is significant viewer involvement and identification with characters in an extended narrative. For this reason, we can expect a feature-length animated drama to have a significant impact, despite its apparently low modality.

The depiction of violence within *The Iron Giant* may be distressing for several different age groups. Younger children may be disturbed by the appearance of the giant, especially when he inexplicably changes from good to bad as his eyes go red and he threatens his friend, the child protagonist. Older children will be frightened by the threat of a nuclear holocaust when the military arrives in force and the presence of the iron giant leads to the detonation of a nuclear warhead, which the younger children will not understand. The narrative context in which the violence occurs operates to maximize the fear response, since it is the good protagonist who also embodies the threat. The narrative is complex, with a strong prosocial message, but an "all ages" rating may be inappropriate especially since the modality markers that signal a move away from reality may tap into a fantasy world of heightened emotional responsiveness for children. Here the potential for identification, confusion, and mimesis is significant, and the complexity of the narrative means that young children may act out undesirable roles portrayed within the film, since the same character can be both good and bad.

The Lion King, another popular film rated as suitable for all ages, illustrates different issues salient to assessing the effects of disturbing content.

The climactic scene of *The Lion King* contains five minutes of violence as Simba, the hero, returns to the pride to confront his uncle, the villainous Scar. As they battle to determine who will be king, thunderclouds roll in and a lightning strike sets the bush alight, turning the sky an ominous red. The scene begins with a flashback to another traumatic moment in the film, Simba's father's death, and progresses through a number of dramatic fight sequences interspersed with dialogue. As Simba argues with his uncle, Scar's character swings unpredictably between cruelty and kindness. "I am family," he says, "It is the hyenas who are the real enemy. You wouldn't kill your old uncle . . ." Such character changes are alarming and difficult for young children to interpret. In a grand finale that sends an ambiguous message about violence as a conflict resolution technique, Simba replies "No, Scar, I'm not like you" and he tells his uncle to leave. However, when the hyenas then close in to kill Scar and he cries for help and mercy, Simba does not intervene. For young children this scene may have a disturbing impact, for despite the fact that Scar is not a good character and we do not see him torn apart by the hyenas, we are still invited to imagine it.

It is revealing to analyze this scene from *The Lion King* with reference to the following points raised by the American Academy of Pediatrics— Committee on Public Education 2001:

Figure 17 The Lion King: *Simba battles Scar as a storm brews and the sky is filled with sparks, flames, and thunder.*

It is not violence itself but the context in which it is portrayed that can make the difference between learning about violence and learning to be violent. (. . .) Viewers learn the danger and harm of violence by vicariously experiencing its outcomes. Unfortunately, most entertainment violence is used for immediate visceral thrills without portraying any human cost. Sophisticated special effects, with increasingly graphic depictions of mayhem, make virtual violence more believable and appealing. Studies show that the more realistically violence is portrayed, the greater the likelihood that it will be tolerated and learned. Titillating violence in sexual contexts and comic violence are particularly dangerous, because they associate positive feelings with hurting others. (1224)

Close attention to the modality markers in this scene, and to how viewers are likely to respond to it based on its position in the overall narrative reveals a great deal about the impact of the potentially disturbing content, and whether the violence portrayed is likely to cause fear, mimesis, or some other reaction. In a broad sense, *The Lion King* has an even lower modality than *The Iron Giant* because the protagonists are talking animals rather than humans, but if we look more closely at the narrative context and at the treatment of the final scene of *The Lion King* the picture becomes more complex. By the end of a feature-length film, it is reasonable to expect that many children will be emotionally engaged with the characters and will identify strongly with the protagonist, Simba. They will be concerned for his welfare irrespective of the fact that he is feline rather than human. He has many qualities that are considered attractive or valuable within the film, and also in human society: he is young, strong, smart, and regal, occupying a position of power and privilege in the narrative world. Children also identify readily with animals, and will be particularly likely to identify with Simba since he is a "child" himself when we meet him as an undisciplined and inquisitive lion cub at the beginning of the film. These factors do not necessarily raise the modality of the text, but they counteract the modality markers and make what is clearly "unreal" acquire a higher degree of relevance for children.

Modality markers embedded in the final sequence may also work against the expectation that the scene will not be disturbing for children. Phenomenologically, the threatening hue of the blood red sky will work on an experiential level to strengthen a fright response rather than weaken it, even though it is unrealistic that the sky would be red. Older children will know that red signifies danger and anger, and younger children will experience the deviation from "normality" as being a sign that something is wrong. Similarly, the loud orchestral music that rises to a crescendo at climactic moments and accompanies sudden movements in the fight sequence further marks out the film as being unreal: the nondiegetic sound track is a cinematic artifice designed to cue or intensify viewers' emotional responses. No orchestra is visible on screen, so the presence of the music is clearly unrealistic, yet it does not function as a modality marker that weakens the realism or, by extension, the impact of the scene. On the contrary, it strengthens the emotional realism, and the scene's overall impact. It will also be likely to augment a child's fear, since loud noises and sudden movement have been identified by Cantor (2001) as universally frightening. The fact that young children are often frightened of animals and characters with scary appearances reinforces the impact of this scene, without undermining identification with the hero, Simba, whose attractiveness and good, humanlike qualities render him nonthreatening.

Slow-motion can also raise the modal force of a scene even though it makes it less realistic (neither lions nor humans actually move in slow motion when they are fighting). Hodge and Tripp observe that audience members interpret slow-motion as a convention involved in the treatment of exceptional moments in screen texts, and that this awareness prevents slow-motion from weakening the modal force of a scene (1986, 109). A phenomenological interpretation of the experiential impact of slow-motion suggests a different explanation, particularly for young viewers with limited familiarity with cinematic conventions. The use of the slow-motion mirrors or describes human experience at certain moments of extreme stress or heightened awareness. At times like a car crash, or when being attacked, victims often report a sense that everything was happening in slow-motion, or conversely, that everything became a blur. The representation of slow-motion experiences in screen media can have a high-modality association with actual experiences of fear, adrenaline, and corresponding hypersensitivity to movement through space and time. Cinema uses "unrealistic" techniques like jump-cuts, slow-motion, and unexpected camera movement to describe or convey human experience, and when the description is accurate the modality of the text is strengthened even if the conventions of realism and the laws of physics are broken.

These case studies illustrate instances when it is appropriate to exercise caution in screening films for children under school-age, and suggest that it may be beneficial to offer consumer advice about frightening content in films as fear can augment responses to violence. They also illustrate the necessity of considering that while "realistic violence" has been shown to have heightened effects, "fantasy violence" should not be dismissed as harmless. What children experience as "realistic" or relevant will be marked by different features than for older audiences, particularly for children under about age eight, whose modality systems are not yet sophisticated.

Humor and Violence

Many films provide light relief by including comic interludes in the middle of tense sequences, and often violence perpetrated by positive characters will be represented as funny (see Villani 2001, 395; Yokota and Thompson 2000, 2720).[9] *The Lion King* is no exception. In the middle of the battle between Simba and Scar we cut away to the minor characters fleeing from the hyenas. They debate whether to hide inside of, or attempt to escape from a "rib cage" as they try to prevent themselves from being eaten by hyenas. In the midst of this combination of sight gags and word play, the tables are turned and the hyenas are defeated after an aggressive attack by one of the funny good guys, "Mr. Pig." Research shows that the combination of humor and violence runs the risk of trivializing violence and desensitizing audiences. It also reduces the modality of the violence, because real violence has real and unpleasant consequences and therefore does not present an occasion to laugh. However, as Nathanson and Cantor point out in relation to their own study of the relationship between humor, violence, and aggression in cartoons:

> Even if children know that the cartoon is not real (as most fifth and sixth graders surely do), it seems that the combination of the attractive, funny perpetrator with no reference to the consequences of violence for victims is sufficient for increasing aggressive inclinations in elementary-school boys. Hence, this project demonstrates that programs that appear as benign as a classic cartoon require some form of mediation to prevent boys from learning aggression from the material. (Nathanson and Cantor 2000, 136)

We might expect that a decrease in realism would lead to a decrease in impact and effect, yet humor is consistently linked to increasing the negative effects when associated with violence. While it is difficult to generalize or to predict how the introduction of humor might modify the effects of watching violent media, in this case a modality analysis sensitive to the experiential response of the audience suggests that humor acts as a safety valve, releasing pent-up tension and offering children some respite from the grip of fear. It works to render the scene more pleasurable, but it would be erroneous to assume that this necessarily trivializes the material and makes it less suitable for children.

The analysis of modality markers above suggests that special effects such as slow motion and the ominous red color of the sky do not necessarily "make virtual violence more believable and appealing," but they may well make it more frightening, heightening its effect. The recommendation by the American Academy of Pediatrics, Committee on Public Education 2001 to "Eliminate the use of violence in a comic or sexual context or in any other situation in which the violence is amusing, titillating, or trivial-ized" (1227) also seems to be misplaced in relation to *The Lion King*, which uses humor in a way that is typical of many children's films and is consis-tent with an all-ages rating. Decisions about how humor moderates the impact of scenes containing violence, fear, or prejudice must be made with sensitivity to the genre and narrative context, considering whether it may trivialize the issue in question, or contribute to desensitization, or lessen the impact of the episode in a way that helps young audiences deal with anger, fear, or other responses. In making such decisions, a phenomeno-logical analysis of the experiential impact of film and an appreciation of the mechanisms of cinematic identification can be useful in evaluating the probable influence of screen media.

Phenomenology, Screen Violence, and Narrative Context

This section draws together points raised above about the significance of narrative content, structure, style, intertextuality, and identification in order to harness both phenomenology and narrative analysis to evaluate the influence and ethical significance of screen violence in *Batman Begins*. The manner in which the filmic material is represented clearly has a signifi-cant impact on how viewers experience and respond to screen narratives and their characters, which underscores the need to develop more sophis-ticated tools for textual analysis and theories of identification. As Robert Stam and Louise Spence write, analysis of spectatorial identification must attend to image scale and duration, which are "intricately related to the respect afforded to a character and the potential for audience sympathy, understanding and identification" (1983, 17). The authors go on to prompt questioning as to "which characters are afforded close-ups and which are relegated to the background? Does a character look and act, or merely appear, to be looked at and acted upon? With whom is the audience permitted intimacy?" (Stam and Spence 1983, 17). The mechanisms of cinematic identification governing how the spectator is positioned in relation to screen characters also include subjective sound and aural perspective, point of view, editing techniques such as eye-line matches, narrative placement of event and character, *mise-en-scene*, depth of field and focus, music, framing, plot and character, and the use of language and subtitles.

Batman Begins opens dramatically with a flight of bats swarming across the sky, their wings beating at the screen itself and bombarding the audience with a cacophony of high shrieks and panic-ridden fluttering. With a flurried match on action, we are again caught up in frantic motion as we segue into the sugar-coated nightmare scenario of an innocent children's game that is aborted when a young boy running through an overgrown garden falls down the shaft of a bat-infested well. Nothing signifies the dream status of this first flashback scene other than the abrupt awakening of our protagonist, the grown version of the young Bruce Wayne. The remainder of the film unfolds in a jumbled chronology of flash-forwards from this point: *Batman Begins* commences with this youthful fear and returns to it often, milking a series of childhood vignettes to heighten the impact, identification, and relevance for young viewers. No sooner has the grown Bruce Wayne (a muscle-bound Christian Bale) awoken from his nightmare than the film catapults us along with him into a rowdy, muddy, bloody prison brawl. The mythology of his invincibility is established as he ruthlessly vanquishes six (or seven) opponents and is thrust "for *their* own protection" into a solitary cell with walls as dank and dark as the well he so recently inhabited in his nightmare. A subtle underscore with sinister stings introduces the looming figure of Henri Ducard (Liam Neeson), a representative of the League of Shadows, who dominates screen space in menacing low-angle shots that foreshadow his pivotal role as the henchman of arch villain Ra's al Ghul. It is with Neeson's character that Nolan's showmanship as a director comes into full swing, complete with an ominous undercurrent of sound, dramatic shadows and shards of splintered light, and black-clad ninja rituals. Ducard and his protégée Bruce Wayne, the Dark Knight, bond over training sequences as they "seek the means to fight injustice and turn fear against those who prey on the fearful."

Batman Begins plays with and comments on the conventions of Hollywood characterization and narration that underpin superhero films, making obvious the narrative process of dialectical synthesis that undermines simplistic polarities of good and evil. Indeed, the League of Shadows' ultimate goal is to purge Gotham City of evil, and Batman's ultimate combat strategy involves harnessing the dark power of his own emotions, drawing on reservoirs of fear, anger, grief, guilt, and hatred in repeated flashbacks to his childhood and youth and in an extended sequence where he lives in the criminal underworld to learn its secrets. Henri Ducard and Bruce Wayne may seem to be polar opposites, yet they have much in common, both having lost loved ones to violent crime. They could well have formed a dynamic duo had Bruce Wayne not baulked at a moral stumbling block when, at a key turning point, he defied a command to execute a criminal and prove his allegiance to the retributive justice practiced by the League of Shadows. Instead, the self-definitional power of Bruce Wayne's seething emotional past becomes more than the key to being a fierce fighter—it enables him to recover the lost ideals and values in defense of which those emotions first arose.

What makes *Batman Begins* interesting from a phenomenological perspective and in terms of its capacity to influence the ethical orientations of young viewers is the ambiguity and darkness surrounding the eponymous character. Taken alone, any scene or sequence in the film could well set Batman up as a dubious role model, especially since much of the narrative frames Batman from the criminals' perspectives. The scene when viewers see through the eyes of characters under the influence of the punningly named *Scare*crow's panic inducing weaponized psychotropic toxin shows black filth oozing from Batman's own eyes and mouth. Visual disturbance and sonic distortion warp the screen in profoundly disturbing ways, making it virtually impossible for the image of Batman as a force for good to remain unshaken. Visual and aural effects used in scenes featuring the hallucinogenic toxin heighten the threat and impact of the violence by working through sensory associations with the experience of drowning in panic or psychosis. The pulsing sound and shimmer of blue light give the impression of a heart pounding underwater, and we are drawn into the disturbed realm of the psyche as the usual clarity of sound and vision are subjectively distorted.

It is the ideological function of the narrative resolution and closure, along with the developing contrast between Batman and the villainous characters that is central to eliminating any moral ambiguity and restoring harmony and justice to the story world. Viewers need to follow Batman's personal journey to the very end to get the message that he is a heroic figure rather than a terrifying, dangerous vigilante. When Ducard says "Compassion is a weakness your enemies will not share," Batman responds by situating himself and "us," the audience, firmly on the side of good,

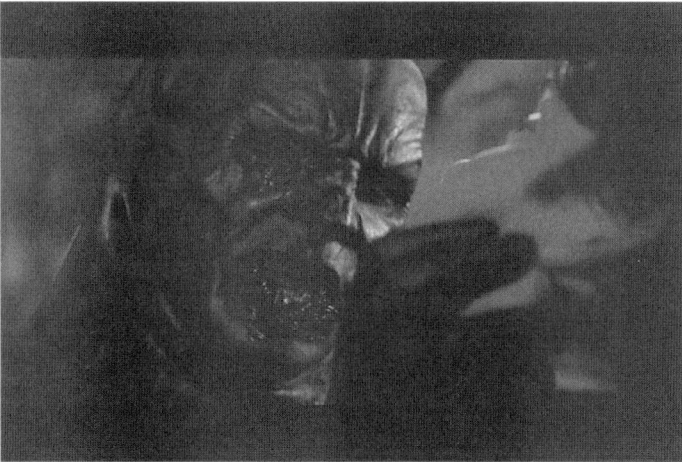

Figure 18 Batman Begins: *Batman threatening Scarecrow whilst oozing black tar, as seen under the influence of the psychotropic toxin.*

whilst implicitly acknowledging the underlying goodness in his opponent's motives when he states, "That's why it's so important. It separates us from them." This line in fact justifies Batman's final act, which would in any moral universe outside of the cinema be considered heinous: Batman coldly stands by and allows a man who once befriended him to die. As a speeding train rushes toward its inevitable destruction Batman tells Ducard "I won't kill you, but I don't have to save you," performing much the same sleight of hand that Simba uses to ward off culpability for Scar's death. In this devious twist, the film simultaneously valorizes Batman's compassion (he has in fact saved Ducard once before, and derailing the train is crucial to save Gotham City), yet legitimates his callous failure to rescue his former mentor *because* his opponent lacks compassion for others. Batman, it seems, is a hero who can masterfully straddle both sides of the dichotomy that "separates us from them."

Research on modality markers and the ways in which young viewers negotiate the fantasy/reality distinction at various ages indicates that *Batman Begins* wouldn't be suitable viewing for Batman's most devoted fans: young boys who wear superhero masks and capes to birthday parties. Certainly up until the first years of primary school most children are likely to find the complex chronology and character transformations alarming and confusing, and are equally likely to emulate "harmful" or "justified" violence. Batman's power and expertise are amply demonstrated in no less than 16 realistic fight sequences cut blindingly fast to emphasize Batman's skill as a warrior.[10] Aesthetic cues such as the style of music, costume, lighting, and the responses of secondary characters that usually establish unequivocally who viewers ought to align themselves with are unreliable in a film as dark as this, with a hero who is wracked by guilt and fear, is shat on from a righteous height by both his girlfriend and his butler, and who is seen to steal, drive recklessly, and kill without remorse. However, the psychological intimacy we are granted through access to Batman's dreams and memories build allegiance with him through establishing a rich and sympathetic understanding of his character. This focalization of the narrative through the experiences of its central character is augmented by the large amounts of screen time and dialogue accorded to Bruce Wayne, and the self deprecating humor and kindness he exhibits in exchanges with his fatherly butler Alfred, Lucius Fox, and the young boy he befriends. For older viewers familiar with Christian Bale's oeuvre, any wholesome reading of the character is likely to be tainted by the actor's other dark and twisted roles in films such as *American Psycho* (Mary Harron, 2000).

Batman's good name is grounded in his "wholesome" connections to, and care for representatives of law and order (Detective Gordan, and the virtuous lawyer Rachael Dawes), then secured in the narrative resolution and reinforced through intertextual links to other stories in the extensive Batman franchise. The problem is that the force of this ending and its considerable intertextual and ideological clout disambiguates what should be an ethically charged life or death decision at the end of the film, rendering uncontestable the brutal model of heroism that Batman embodies. This underscores both the power and the problems of narrative as a mode of facilitating ethical understanding. On the one hand, film narratives are fairly reliable in guiding audience members to align themselves with positive characters and to feel satisfied when negative characters are vanquished and justice is served. Grievously unethical behavior seldom goes unpunished in popular cinema, so in broad terms narrative typically functions to uphold the moral order or to make audience members desire that it be upheld. Consequently, concerns about screen violence encouraging viewer aggression are often misplaced as long as consumer guidelines about ageappropriate viewing are observed.

On the other hand, the satisfying closure offered in narrative resolution may often discourage viewers from thinking further about the issues and actions screened in the narrative, leaving the impression that the problems of the text have literally been resolved and the protagonist's actions and conflict resolution strategies are legitimated. Some critics argue that "depictions of justified violence by heroes who are rewarded, not punished, are in fact worse than gruesome violence by villains who get their comeuppance in the end" (Heins 2006, 175). For instance, Gerbner considers what he calls "happy violence" to outweigh responsible depictions of violence and to be problematic: "This happy violence is cool, swift, painless, and often spectacular, even thrilling, but usually sanitized. It always leads to a happy ending. After all, it is designed to entertain and not to upset" (2006, 46). Ultimately, Batman's 16 battles and the explosive ending add up to "happy violence" and legitimate the use of force to resolve conflict.

It is partly due to the falsely reassuring nature of "Hollywood endings" that the lack of closure in the nontraditional narrative structures of films made for mature audiences may have special role in ethical understanding because they challenge the audience to activate our cognitive, deliberative faculties more vigorously, whilst retaining the sensory, imaginative, and emotive power of film. To an extent *Batman Begins* does leave the door to transgression and disruption of the ethical and social order open, signaling unresolved tensions between good and evil not just within Batman himself, but between the forces of justice and criminal figures such as the Joker. This is necessary to set up the sequel but it also has an important function in encouraging audience members to engage with ongoing questions concerning the violation of norms.

The relatively predictable ethics of *Batman Begins*' good versus evil action genre storyline that abides by classical narrative norms of conflict and its resolution can be rendered more complex by elements such as a nonlinear, fragmented chronology and aesthetic factors like the powerful score by Hans Zimmer, with incredibly fast editing that augments the action sequences, and shadowy sets. Opportunities for identification and empathy are affected by the intersection of the viewer's own identity and experiences with characters' transformations, appearances, dialogue, and decisions. These influences may be inflected by viewing contexts such as parental or peer guided viewing at home or in the cinema, intertextual knowledge of other installments of the Batman story and extratextual knowledge of the stars involved. As the *Batman Begins* example has illustrated, the message and influence of a film can be complicated by its narrative structure, style, content, contexts, intertexts, and various character-audience identifications.

****

This chapter has extended consideration of the ethical impact of film to include factors that facilitate or impede identification with screen characters and that have a bearing on media "effects" related to the development of intergroup hostility or prejudice, and the adoption of role models and behavioral scripts. While the potential for film texts to have adverse effects is acknowledged, generalizations about the corrupting influence and moral dangers of screen media, and claims that individual movies cause viewers to mimic ethically undesirable behaviors remain difficult to substantiate. The discussion above is intended to contribute to a better understanding of the kinds of impacts that film can have, applying the insights of screen theory to enable an informed analysis of how particular texts might influence audiences. I have argued that questions about the relationship between realism, fantasy, and the impact of humor within violent content must consider modality markers within the text itself, as well as attending to the developmental phases that children move through as they come to grips with the fantasy/reality distinction. In each case, the degree of identification with screen characters plays a significant role in determining the nature and extent of a media text's influence.

As demonstrated above, a phenomenological approach to film helps to describe the experiential and affective impact of particular texts. Some audience responses are related to contextually specific factors and to the developmental level of the viewer (for instance, modality markers are interpreted differently by different age groups), but many are not (e.g., sudden movements and loud noises are universally shocking or frightening). Phenomenology has limitations in terms of predicting long-term cumulative effects or in assessing the impact of textual content that has psychologically or culturally contextual meanings and effects, such as what might be defined as violent or illegal or prejudiced. Phenomenology is much more useful when applied to the responses of spectators of all ages in what Linda Williams terms "sensational" films (1995). Williams uses the term "sensational" to refer to films of the horrific, pornographic, or melodramatic genres that rely on eliciting a "gut reaction" that directly relates to the affect of fright, arousal, or tears demonstrated by screen characters:

> The body of the spectator is caught up in an almost involuntary mimicry of the emotion or sensation of the body on the screen (and) the success of these genres seems a self-evident matter of measuring bodily response. (. . .) What seems to bracket these particular genres from others is an apparent lack of proper aesthetic distance, a sense of over-involvement in sensation and emotion. (1995, 143–144)

Attention to bodily responses can be extended to evaluate the impact of films that do not necessarily fall into a particular genre but do contain elements of fear, sex, and melodrama, and those that contain comedic elements which may trivialize violence. The ethical significance of such affective and emotive responses to film is elaborated in the next chapter. Since classification boards assess films on a case-by-case basis, attending to content-specific, direct effects that may reasonably be expected to arise from watching the film, a phenomenological understanding of the experiential impact of the cinema's mechanisms of identification and its modal and affective cues may prove useful, especially if informed by knowledge of how viewers react at different developmental levels.

Virtually all films contain instances of violence that send mixed ethical messages and can be interpreted as destructive or instructive. Even the powerful critique of violence and racism mixed with disturbing undercurrents of misogyny and homophobia in *8 Mile* is preferable to the construction of a sanitized, politically correct narrative world with a didactic ethical message. While the contextualized analyses of narrative style and structure undertaken here can help to understand how screen violence might be experienced and interpreted, it cannot predict its effects. The best suggestion for moderating the influence of screen violence that this research has unearthed is that viewers *renarrativize* the violence, thinking through causes and consequences that may or may not be portrayed on screen. This means encouraging audiences to think critically about their own affective responses and about the ethics implicit in the text, considering alternatives to decisions enacted by characters rather than accepting rationales embedded in the narrative. Encouraging fictional involvement with the victims depicted in violent media and thinking critically about the consequences of violence from a victim's perspective can have a significant impact on interpretations of screen narratives and their characters, according to research conducted by Dubow and Miller (1996, 140) and Nathanson and Cantor (2000, 127). If, as such research suggests, thinking critically about the consequences of violence inhibits aggressive responses as effectively as actually depicting the consequences of violence, it might be a good way to prevent the development of aggressive attitudes and behaviors from media violence (Nathanson and Cantor 2000, 135).

Notes

1. Screen violence is far from the only element of narrative film that has been associated with moral panics about the negative influence of the media, but it has been chosen for the focus of this chapter as it is often more directly related to ethical issues than, for instance, concerns about depictions of sex, nudity, or crude language. While restrictions on screening sexual material involving minors, pornography, or violence are unquestionably tied to

ethical values and the protection human rights, many concerns about expressions of "obscenity," sexuality, nudity, and blasphemy are related to religion, politics, and taste rather than to ethics. Perhaps the most significant influence of screen media occurs in the impact on consumption behavior and attitudes toward materialism, but while this has ethical importance, it falls outside the scope of the current study and relates to broader ideological and economic functions of the media.

2. For more on prosocial effects see Bickham et al. (2001); Huston and Wright (1996); Mares and Woodard (2001); Milavsky et al. (1982); Naigles and Mayeux (2001); Singhal et al. (2004); and Van Evra (1990).

3. Although *8 Mile* was not classified as suitable for children, its star, Eminem has a young fan base and the film focuses on members of a youth subculture apparently in their late teens. This indicates that it addresses a young audience regardless of its rating. For precisely this reason, it makes an interesting case study. Similarly, *Batman Begins* may be rated as appropriate for "mature audiences," but its appeal to and likelihood of being watched by children is very high given Batman's privileged place as a superhero in children's culture.

4. Television and film are viewed in different contexts, they have different production imperatives, visual styles, and narrative structures, and audiences typically spend much more time watching television than going to the cinema, thus the two media do not have identical effects on their audiences. However, since most films end up on television, video, or DVD, this study includes some relevant television research.

5. Copyright 2003–2005 Rod Hilton. http://www.the-editing-room.com/8mile.html (accessed March 25, 2008).

6. The *8 Mile* DVD special features includes the music video for Eminem's song "Superman." The catchy lyrics (containing sentiments attributed to Eminem's alter ego Slim Shady) refer to the woman in the song as a bitch, a liar, a ho, and a motherfuckin' slut. In an innovative manifestation of misogyny, the singer threatens to "Put anthrax on a tampax and slap you till you can't stand."

7. In her work on trauma cinema, Janet Walker claims that films dealing with traumatic events are often shot in "a nonrealist mode characterized by disturbance and fragmentation of the films' narrative and stylistic regimes . . . drawing on innovative strategies for representing reality obliquely, by looking to mental processes for inspiration, and by incorporating self-reflexive devices" (2005, 19). Walker's work deals specifically with incest and holocaust narratives, and is best applied to films such as those directed by Alejandro González Iñárritu—*Amores Perros* (2000), *21 Grams* (2003), and *Babel* (2006)—in which the fragmented narrative structure articulates experiences of trauma and loss. However, her comments about the representation of intensely disturbing moments are relevant to the violation of realist editing conventions in *8 Mile's* confronting rap battles and to the violent, psychotic ruptures of *Lost Highway*, as discussed in the previous chapter.

8. Perspective taking, empathy, and critical viewing skills are unlikely to benefit children under seven because they lack the sophisticated moral reasoning required to think about the justifications for violence, or the ability to imagine the consequences of violence

from a victim's perspective, if these aspects are not explicitly represented in the narrative (see Krcmar and Valkenburg 1999, 612; Nathanson and Cantor 2000, 137).

9. The paint gun sequence in *8 Mile* and the scene when Cheddar Bob shoots himself could be interpreted in this light.

10. The fight sequences in *Batman Begins* are staged to augment the realism of the violence and heighten its threat by showcasing the martial arts skills of the actors themselves (rather than featuring stuntmen and wirework). Christian Bale states in the DVD special features that he could not have pulled off the savage fight scenes unless he "literally became a beast" when clad in the Batsuit.

5

Resistance and Responsiveness: Emotion and Character Engagement

Narrative is implicated in ethical life by virtue of its content, form, and structure. In addition, the kinds of interpretive resources stories call into play and the responses they give rise to can also be of ethical significance. This chapter offers an understanding of the characteristics of emotional engagement with film narratives, as well as a clarification of the nature of emotion. It addresses the ethical dimensions of emotional engagement with narrative films and film characters, working from general aspects of the importance of emotion and a defense of the value of emotion in rational ethical evaluation, to specific mechanisms by which film invites an emotive response.

According to Jack Katz, author of *How Emotions Work*, an influential phenomenological study of emotion:

> Emotions, which have so often been treated as opposed to thinking, are paradoxically self-reflective actions and experiences. But the self-reflection in emotions is corporeal rather than a matter of discursive reasoning. Through our emotions we reach back sensually to grasp the tacit, embodied foundations of our selves . . . through them we seek to articulate the corporeal metaphors that operate implicitly at the foundations of all our conduct. (1999, 7)

Following Katz, this research will emphasize the sensual and embodied aspects of emotion as well as exploring its relationship with cognition, belief, and ethics.

Film's importance in furthering understanding of the nature and role of emotion in ethical life is threefold: it portrays emotions embedded in a narrative context; it allows spectators to see, hear, and reflect on the affective displays of screen characters and, finally, it elicits felt responses from spectators. I will draw on two Australian films directed by Rowan Woods, *The Boys* (1998) and *Little Fish* (2005) in order to illustrate how emotions are involved in ethical life. In working through the characteristics and consequences of emotional engagement with these films, a narrative structure within emotions (and within which they are embedded) becomes evident, as does the ethical significance of emotion understood as a form of perceiving and attending to salience, and as felt, experiential knowledge.

Like most films, *The Boys* shows characters expressing strong emotions, uses narrative structure and plot devices to amplify the audience's investment in the fates of the characters, and makes use of the specific capacities of the audiovisual medium to represent the emotional drama of the story world. However, *The Boys* is interesting partly because it offers *few* opportunities for spectators to relate to or develop a sympathetic rapport with the characters. At the same time, the emotive charge of the film and the quality of character engagement that does occur deepens the audience's feeling for the nature and extent of the ethical and social problems dealt with by the film, in thought-provoking ways.

Many accounts of emotional responses to film and identification with characters in film presuppose that the spectator must experience empathy, mirroring the characters' emotions (Neill 2006), or must care for the characters (Gaut 2006, 261). Noel Carroll argues that "the narrative must invest the viewer with certain concerns about the fictional characters and events (and their prospects) in the film. These concerns or pro attitudes function like the desires that are found in many everyday emotions" (2006, 223). Carroll goes on to claim that when our desire for a good outcome for a character is thwarted, we tend to feel dysphoric, and when a bad character is punished in the narrative we tend to feel euphoric (2006, 224). Rowan Woods' films elicit emotional responses that cannot be adequately explained by such accounts, partly because they feature complex, damaged protagonists. For this reason, I have chosen Woods' films as case studies on which to build a more nuanced understanding of emotional engagement with screen characters. *Little Fish* is important to this analysis because it uses music much more extensively than *The Boys* to orchestrate the emotional ups and downs of its protagonists, and the screenwriter Jacquelin Persky has scripted a more sympathetic range of characters.

The Boys takes up the story of Brett Sprague (played by David Wenham) and his family on the day Brett is released from a year in prison for assault with a deadly weapon (a screwdriver) and grievous bodily harm. Later we learn that in the bungled attempt to burgle the local liquor store for which

Brett was incarcerated, he was more seriously wounded than his victim was. The film spans only 15 hours, but it flashes forward in time up to six months later, depicting the events of that day and underscoring their consequences. As spectators we witness the mixture of emotions that Brett's extended family feels upon his return, and the anger and pain he feels at having being excluded from their lives. We also feel the tension surrounding the volatile mixture of his celebration of freedom enmeshed with his rage about being locked away, and about the social injustice that he believes underwrites his situation. Suspense and confusion builds throughout the film in response to the menacing, conniving nature of Brett's character as we wait with anxiety and dread for the second violent crime signaled in the flash-forwards. The complexity of emotional responses to *The Boys* arises partly because the film thwarts narrative conventions and expectations with its disjunctive chronology (depicting the effect—another jail sentence—before the unspeakable crime that caused it), and partly because it features an unexpectedly dark and emotionally manipulative character as the central protagonist.

Little Fish begins with fleeting childhood images of the central character Tracy Heart playing at the beach as the waves wash up on the sand in a dazzle of light. The melodic notes of the instrumental theme are interwoven around these shots of young Tracy at the beach, interspersed with fragments of a journey along a road late at night, which we later discover leads toward the crisis in the final act of the film. Then, quite suddenly, we are with the adult Tracy (played by Cate Blanchett) on the day of her 15-year high school reunion. Though these brief images from Tracy's youth haunt the narrative and invest it with the poignancy of lost possibilities, the plot follows a linear logic from this point forward, hinging on the interplay of hope, remorse, and fear. Tracy's story is that of a recovering heroin addict in Cabramatta, the same area of Sydney in which *The Boys* is set. Tracy's goal is to secure a bank loan so she can own her own business instead of continuing to work in a video store as she has done for four years. Of course, the loan is refused and her aspirations are crushed as the bank tells Tracy it "cannot approve an unsecured loan for someone with your history." In desperation, she is then drawn into temptation, lies, and crime as three men who were close to her during the time she was an addict threaten to drag her back into their world. Hugo Weaving plays Lionel Dawson, Tracy's father figure, a washed-up former professional rugby player who is trying to kick his own addiction and turn his life around. Despite the fact that he is the man who introduced her to heroin, the two have a close, affectionate bond. Early in the story Tracy's aimless but affable brother Ray (Martin Henderson) uses her video shop as a drop-off point for a packet of drugs shaped like little fish, and invites his mate, Tracy's ex-boyfriend and former dealer Jonny (Dustin Nguyen) home for dinner. To the mounting distress of her mother Janelle (Noni Hazlehurst), the three men that Tracy loves involve her in their dealings with two far more dangerous figures in the criminal underworld: Brad "The Jockey" Thompson (Lionel's former lover, played by Sam Neill) and his corrupt lieutenant, Steven Moss (Joel Tobeck).

In order to see how the different levels of emotion relate to spectatorial identification, narrative engagement, and ethical evaluation in *The Boys* and *Little Fish*, a clearer understanding of emotion is first required. I will take as my starting point a broad definition of emotion that acknowledges (in addition to other important elements) emotion's cognitive component and its contribution to rational deliberation.

An Account of Emotion

The philosopher Justin Oakley understands emotional states as "complex phenomena involving dynamically related elements of cognition, desire and affectivity" (1992, 2). Oakley demonstrates that conceptions of emotion that are limited to any one element or any pair of these three elements do not provide a basis to distinguish consistently between emotional states. For example, the affective aspect (the physiological dimension of emotion that we experience as a "feeling") of excitement might be expressed in ways that look like anxiety and create similar physical effects such as a rush of adrenaline. Similarly, a happy smile might be mistaken for a derisive smirk, but each emotion is linked to quite different beliefs, which in turn relate to different desires (desire being the action-oriented dimension of emotion). Without taking the complexity of the relationship between these three constitutive elements of emotion into account, we cannot fully understand or interpret emotional responses.

In *The Boys* Brett's mother, Sandra (Lynette Curran) exhibits what appears to be excitement and joy upon his return home. The cognitive component of her emotion is knowledge that Brett's release from jail warrants celebration, based on the belief or hope that he has "learned his lesson" by doing time. She also exhibits the desire to make Brett feel welcome, and the conjunction of cognition and desire are expressed affectively by squeals of delight, a broad smile, and a warm hug as he walks in the door. We find as the film progresses that Sandra's demonstration of affection was inflected with anxiety as the desire to be welcoming blended with her wish not to offend or aggravate her volatile son, and the hope that he learned his lesson was offset against the fear that he would punish his family for their failure to visit him in jail. The affective experiences and displays that characterize particular emotions are largely consistent across different cultures, as the work of Paul Ekman in *Emotions Revealed: Understanding Faces and Feelings* (2003) demonstrates, yet signifiers of surprise, excitement, and fear are easily confused and the possibility that people may attempt to mask or fake emotions, or may express compound emotions, creates room for misinterpretation. This suggests that interpreting an emotional response such as Sandra's requires an understanding of the narratives in which the three elements that Oakley ascribes to emotion are embedded.

This association between emotion and narrative is taken up by theorists such as Ronald de Sousa, Nussbaum, and Oakley who argue for the social construction of emotions as learned responses to situations. In *The Rationality of Emotion,* de Sousa claims emotions are constructed in circumstances that he refers to as paradigm scenarios: "We are made familiar with the vocabulary of emotion by association with paradigm scenarios. These are drawn first from our daily life as small children and later reinforced by the stories, art, and culture to which we are exposed" (1987, 182). As with the "cognitive scripts" in Bandura's observational learning theory of media effects, a paradigm scenario is like a dramatic scene in which roles, responses, and feelings are composed into an intelligible pattern and given definition in relation to one another.

In a passage that echoes de Sousa's approach, Nussbaum says:

> A child does not learn its society's conception of love or of anger, by sitting in an ethics class. It learns them long before any classes, in complex interactions with parents and society. These interactions provide paradigms of emotion and teach the cognitive categories that underlie the experience of emotion. And, since we are all tellers of stories, and since one of the child's most pervasive and powerful ways of learning its society's values and structures is through the stories it hears and learns to tell, stories will be a major source of any culture's emotional life. (1990, 293)

Since judgments and values are able to be modified by an alteration of beliefs (by seeing from another perspective; by telling a different story), the script that an emotional response follows is "a pattern that can be unraveled, a writing that can be unwritten, a story that can be ended"

(Nussbaum 1990, 287). Potentially, narrative films can help to rewrite such scripts, presenting avenues for understanding our own "scripts" and those of others. I will discuss this in more detail, after establishing the ethical significance of emotion and working through some of the problems associated with emotional responses to film narratives.

The Problem of Belief

There are a number of differences between emotional responses to fiction and "real life." Cognitivist theories of emotion focus primarily on the significance of belief to the possibility or legitimacy of an emotional response. Such a view is sometimes used to suggest that we do not actually experience emotional responses to fictional narratives at all because emotions are reliant on the beliefs underwriting the situations in which they arise: for example, fear is based on the belief that a threat exists and poses a danger to me or to that which is dear to me. In theories of emotion emphasizing cognition, responses to fiction are often called "quasi-emotional," as Gregory Currie dubs them in his book *The Nature of Fiction* (1990), or "make-believe emotions" as Kendall Walton terms them (1990; 2006) because they do not rely on the belief that the fictional occurrence actually happened to a real person, or is occurring at the time of watching the film. By such accounts, when the cognitive content of an emotion is invalid and this is known to be the case, it is not a true emotion. For instance, from a cognitive perspective, responses that do not hinge on appropriate beliefs can be explained as bodily reactions or impulses: affects or desires. A cognitive film theorist might interpret the response to an impending disaster on the screen as an adrenaline rush induced by audiovisual stimuli. Such a physiological response can be explained away as a purely affective reaction, rather than a real feeling of fear or anxiety (knowing, as the spectator does, that characters in the film are played by actors who are in no *actual* danger). This form of reaction to film is considered in cognitive accounts to fall short of a full emotional response (since, in fact, the audience is aware that the character does not exist and it therefore matters little whether things go well or badly on the screen).[1] I will argue that any account that denies spectators experience emotional responses to fiction film must be based on an inadequate understanding of emotion. A broader view of how fiction engages the cognitive aspects of emotion is necessary.

Nussbaum claims that fictional narratives elicit a range of emotions that are pegged to the concrete circumstances of particular characters but that may also relate to beliefs about the reader or spectator's own life possibilities.

In addition, emotions extend outward from the text to "bridge the gap" between the character's circumstances and those of real people as spectators make a "judgment of similar possibilities" (Nussbaum 2001, 320–321). For instance, knowing the characters in *Little Fish* don't represent real individuals does not lessen my emotional response as I believe that the issues, hopes and fears, decisions and desires they struggle with *could* occur in reality and are important whether they occur in Tracy's life, in my life, or the in lives of real people in Cabramatta. This suggests that although spectators remain aware that we are watching a fiction, our emotional responses do relate to beliefs about the real world. It is easy to see how this applies to a realist drama, but to show how we can respond emotionally to less plausible films like science fiction narratives, we need an account of the cognitive component of emotion that acknowledges the richly intersubjective[2] experience of identification and that is less dependent on logic or on beliefs about truth, than on imagination and beliefs about possibility and *value*. De Sousa's theory of paradigm scenarios suggests this very thing, presupposing that emotional reactions are informed by general beliefs and attitudes about how it is right or wrong to treat a human being.

The cognitive component of responses to film texts is a far more complex matter than believing that the story is real or fictional. The cognitive dimension of emotion involves an appraisal or evaluation of an object's salience or value which does not necessarily take a propositional or linguistic form, as Nussbaum points out (2001, 23). Cognition cannot be reduced to a single structure: it entails thoughts, memories, imaginings, apprehensions, and speculations as well as evaluative perceptions and beliefs (see Oakley 1992, 15). In an emotional response to a fictional narrative the cognitive component of emotion is frequently imaginative, rather than directly belief oriented, as Alex Neill argues in "Empathy and (Film) Fiction" (2006). As discussed in the next chapter, the metaphoric or symbolic understanding that narratives evoke and that imagination allows access to can communicate truths about human experience, even though we apprehend them or come to understand them through something that we do not believe has actually happened or is likely to happen.

Emotional responses arise in relation to a dynamic array of stimuli that are internal and external, conscious and subconscious, past and present, fictional and factual. For example, when Brett's impotent rage is unleashed on his girlfriend in *The Boys*, spectators may experience the desire to see Michelle safely escape the violent assault. This desire is narratively embedded within an emotional response that could include fear and anger on the part of the spectator, empathizing with Michelle. These feelings are characterized by actual bodily tension, and based on justified beliefs about it being wrong to assault another person, and a realistic recognition of the danger a woman would face if a violent, strong man intended to break a wall with her head. The reality of the spectator's desire to see things go well for Michelle is not compromised by the fact that we know we are viewing a fiction film, or that we are unable to intervene in the narrative and extend help to her in the story world or on the film set. When we are viewing the film, at the point where Brett's rage and frustration escalate, endangering Michelle, part of our emotional response is to actually desire that Michelle escapes harm. The emotional turbulence that spectators may experience with and for Michelle is not undercut just because, given the opportunity, few of us would wish to rewrite the script so that the story unfolded differently, omitting the dramatic tension. This desire exists in the context of the film and is related to feelings that the story and its characters invoke, as well as to our own experience of and imaginings, construals, and beliefs about the world we actually live in and about the story world. Our emotional response, which includes bodily reactions, complex cognitive dimensions, and contextually specific desires, indicates our alliance with Michelle's best interests and it reflects a participative understanding and evaluation of the narrative as a whole. This includes an understanding of the ethical issues involved in such situations, which can also be brought to bear on actual situations that we might perhaps encounter.

The Significance of Emotion in Ethical Life

Justin Oakley defends the value of emotion in ethical life by reminding us that we regard each of the components of emotion (certain cognitive and affective functions, and desires) as individually bearing moral significance (1992, 43). For example, we recognize the ethical significance of *beliefs* about human rights and responsibilities, and of the *desire* to relieve suffering, and we also acknowledge that the *affective* experience of emotion (feelings of compassion, outrage, remorse, or shame) may motivate ethical action. Unless these component elements are considered together, we can only provide an incomplete account of the ethical significance of emotions (Oakley 1992, 45).

Many traditional accounts of rationality either explicitly exclude emotion from the domain of reason altogether, admit the value of restricted categories of emotion (such as compassion), or relegate emotions to a motivational or instrumental role in which they catalyze certain actions. Restrictions on both the variety and function of those emotions that are accorded significance in ethical decisions are representative of the ways in which emotions have been seen as problematic within much of Western analytical philosophy; emotion has also been deemed unreliable and aligned with irrationality and a lack of volition.[3] A detailed working through of the different arguments that have been used to exclude emotion from the domain of ethics and rational deliberation has been undertaken elsewhere.[4] Though the value of emotion is defended from some of these critiques at intervals throughout the chapter, systematically revisiting such debates here would add little to an attempt to understand the role that emotional engagement with film narratives has in ethical life. A richer appreciation of emotion, the various elements that make it up, and the contexts within which it is embedded, makes it easier to recognize how "emotions may contribute in important ways to our achieving the virtues of clear perception, keen judgment, and depth of understanding, and this shows an important dimension to the moral significance of emotions" (Oakley 1992, 53).

An example from *The Boys* clarifies the links between emotional responsiveness and the cognitive grasp of ethical salience. Early in the film we discover that Brett's youngest brother Stevie met and became sexually involved with a young woman called Nola. She fell pregnant while still a teenager, and when her father threw her out of home she came to live in the Sprague household, despite the fact that Stevie indicated that he did not care for her and exhibited reluctance to take responsibility for his unborn

Figure 19 The Boys: *Nola (unfocused in the background), Glenn and his partner Jackie (foreground), and Stevie drinking beer.*

child. Nola, who appears to be in the second trimester of pregnancy, is a quiet, sensitive creature; she is often a little out of focus as she hovers in the background and on the edges of the frame. These techniques make it evident that she feels like an outsider, uninvolved in the family drama and neither seen nor heard by those around her with any clarity.

After an unsuccessful attempt to connect with Stevie when he fetches Brett from prison, Nola timidly suggests she might leave. When Brett's brash girlfriend, Michelle (Toni Colette), asks a few pointed questions and it emerges that Nola has no money and nowhere to go, she bursts into tears. Brett, who has only just been introduced to Nola, moves to hug and comfort her, telling her "You're one of us now Luv . . . You're carrying Mum's first grandchild." Stevie looks on silently and dispassionately from a distance. Gesturing to Brett's attempts to soothe Nola, Michelle snaps at Stevie, criticizing his heartless failure to respond to Nola's suffering and his refusal to take responsibility for his own actions, saying "That's what you should be doing!" Stevie's emotionless response is indicative of a corresponding moral deficiency, as he fails to grasp the gravity of Nola's situation as a homeless, unsupported, unskilled, pregnant young woman with little hope and few prospects. This failure to understand (which may be associated with a lack of moral maturity) leads to a failure to rationally deliberate about the ethical values and responsibilities arising from the situation.

This scene from *The Boys* helps to illustrate that emotion is often characterized by a particular sort of cognition, specifically linked to the discernment of value and the ability to perceive which aspects of a situation have ethical salience. The relationship between beliefs and judgments concerning salience and value is one of the principle links between emotion and ethics.[5] In this capacity, emotions play an epistemological role that is crucial to ethical insight. By revealing beliefs and values, the kind of understanding made available via emotional perception and response is a form of *embodied perception*, hence emotions can be described as narratively embedded, embodied experiences that shape our understanding and provide ways of making sense of situations (see Katz 1999).

Consequences and Instrumentality

Another way in which emotional engagement has been understood to be morally significant is in terms of the transformative potential of emotion in *motivating* ethical action.[6] Of the emotions that are readily recognized to motivate ethical action, compassion for the plight of others is among the most important. Often when we view a film, compassion arises as a result of the increased sensitivity to and understanding of others. Such a compassionate response embraces the screen characters we relate to, but may also inform our responses to people and situations outside the cinema. Nussbaum advocates the "cultivation" of compassion as a "bridge" between people that is based on thought and evaluation regarding the "wellbeing of others" (1996a, 28).[7] By contrast, Oakley observes that though we may be able to "cultivate" or restrain certain emotional states, it is our *lack* of conscious control of emotions that gives the perception of value and ethical salience the uncontrived, honest nature of a "gut reaction." He suggests that "It is often a good thing that we cannot (or cannot usually, anyway) stop ourselves having emotions at will, for this reminds us of the importance of the authenticity and responsiveness of our emotions in relation to the world around us" (Oakley 1992, 132). Since emotion is in some respects involuntary, and in other respects subject to conscious influence, the difficulties inherent in attempting to hold moral agents responsible for their emotions (and whatever effects those emotions might have) suggest that we need to find another way of understanding ethical agency in relation to emotions. While emotions are nonvolitional states in some ways, we do remain answerable or accountable for our emotions and the various ways in which they find expression, to some degree.

Framing the ethical aspect of emotion in terms of responsibility can lead in two inappropriate directions: blame, or a kind of façade that masks or bottles up authentic emotional responses. In *The Boys*, Stevie feels revulsion, not compassion for Nola in her pregnant state. Can we really blame him for his gut reaction? Would it really be better if he pretended to feel compassion and therefore behaved with more outward civility toward her? She may then be deceived into remaining in a dangerous and degrading situation. The process of reflecting on one's emotions is a process of constructing a story, and a way of becoming ethically accountable. If Stevie were in the habit of self-reflection or of cultivating empathy, then his own story might take a different turn. He might, for instance, recognize his feelings as originating from a fear of responsibility, or regret for irresponsibility, if not some deeper pain about the absence of his own father. In the process of developing an honest account of emotions, the emotions themselves often shift and change, eventually leading to other transformations and extending into action. Taken further, Stevie's feelings, which indicate the lack of value he places on Nola, their relationship, and their unborn child, might let him know what the right course of action would be. As Oakley suggests, the ability to control something is not the only way of taking responsibility for it.

Emotions also motivate action because perceiving events through the lens of feelings like hope or fear can affect ethical character and conduct. For instance, in *Little Fish* Janelle's fear for her children's well-being is an emotional lens through which she sees herself and those she loves as threatened, based on past experience. This emotional perspective influences the course of action Janelle takes. She perceives Lionel and Jonny to be leading Tracy and her brother Ray astray. Tight lipped and cold Janelle voices recriminations about the night Ray lost his leg when Jonny crashed a car while on drugs, and she orders Lionel to stay away from her kids, refusing to listen when he comes to tell her he has willed his estate to her family. While Janelle's negative feelings are grounded in concern for her children and can be seen to have positive ethical implications (since her emotional response registers beliefs about what she values), they are ultimately expressed in angry, judgmental ways with the inadvertent consequence that her children fear her disapproval and feel unable to confide in her as they are drawn deeper into trouble.

Problems with Narrative's Propensity to Generate Emotion

The concern may arise that in becoming sympathetically and empathetically involved in a character's life, spectators can be blinded by emotions to other, perhaps more objective ways in which the ethical dimensions of the situation might be viewed. One of the principal reasons for the exclusion of emotions from moral reasoning is that they are thought to compromise the ability to remain objective, impersonal, or impartial.[8] Partiality is characteristic of emotional relationships with others and it is held to be problematic because it may narrow the sphere of moral concern to exclude people who are distant from us and whose circumstances are known only vaguely or not at all. Emotions themselves generally have a "self-referential element" related to persons, objects, and goals that have importance to the person experiencing the emotion: "Emotions look at the world from the subject's own viewpoint, mapping events onto the subject's own sense of personal importance or value" (Nussbaum 2001, 33). For this reason, outwardly directed emotional states such as empathy, sympathy, and compassion have special ethical relevance. Furthermore, other criteria and guides are useful as a counterbalance to emotional intelligence, for instance, the principles and rules of justice and the legal system should have guided the Sprague brothers and the characters in *Little Fish* when they were in the grip of emotions that influenced their choices.

Another potentially adverse aspect of engagement with narrative, particularly those narratives with persuasive characters, is that the attitudes,
values, and views in the text are communicated with the authority and conviction of personal experience. An example of this form of criticism of
emotional engagement with the characters in narratives is found in the
work of Daryl Tress and Adrienne Fulco (1995). Such critics argue that
narrative form *undermines* the interpreter's efforts to critically engage
with the content of the story, claiming that the narrative form repels
doubt, critical analysis, reasoned debate, and skepticism (Tress and Fulco
1995, 274). More specifically, it is the sense of personal closeness with
characters that narratives can encourage that is deemed to be problematic
because "the fictional suggestion of familiarity dictates the response
appropriate among friends who already know the particulars and the
people involved, namely, nodding in sympathetic agreement" (Tress and
Fulco 1995, 274). While it is correct to say that the story-telling form
often "emphasizes and legitimizes the emotional and more subjective
dimensions of communication and understanding,"[9] emotional responses
to narratives are complex, varied, and difficult to "dictate." (For instance,
I first saw *Little Fish* with a friend who felt the ending was uplifting whereas
I wept, despite the fact that we share similar values and occupations, and at
the time both had daughters roughly the same age as little Tracy, who is
seen playing at the beach in the closing images of the film.) The sense of
familiarity that narrative can foster between reader and writer, or characters and viewers, does not render it immune to questions and criticisms
(though in particular instances that may be the case). Instead, the more
informed we are about narrative context and causation, the deeper our
understanding and the more likely we are to offer a thoughtful interpretation and to ask the most helpful, provocative, or sensitive questions. The
more likely we are, in short, to be able to understand and reflect upon and
come to a rational evaluation of the ethical issues involved in the situation
or story.

Responsiveness and Resistance

As I have argued, an important means by which we interpret the significance of particular stories is by moving back and forth between a sense of
involvement with their characters and details, and taking recourse to more
general values and perspectives found in broader life experiences. The
reservoir of personal experiences and commitments to general values
provide the guidelines for discerning good from bad in the narratives we

are exposed to. Within the structure of film texts and the conditions of spectatorship, films provide opportunities for critical distance. Patterns of empathy or close audiovisual identification with a particular character are fragmented by means of the inclusion of shots from other character's perspectives or an "omniscient" viewpoint. Most importantly, spectators bring their previous ethical beliefs and values with them into the cinema. We interpret the actions of characters on the screen in relation to these preexisting ethical commitments, evaluating characters' behavior in relation to our own values. In the process of emotional simulation involved in empathy, "we do not lose ourselves in the other, but imagine possessing certain predicates of the other" (Smith 1995, 97). In imagining and, to a certain extent, experiencing how another person feels within a narrative context, we access the significance or value of events and issues *to them*, without losing sight of our own ethical standpoints.

An important feature of narrative interpretation is the shifting balance between responsiveness and resistance to the messages the story conveys, including those messages that we come to "know" through feeling the emotions inscribed in or instilled by the text. The structure of spectatorial engagement enables film to be a source of ethical development because of similarities with an ideal of moral engagement and attention involving a dynamic equilibrium between partiality and impartiality, the particular and the universal, concrete and more abstract details of the situation, identification and evaluation. Narrative film has the capacity to bind us to the moral projects of the characters whilst allowing us to discern the patterns of moral complexity with a clarity and distance unavailable to us as agents involved in our own problematic lives, lacking perspective, foresight, or hindsight.

Spectatorship and Attention

De Sousa claims "Emotions are in part, patterns of attention. Therefore one might expect a change in patterns of attention to entail changes in emotion" (1987, 243). Because emotions are a kind of perception and interpretation of value, intimately bound up with practices of attention, the ways in which cinematic narratives focus and direct attention can cultivate the emotional responses of spectators in ethically significant ways. On the relevance of perception and attention to emotion, Carroll writes that perception can become emotionally charged in a film narrative because emotion can act like a "searchlight": "It casts the cause or the object of our state in a special phenomenological light; it fixes our attention on it and

alerts us to its significance" (2006, 221). In this sense, the emotions organize or direct perception and manage our attention, "guiding both what
we look at and what we look for" (Carroll 2006, 221). Carroll makes the
important point that in fiction films the salient details of situations are
foregrounded for the audience by the narrative structure, characterization,
the reactions of surrounding characters, music, performance, cinematography, and so forth; hence, the audience's emotional reactions are predeter-
mined or "prefocussed" to a certain extent. Prefocussing happens when
criteria appropriate to given emotions generate and manipulate those
emotions. This relates to what Paul Ekman terms the "blind spot" or
"hot spot" of emotional immersion caused by a refractory period when
information incompatible with the emotion is briefly unavailable to us
and details relevant to the emotional state are foregrounded (2003, 122).
According to Ekman's research, in the grip of an emotional state "expectations are formed, judgments are made, that typically serve to maintain
rather than diminish the felt emotion" (Ekman 2003, 63). Hence Ekman
suggests that we need to cultivate the ability to impose a reflective distance
from emotional triggers instead of responding in the heat of the moment
in order to exercise greater control and choice (2003, 121). Like the refractory period of emotions themselves, the way a situation is framed in a film
can direct emotional perception, zeroing in on things relevant to that
emotional state and excluding other details from our attention. As Carroll
puts it, "Our attention is glued to those features of the object of the
emotion that are appropriate to the emotional state we are in" (Carroll
2006, 223). To ensure the success of this emotional "prefocussing," the film
sets us up to respond in a certain way by investing the viewer with
concerns and preferences about the fictional characters and the way events
are resolved (Carroll 2006, 223). Hence, the particular view of life that the
film offers will direct our attention in certain ways, cultivating particular
emotional responses.

Like Ekman, de Sousa suggests that a conscious redirection of attention,
perhaps from consequence to intention, or from positive to negative aspects
of a situation can lead to reinterpretation, helping us to see something in a
different light, rather than simply "apprehending the world as we find it" or
accepting the way a narrative guides our emotional perception (de Sousa
1987, 324). The cinematography in *The Boys* certainly directs attention
to certain aspects of the narrative situation, often using differential focus,
a long lens, and unusual camera placements. There is one scene that is particularly disturbing because attention is directed to the menacing nature of
Brett's character. For the second time that day Nola is gathering together

her belongings and mustering the courage to leave the Sprague household. Brett corners her in his bedroom and interrogates her as to whether she called the police earlier that day when he was abusing Michelle. In one of the devious shifts that marks Brett's character and makes him so unnerving, he suddenly becomes gentle and begins to soothe the tearful Nola once again. He sits beside her on the bed, extracts a confession from her about phoning the police, and proceeds to convince her that although she has done the wrong thing, he is not angry. He claims to understand and to forgive her, saying "we all make mistakes, don't we now." This scene is unsettling because a dangerous and unpredictable character is soliciting the trust of a naive girl, desperately in need of someone to rely on. Viewed in confronting close-ups and often shot from a low angle, Brett's presence dominates the screen. This, in conjunction with convincing emotional performances by the actors, succeeds in conveying a strong sense of how intimidating it would be for Nola to be in such close proximity to him.

At the point when Nola is both physically and emotionally vulnerable to Brett, he leans forward and kisses her on the forehead and the film shifts into slow motion until he moves away.[10] Significant sections of this scene are shot from Nola's point of view, with the camera aligned so closely to her line of sight that her head sometimes moves into frame, obscuring the spectator's view and forcing us to literally try to *see through her*. Significantly, the shot where Brett leans in to kiss her shows Nola herself in the

Figure 20 The Boys: *Brett discusses Nola's call to the police, and her intention to leave the Sprague household.*

frame: here the film simultaneously invites us to participate in Nola's subjective experience and to view her from a more omniscient perspective. Even as it reveals her expression in extreme close-up, by casting her in soft focus and dim light it points attention toward the more harshly lit figure of Brett. The temporal deceleration due to the subtle change in frame rate represents Nola's subjective perception of his movement as threatening and directs the audience's attention to the danger Brett represents as a menacing, manipulative, duplicitous character. Our perception is slowed down to register the heightened significance of the scene, and our emotional response is potentially intensified by sharing in Nola's emotional experience, and also by seeing the emotions expressed on her face and Brett's.

Engaging Characters

In his fascinating book *Engaging Characters*, Murray Smith states that "character structures are perhaps the major way by which narrative texts solicit our assent for particular values, practices and ideologies" (1995, 4). Both empathic and sympathetic emotional responses to the stories of other people's lives require imagination to a large extent, so the emotional and imaginative components of spectator-character relationships are often difficult to disentangle from one another.[11] It is the emotional response, together with the process of connecting with and relating to characters through projection, metaphoric understanding of their situation and other imaginative means, that constitutes character engagement. What follows is an investigation of the nature of the relationship between the spectator and screen characters that aims to show how film narratives engage spectators with the values, behaviors, beliefs, and ideologies they depict.

Smith's careful breakdown of the structure of sympathy and empathy does much to reveal how engaging with a character doesn't simply mean identifying with the heroes, feeling badly for the victims, and becoming influenced by a subject's moral perspective when the camera shoots from their point of view. Working with a text like *The Boys* in which there is no heroic protagonist, and rapport with the characters is *not* explicitly established gives insight into other layers of emotional responsiveness and resistance to a narrative that are often overlooked when we think of films in terms of whether they make us cry, or laugh, or feel as though we have related to or identified with the characters.

Character engagement occurs as spectators respond empathetically and sympathetically to screen characters and their circumstances. Though philosophical conceptions of sympathy and empathy vary considerably, they can be understood as two responses to character that Smith loosely describes as "feeling for" and "feeling with":

> In the case of sympathetic responses, we cognitively recognise an emotion and then respond with a different but appropriate emotion based on our evaluation of the character, while in the case of empathic responses, we simulate or experience the same affect or emotion experienced by the character. (Smith 1995, 102)

Following Smith's distinction between sympathy as "feeling for" and empathy as "feeling with" others, I will first consider sympathetic engagement with screen characters.

Sympathetic Understanding

Sympathetic responses to fictional characters are emotional reactions in which the cognitive component of emotion is prominent. As well as recognizing, reflecting on, and evaluating what is going on for the character emotionally, we are also able to sympathize about more external difficulties such as their fate and circumstances. Sympathy, Smith says, has three levels of imaginative engagement: recognition, alignment, and allegiance.

Recognition is in Smith's words, "the identification and assignment of traits to characters" (1997, 415). We can recognize animated and nonhuman figures like Shrek as characters with human traits, inviting our sympathy. In the cinema, spectators can occupy audiovisual standpoints which seem to be "in line" with those of certain characters. The term "alignment" refers to the ways in which a film positions spectators in the story space along with screen characters, directing our attention toward a particular character's reception of information by making that reception mutual (point-of-view shots, subjective imagery, and nondiegetic sound, especially interior monologues and musical indications of mood, are techniques commonly used to foster alignment). Characters can be understood partly as the vehicles that transport certain kinds of information to the spectators. For example, scenes shot from a particular character's point of view create visual or sensory alignment of the spectator with that character. In *The Boys* spectators may experience a sense of alienation because we are often aligned with Nola's point of view, as she hovers on the fringe of the Sprague family, standing in doorways and looking on. Often, in the process of becoming visually aligned with a screen character, the spectator literally comes to see things from another person's perspective, when the

camera presents the spectator with an image or a story shot from a particular character's point of view. Thus the prevalence in the early scenes of *The
Boys* of visual alignment with Nola may enhance the sympathy spectators
feel for a character it would otherwise be all too easy to ignore.

As well as the obvious audiovisual alignment of spectators with a character, the film can also align us with its own particular way of seeing and
interpreting the narrative (another way of saying this would be to claim
that spectators can become aligned with the narrator of a story, even when
that narrator is not embodied as an on-screen or in-text character). For
example, the opening sequence of shots in *The Boys* expresses and gives us
access to a way of seeing that leaves a distinctive impression. Together with
the pixilated video footage spliced into the film, it gives the impression of a
shift in attention from external events to a distorted inner world, experienced by a subject with a loose grip on reality. This world view becomes
progressively more confronting as the boys drink beer and drop acid, and
as the telephoto lens lurches ever closer to the action in the disequilibrium
of the second act.

The camera in *The Boys* is often unsteadily hand-held, it moves rapidly
with whip pans, seeming to jerk its head around as though startled or suspicious. The opening shot of the film is hand-held and grainy like the
footage from a surveillance camera, and video surveillance is a recurring
theme throughout the narrative. The Sprague "boys" are literally being
watched. They are watching their backs, they are watching each other, the
women in their lives are represented as prying or spying, and they are being
watched by the police. Everyone is waiting to see their next mistake.

The entire film is shot around corners and obstacles, using different
planes of space in the house to show how characters in the background
respond to a drama that is playing out in the foreground or revealing someone eavesdropping while concealed by a door or wall. Our view of the
action is almost always partially obscured by doorways, shoulders, or walls
so that we feel that we must strain our eyes and crane our necks to properly
see what is going on.

The way of seeing that we (as spectators, and as subjects engaged in
the film's own visual agency) participate in fractures the spaces within the
film. The obstacles that are constantly separating the seer from the seen
work in conjunction with the fragmented, nonlinear narrative structure to
inflect the domestic and social spaces inhabited by the film with a sense of
sneakiness, suspicion, and disunity. The barriers impeding our vision prevent us, as spectators, from feeling included in the familial space, and
surveillance cameras mediate our vision of public spaces. Although we

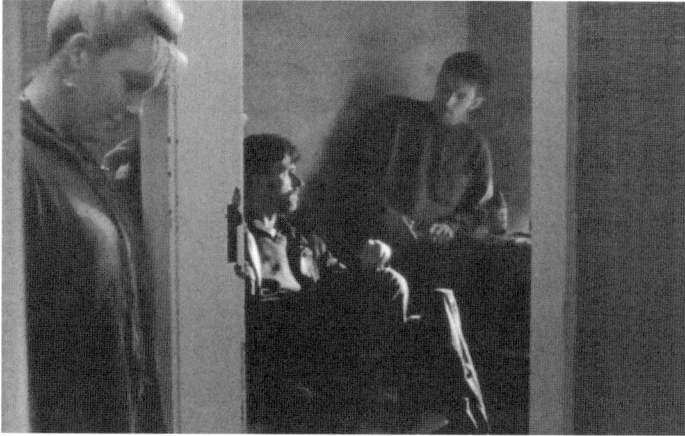

Figure 21 The Boys: *Michelle eavesdropping on Brett and Glen.*

Figure 22 The Boys: *Brett being watched by a surveillance camera.*

experience transitory visual alignments with the perspectives of each of the characters in the Sprague family, the visual style of the film conveys the impression that the characters feel as much like outsiders in their own world as we do. The shallow focus and flash-forwards that intersperse and disrupt temporal continuity throughout the film suggest that for those within the story world, there is no continuous or clear picture: the characters' understandings of their own situation are hazy and intermittent, disjunctive, oddly angled, and de-centered.

Figure 23 The Boys: *Looking past obstacles at Brett with a low-level camera and a long lens.*

As the example above illustrates, the effect on spectators of the film's own vision or version of events must not be underestimated. We are not only aligned with and influenced by the characters in the story, though when we are, the impact can be moderated due to the way of looking established within the film as a whole. Along with character alignment, sensory alignment with the film's body works in ways that are virtually indissociable from narrative style and structure to inform spectators' emotive responses to a text and its occupants.

Allegiance, the third way in which sympathetic engagement with film characters functions, operates in relation to narrative content and context. Allegiance requires the ethical evaluation of characters on the basis of the values they embody, values that the spectator may experience resonance with or repulsion from. More than just understanding or experiencing a sense of fellow feeling, allegiance entails "evaluating and responding emotionally to the traits and emotions of the character in the context of the narrative situation . . . without replicating the emotions of the character" (Smith 1995, 84–85). The spectator's responses of allegiance are evaluative in a cognitive sense due to the extent of our knowledge of the context in which the character acts, in an affective sense because we are connected (via embodied understanding or attunement) to the subjective state and feelings of the character, and in terms of desire, because either we experience an attraction or an aversion to the direction and object of the character's own desires.

In the scene where Brett breaks the conditions of his parole to revisit the scene of his crime and confront Graham Newman, who defended himself and his store by sticking a carving knife into Brett's belly and calling the police, the spectator's sense of allegiance shifts uneasily. Brett is clearly not a paragon of virtue, but when we encounter Graham Newman we experience no urge to ally ourselves with him either. Our aversion to him begins to help us understand Brett's actions a little better, though we retain our evaluation of burglary as being wrong. However, when the Spragues hurl unprovoked racist insults at a couple of Newman's Asian customers as they leave, our allegiance turns away from them even though we are aligned with their visual perspective. Ideally, spectators are moved to evaluate the values the Sprague brothers embody as being unethical and unlike our own. In consequence, the audience is likely to feel repelled from and judgmental of Brett. The cinematic techniques in this scene position spectators such that we tend to evaluate his behavior negatively.

The three aspects of sympathetic engagement Smith identifies indicate that, to a certain extent, the spectator's viewing position in relation to screen characters is dictated by the position of the camera and by other cinematic techniques, but in other senses the response to screen characters depends on factors within the world of the narrative and within the moral and political terrain the spectator inhabits. The spectator is positioned in the text in multiple and transitory ways that may facilitate or inhibit character engagement. On one level, the camera position defines the spectator's implied location in screen space (we experience the action from where the camera and microphone are positioned, which entails perceptual identification with the film's own point of view). In addition, the camera often adopts the position of screen characters, which locates the spectator within an audiovisual viewpoint and invites identification with their psychological and physiological experiences by means of point-of-view shots and subjective sound and imagery. The spectator is also implicated in the acts of judgment undertaken by the characters, witnessing as they evaluate each other, and responding as we imagine ourselves in social situations. For this mode of identification we need expressive reaction shots that show the body language of screen characters, as well as shots viewing the world through their eyes, since point-of-view shots on their own give access to perceptual subjectivity but do not necessarily foster identification or an affective response.

Nick Browne argues that the position of the spectator is defined:

[N]either in terms of orientation within the constructed geography of the fiction nor in terms of social position of the viewing character. On the contrary, our point of view on the sequence is tied more closely to our attitude of approval or disapproval and is very different from any literal viewing angle or character's point of view. (1992, 219)

This understanding of spectatorial identification privileges the audience and what they bring to the narrative in the act of interpretation over the film, and the way it invites the audience to share its world view. In this sense, Browne prioritizes allegiance over alignment, whilst recognizing the intersubjective dialectic that characterizes the spectator's relationship to screen characters. This relationship hinges on the unique ability of film to locate the spectator in the interchangeable positions of the one seeing and the one being seen—a dynamic that is particularly obvious in shot-reverse-shot dialogue sequences but that is also implicit in all shot sequences. "Identification," Browne writes, "asks us as spectators to be in two places at once, where the camera is and 'with' the depicted person—thus its double structure of viewer/viewed" (1992, 219).

The important point to emerge from the accounts of emotion and character engagement discussed here is that identification with screen characters is "*aspectual*" rather than totalizing, as Berys Gaut points out in an article entitled "Identification and Emotion in Narrative Film" (2006, 263). We don't become another person during cinematic identification, and we don't have to feel what they feel or agree with their actions or opinions in order to imaginatively identify with their situations or their aspirations, as Smith's work has shown. Rather than taking on a character's subjectivity wholesale when we watch a film, different cinematic techniques invite a shifting intersubjective experience in which we share in the optical, affective, motivational, evaluative, or epistemic perspective of particular characters (or of the film itself, and its implied narrator) at various points in the narrative. Of these aspects, affective identification or empathy affords a particularly deep level of identification and therefore warrants a more detailed discussion.

Empathic Understanding

Alex Neill's account of empathy and film fiction casts empathy as a form of affective imagination, understood as "feeling with" a character in a way that "depends on our imagining what her beliefs, desires, and so on might be [. . .] empathizing with another is at least partly a matter of *understanding how things are with her*" (2006, 252, original emphasis). The role of imagination in character engagement and film spectatorship is dealt with in the next chapter, but here I would like to explore the affective, visceral dimensions of empathy. With the exception of sensory alignment with the film's body, which I discussed above, Smith's analysis of the structure of sympathy as a means by which a text's audience engages with its characters is more or less applicable to other forms of narrative such as spoken, performed, and written stories. It is when we delve into the structure of empathy that we unearth qualities of character engagement that may be specific to the cinema. This in no way privileges empathy over sympathy in terms of the contribution to ethical insight or suggests that empathic engagement is restricted to cinematic narratives. We can certainly empathize with characters in novels and in the narratives of everyday life; however, Smith's account reveals some ways in which film solicits empathic responses from its spectators that are unavailable in literature.

Where sympathetic engagement emphasizes cognition, in experiencing empathic engagement with screen characters the spectator is more involved in the affective dimension of emotion. This is very important in relation to the embodied or experiential nature of ethical responsiveness. In Smith's account of empathy, three distinct reactions can be discerned in spectatorial responses: affective mimicry, autonomic reactions, and emotional simulation.

Affective mimicry[12] is a reaction involving mirroring a character's feelings via "perceptual registering and reflexive simulation of the emotion of another person" (Smith 1995, 99). This kind of affective reaction may consist of "involuntary neuromuscular response" or "kinaesthetic mimicry" such as smiling when Sandra smiles as Brett first walks in the front door, or feeling moved to tears when Tracy is weeping. Close-ups of faces often cue an empathic response, though they can also give rise to a different emotion or a sympathetic reaction if we are strongly aligned with another character from whose viewpoint we gaze at the face in close-up, as when we respond to the sight of a character's angry expression with fear or concern rather than mirroring their rage. In cases of mimicking the physical expression of a character's emotion, the spectator's own "subjective experience of the emotion is intensified" (Smith 1995, 100).[13] Hence, in Smith's explanation of affective mimicry, film spectators empathically experience the emotions of characters in a stronger form than they might without audiovisual stimuli, but in a weaker form than the character expressing the emotion supposedly does.

Smith notes that "mimicry pertains to only those basic affects which are distinguishable physiologically, and via feedback, subjectively" (1995, 101). Thus, the term "affective mimicry" may not apply to responses to someone else's feelings of guilt or shame as these emotions have complex physiological expressions that might not be readily recognizable. Affective mimicry would also be an inaccurate description of emotive responses to nonaudiovisual narratives, such as novels. In these cases (where the nature of the affective response is not readily discernible, or simply not available to the senses), an empathic response might better be described as affective resonance or affective evocation, if it does not fall into one of the other aspects of empathy that Smith identifies.

Autonomic reactions are involuntary: as spectators we are linked to the characters on screen because situations arise in which we experience identical shocks to them (Smith 1995, 102). This occurs in response to sensory stimuli common to the screen world and the cinematic environment. When the camera is aligned with a character's point of view and something abruptly springs toward that character's face, spectators also experience the sense that something is springing up in front of our eyes.[14] For example, if we flinch along with Michelle when Brett suddenly raises his fist to her or slams her head against the laundry wall, we are experiencing an autonomic reaction that enhances one aspect of empathy for Michelle.

In a literary narrative none of the sounds or sights in the world of the novel can actually be available to the senses of the reader as they are in film (though they may be vividly brought to life in the reader's imagination). In film we frequently physically hear what the characters hear and see what they see. Smith claims that our reactions to such shared sensory stimuli do not arise "from an engagement with the character, as it does with simulation and mimicry, but directly from the represented visual or aural environment in which the character moves" (1995, 102). As spectators, our autonomic reactions are masterfully manipulated by films, especially in the horror, action, and thriller genres where we often find ourselves flinching and gasping in response to the sudden appearance of monsters, explosions, and slamming doors.

Emotional simulation is closest to the commonly accepted understanding of empathy. It involves "centrally imagining" and simulating an emotion through forming hypotheses about how one might feel or respond to a situation using practical reason (to predict and understand behavior) and imaginatively projecting the self into a character's situation. The grief spectators may feel when Lionel dies of an overdose at the end of *Little Fish* and Tracy takes him to the beach one last time is a form of emotional simulation. We might share Tracy's bereavement, feeling it prickling our eyes and tightening the back of our throats because we have been involved in her relationship with Lionel and seen the love between them, and because the film layers her experience of loss with the song "Flame Trees," and flickers of memory showing the lost promise of childhood when Lionel took her and her family to the beach. Empathic reactions "are a means by which we establish bonds with others, even with total strangers. These feelings make you care about [others'] suffering, and they make you want to help" (Ekman 2003, 96). This is important in terms of the ethics of cinema as it is one of the ways in which responses to film extend themselves outside the cinema through the impulse to help, if the suffering depicted on screen is of a nature that connects to that encountered in extracinematic life.

A more complex (and rare) moment of empathy is buried in the scene when Brett menaces Nola in *The Boys*. Although we are not visually aligned with Nola at that particular point in the film, we feel a much stronger sense of allegiance with her than we do with Brett (the evaluative aspect of our sympathy lies with her). Up to the point where Brett kisses her, our emotional response is likely to be purely sympathetic: we may feel concern in response to Nola's feeling of despair and vulnerability because we know more about Brett's character than she does. When the film moves into slow motion it signals an alteration in Nola's sense of her personal situation; the shift in her emotional response from distress to fear corresponds with her perception that she is in danger rather than merely in difficulty. At this point, the spectator's emotional response might mirror Nola's as the menacing nature of Brett's proximity,[15] emphasized by the use of slow motion and tight framing, confronts our senses in a way that expresses Nola's experience, and allows us to feel what it might be like for her.

Empathy brings us into relation with others by centrally involving us in their lives, and it offers a felt, experiential understanding of their situation, their values, and the impact of their circumstances. Such vicarious or borrowed experience is valuable in three senses. First, it enhances our potential sensitivity to (and the accuracy of) our perception of that person's situation. Second, it provides us with an understanding that we may be able to extend to or draw upon in other similar situations that we encounter in our own lives, and third, it offers the opportunity to practice working through challenging ethical scenarios without requiring us to experience them first hand because it enables us to emotionally experience a kind of felt understanding or visceral knowledge (see de Sousa 1987, 321 and Neill 2006, 250).

Smith maintains that (with the exception of emotional simulation) empathic reactions, unlike sympathetic responses, do not require comprehension of the narrative situation or engagement with the characters (1995, 102). It seems clear that the structure of sympathy as Smith presents it requires a more profound level of character engagement than the mimetic and autonomic levels of empathy; however, this does not fully recognize the extent to which bodily reactions to sensory stimuli are enhanced (if not constituted) by the spectator's involvement in the web of narrative causation and contextuality. Narrative situates emotion and makes it significant; also, empathic responses can be moderated or amplified depending on other forms of engagement already established in the narrative context. For instance, in cases of rage and malicious expressions of emotion such as Brett's attack on Michelle, the spectator's potential emotional response to or identification with the perpetrator may be averted. Even when we are visually aligned with Brett's perspective and involved in "his" story, we have already established sympathetic allegiance and an empathic connection to the victim, Michelle, through emotional simulation and mimicry.

Whether the full narrative is required or not, these experiences of empathy most commonly occur in the context of a narrative, and therefore become meaningful in that context in a way that they would not be if divorced from it. Furthermore, if a spectator were to experience a sudden surge of affect if they saw a visual image that was not embedded in a narrative context (for instance, a decontextualized photo of a man kissing a weeping young woman on the forehead), it may be that (rather than simulating the emotions of figures in the photo), the viewer is drawing on a narrative from his or her own experience to flesh out the context and thus establish narrative grounds for empathy.

This suggests that emotional structure is of a narrative nature. In *Love's Knowledge* Nussbaum articulates an intricate interconnection between narrative and emotion.[16] Narratives, she says:

> [A]re essential to the process of practical reflection: not just because they happen to represent and also evoke emotional activity, but also because their very forms are themselves the sources of emotional structure, the paradigms of what, for us, emotion *is*. This gives us an additional reason to say that we could not acquire the rich information we seek by simply adding to abstract theoretical treatises a few examples of emotion and a few emotive appeals: for the whole story of an emotion, in its connection with other emotions and forms of life, requires narrative form for its full development. (Nussbaum 1990, 296)

This study of *The Boys* and *Little Fish* has built on Nussbaum's insights by investigating the links between ethical life and emotion, narrative, and character engagement. Film shares the ethical relevance of other forms of storytelling, with the additional value of emphasizing the affective component of emotion by making it available directly to the senses and evoking particular forms of empathy in spectators including mimetic and autonomic reactions. This extra level of emotional experience has the potential to enhance the ethical value offered by engagement with fictional characters if we practice attuning our sensitivities to the stories and concerns of others, explore examples of human character, circumstances, and possibilities; and reflect on and develop our own moral character in response to the ethical approaches and situations in which we become vicariously involved.

Haptics and Subsonics

Film can also elicit responses that have little to do with identification, or with responses to the emotions characters express. For instance, Laura Marks' work in *The Skin of the Film* (2000) and *Touch* (2002) explores how screen texts can evoke affect through the tactility of vision and sound. An interesting example of this occurs in the opening sequence of *The Boys*, which is not shot from any particular character's point of view and occurs before we recognize anything resembling a human being on the screen. In this opening sequence we hear low, atonal, disturbing music and see what we eventually identify as a television slowly come into focus, remain in focus momentarily, then fade out. This pattern is repeated with a number of light fittings (all offset from the center of the frame and shot from peculiar angles), the clogged drain of the kitchen sink, an unfastened padlock and its key, and other miscellaneous aspects of an unremarkable domestic environment. Cut-aways to these domestic details recur throughout the film, for no apparent reason. The effect of fading in and out of focus gives the viewer a sense of moving in and out of consciousness, losing clarity and perspective.

According to Marks, optical visuality is the familiar mode in which we respond to most screen images. It relies on separation of subject and object as it involves seeing things from enough distance to objectify and classify the object of vision (Marks 2000, 162). Haptic images and sounds lack clarity and focus and do not have readily identifiable relationships to objects; hence, haptics "denaturalizes" the object of vision or the source of sound, bypassing conditioned assumptions and judgments. With haptic images there is little sense of depth, and a tactile perception of texture overwhelms and takes precedence over form. Similarly, the aural mode by which we ordinarily perceive screen texts relies on identifying conceptual links between sounds and their physical sources; it requires cognition and narrative comprehension (Marks 2000, 162). Haptic sound includes undifferentiated ambient noise and unidentifiable sounds where the relationship between sound, source, and image may be disjunctive and complex: such sounds evoke emotion and grasp at the audience's attention as they bypass cognition and categorization (Marks 2000, 183).

Describing the effects of rare haptic moments such as the opening sequence of *The Boys* requires paying attention to the viewer's own body when recognition of sound and image dissolves and invites the investment of every sense in the act of perception (Marks 2000, 189). Marks suggests that in the haptic mode of perception, the textuality of the screen touches the viewer's body in a direct, affective manner, rather than working through identification with characters or through acts of narrative interpretation (Marks 2000, 164). Haptic visuality, she claims, is an intensified relation that "muddies intersubjective boundaries," it is "a kind of visuality that is not organized around identification, at least identification with a single figure, but that is labile, able to move between identification and immersion" (Marks 2000, 188).

The scene where Brett tells Nola "we all make mistakes" is the first time since the credit sequence of *The Boys* that nondiegetic music is used to underscore the narrative. In the latter scene, the unsettling, ominous music with its undercurrents of sonic disturbance articulates Nola's feeling of dread and amplifies the spectator's own emotional response to the scene. The DVD commentary by director Rowan Woods reveals that ultra low frequency and subaudible sounds emitted from high tension electrical wires were recorded by sound artist Alan Lamb and woven into the soundscape to augment the unsettling effects of performance, music, and cinematography in the credit sequence and the scene where Brett manipulates Nola. This sound design strategy, reprised in the disturbing climax of *Little Fish*, sets the emotional tenor in the opening sequences of both films when the murky, low electronic hum is almost imperceptibly layered underneath other sounds and images. The use of subsonics is becoming increasingly common in films that seek to exploit the technological sophistication of cinema sound and digital editing to create an affective soundscape.

The director Phillip Noyce reminds us that sound is a sensation that is felt as a physical vibration. Our bodies respond even when we can't consciously identify the source or meaning of a noise as the sound mix can include subterranean sound registers below human perception. Discussing his own use of digital sound technology to generate incredibly low, virtually inaudible subsonic effects, Noyce argues that sound manipulation is moving into an era where the audience can be affected emotionally without being consciously aware of it:

> Sound goes directly to the central nervous system. It doesn't need to be decoded. So you can, for example, use a bass rumble that just sort of shakes you, without you being completely aware of it. People get a disturbed feeling in their guts, they know something's up but they can't hear it. They just feel it. For music too, you now have a much more elaborate, dynamic range possible, and high-pitched notes can affect an audience in a very, very emotional way. We're continually refining the sonic range that we're working with as we experiment with trying to create new sounds at the highest pitches and at the lowest bass levels. Those are both primitive and spiritual in terms of their invisible effect on audience responses. (Noyce 2001, 20)

Noyce's ideas about subsonics and the use of sounds that cannot be readily identified or consciously classified has some interesting connections with concepts that are emerging in the production and analysis of experimental film and video art. For instance, Laura Marks' work explores the ways in which screen texts are able to trigger sensory perceptions and responses that extend beyond sight and sound.[17] Because touch and other senses play a part in audiovisual experience, our perception of cinema is necessarily multisensory (Marks 2000, 22). According to Marks, the intersensory links in screen media can be termed synaesthesia, which is "the perception of one sensation in terms of another, such as the ability to distinguish colors by feel" (2000, 213).

Synaesthesia can also be described as a "bodily way of translating information among modalities, a kind of embodied thinking" (Marks 2002, 149). One need only listen as fingernails screech down a chalkboard in order to understand what synaesthesia means kinaesthetically and to grasp how sound can communicate tactility. It is likely that your body will *feel* the sound of fingernails on the chalkboard setting your teeth on edge, and that you will hear it not only with your ears but with your own fingertips. Marks writes:

> By appealing to one sense in order to represent the experience of another, cinema appeals to the integration and commutation of sensory

experience within the body. Each audiovisual image meets a rush of other sensory associations. Audiovisual images call up conscious, unconscious, and nonsymbolic associations with touch, taste, and smell which themselves are not experienced as separate. Each image is synthesized by a body that does not necessarily divide perceptions into different sense modalities. (Marks 2000, 222)

For example, in Darren Aronofsky's mathematical thriller *Pi* (1999), the protagonist suffers severe migraines. Through the use of intense subjective sound the film literally enables audiences to *hear* the pain he experiences. Pain itself is silent, yet migraines are often accompanied by photosensitivity and a heightened sensitivity to sound. The skull-splitting experience of a migraine is communicated by means of a dull, throbbing *doight-doight-doight-doight* noise that feels like blood pumping through constricted vessels. This noise is then punctuated by a searing, high-pitched electronic shriek that attacks with sonic ferocity like a hot blade piercing an eye. As a result, audience members not only hear the protagonist's headache, but may develop one of their own. This experiential use of sound to generate an embodied, sensory response can be termed synaesthetic sound. It represents another level on which the technology of the cinema can evoke an affective response, and it reinforces the importance of understanding how sensory perception relates to emotional engagement with characters and identification with their experiences, and how the physicality of narrative film is central to its impact.

Music and Emotion

Music is another powerful way of articulating emotion, encouraging identification, and eliciting an affective response from listeners—as such it can encourage audience members to engage with the emotional experiences of screen characters.[18] Film music can work as a mechanism to facilitate identification with protagonists via "affiliation" or "assimilation" with the subject positions offered in the story world. In *Hearing Film* (2001), Anahid Kassabian argues that different types of music facilitate identification with screen characters in various ways: the underscore or composed score (usually music without vocals created especially for the film) prompts assimilating identifications, whereas the compiled score (usually consisting of familiar songs already circulating in popular culture) prompts affiliating identifications. Familiar music in a film's compiled score can open onto many different paths for identification by triggering personal associations with memories, favorite artists, and so forth; whereas the term "assimilation" implies that a person is immersed in something that tends to overwhelm their individuality, encouraging them to accept the subject position into which they are being interpellated. What is interesting about Kassabian's work is that it details how different types of film music, diegetic and nondiegetic, the compiled soundtrack, and the artfully composed underscore, can work on different levels to involve spectators in the experience of characters like Tracy or Lionel, even though the identity of a vulnerable, recovering addict or an ageing, homosexual ex-football star might be dissimilar to the spectator's own identity.

Diegetic music takes us into the worlds of particular characters and tells us something of their personality and preferences, and the cultural landscape they inhabit. This is most obvious when Lionel and Tracy compile and play CDs for each other in the first scene we see them together. Our first introduction to Lionel sets him up in an ambiguous way, making it appear that he could be Tracy's lover rather than a father figure as she lies on his bed and he dances above her, shirt open, to the Hoodoo Gurus track "A Place in the Sun," a song from her high school years. As a graduate from an Australian high school in the class of '89 myself, the sound of the Hoodoo Gurus draws on scenes from my past, as it surely must for Tracy and Lionel, creating an affiliation with the characters that leads outward from the text, as Kassabian suggests. The pathways of affective identification differ for everyone, but most viewers will register how the physicality and the brash, masculine sound of the music define Lionel in contrast with other source music like the Vietnamese divas we later come to associate with Jonny, or the slow chords and nostalgic lyrics of the song "Flame Trees" that speak to Tracy.

Lionel switches off the Hoodoo Gurus when the beep of a car horn outside and a subtle change in sound design indicate that Sam Neill's character, Brad, has arrived with a delivery of heroin. While this interaction takes place in the other room, Tracy's eyes wander over a series of photographs that hint at the back story between the characters. The *Little Fish* theme tune then creeps in, leading her memory to the moments at the beach that we saw in the opening sequence of the film.

The *Little Fish* theme and its variations (scored by Nathan Larson) are liquid tunes with just enough reverberation to make the tinkling notes sound like water droplets falling into a deep pool. This musical theme has a sad but hopeful quality like Tracy herself, and it sneaks in to augment

Figure 24 Little Fish: *Little Tracy at the beach. A snapshot triggers a memory underscored by the* "Little Fish" *theme tune.*

emotional turning points. The music underscores moments that bring memories of Tracy's past to the surface, and that have associations with the water motif that runs through the film, associated with "diving in" to love, and with cleansing and washing away the residue of past mistakes. The music invites immersion in Tracy's emotions, gently assimilating the audience into her subjectivity as Kassabian suggests. Almost invariably, this underscore is accompanied by intimate, hand-held close-ups of Tracy with shallow focus drawing attention to the emotions playing across her expressive face.

Other tunes in the underscore sound much darker in timbre, lower, sadder and more ominous in tone. The music "I Can't Score For You" merges with the shriek and rumble of trains at the Cabramatta station and the patter of rain when Tracy does score for Lionel, and is tempted to use heroin again herself. Stark, dramatic low key lighting literally casts a shadow over these fraught moments. The key turning point is explicitly orchestrated by music. As Tracy ducks into a hall to shoot up in the public toilets, she walks in on a school choir rehearsing "Flame Trees." The cinematography moves into slow motion as she is arrested by the wistful music and the children singing it, lights flare against the lens, and the dark undercurrent leaks out of the sound design.

Figure 25 Little Fish: *Tracy waits for Jonny, underscored by the* "Little Fish" *theme tune.*

Figure 26 Little Fish: *Tracy listens to the school choir singing* "Flame Trees."

****

Little Fish shows the difficulties faced by characters as they try to overcome a past polluted by drug abuse, reaching toward aspirations of a financially and emotionally rewarding future. By the end of the story spectators possess a more acute and deeply felt understanding of the complex nature of questions of responsibility and agency, which may lead to the capacity for fairer judgments and responses. Whereas, before viewing *Little Fish*, the reactions of audience members to the crimes of theft and drug dealing may have been judgmental and punitive, increased sensitivity to the degree of responsibility of each individual in the story may temper that response, and perhaps suggest ways of circumventing such a situation.

At the beginning of the chapter I suggested that although we do not necessarily bond with the characters in *The Boys*, the nature of the character engagement that does occur is ethically significant because it has the potential to deepen the audience's feeling for and understanding of the ethical and social problems in the film. Philip Butterss explains the actions of the protagonists in *The Boys* in terms of "protest masculinity," a violent, antisocial response to disempowerment and economic marginalization (Butterss 1998, 40). He argues that for working class men like the Sprague brothers feeling threatened by immigration, feminism, and unemployment, "Their response to feelings of alienation and powerlessness is to live out a kind of masculinity which involves exerting physical force over each other, to some extent, and, more importantly, over those with less power than themselves—women, gays, and ethnic minorities" (Butterss 1998, 41). The detailed narrative understanding of the life circumstances experienced by the Sprague brothers includes a heightened awareness of their lack of opportunities and inner resources, and of the circumstances within which their choices are made. Knowing the story behind their actions, we are sensitive to the fact that all three men experienced rejection by women immediately prior to committing a crime against a woman; all three are poorly educated with meager prospects for employment. We are also aware from both the content of the narrative and the visual style of the film that society expects misbehavior from these men and is watching them, waiting for them to make mistakes. Though this information may help us to see the situation more justly, it gives no reason to either excuse or emulate the Sprague's behavior. There are important differences between understanding a person's motives or actions, emotionally reacting to them, evaluating them, and actively endorsing them.

I have argued that our emotional affiliations with screen characters, our emotional responses to them, and our narrative understanding of their situations are all closely intertwined, and inseparable from the capacity for rational ethical evaluation. The structure of emotional responses and the ethical connections we form with others are reliant on narrative. Reliant, that is, on an understanding of causes and consequences, motives, and mitigating circumstances within an interconnected pattern that develops over time and enables us to account for and explain the way in which we perceive a situation and evaluate its ethical implications. Emotional engagement with fictional characters is to a large extent dependent on the narrative depth and detail with which we understand their predicaments and positions. other people's Empathy enables us to better understand other people's circumstances in a felt, experiential, embodied sense as well as to imagine how life is for them. The empathic dimensions of character engagement are ethically important because they help us to perceive a situation from outside the limitations of our habitual subjective standpoint. Emotions are of ethical value because they are indicative of our values and beliefs about what is important. Narrative films draw out and reveal this sense of salience as we experience it emotionally ourselves, and as we experience it vicariously through our connections to characters whose circumstances differ from our own, yet whose common humanity we recognize.

Notes

1. It is interesting to consider whether spectators would feel differently if they believed that *The Boys* was based on a murder that really happened, such as the actual gang rape and murder of Anita Cobby by three brothers in Sydney in 1986. I did not think *The Boys* or *Dead Man Walking* referenced real events when I first watched them, yet they elicited strong emotions. In later viewings, knowing of the films' relationships to actual people and events, my emotional response has remained essentially the same in nature if not in intensity. This suggests that spectators are capable of experiencing genuine emotional responses to both factual and fictional material, though the duration, intensity, and action associated with the responses may vary depending on the modality of the text.

2. In *How Emotions Work* (1999), Katz's account of emotion suggests that identity is intersubjectively constituted in and by narrative connections with others. Katz explores the dynamic nature of subjectivity and objectivity in the process of "social metamorphosis" effected by emotional expression, and the intersubjective position switching this entails. For instance, he describes the experience of "seeing oneself from without" when one is "treated as an object" and insulted by someone. Responding to the insult, perhaps with anger, we experience ourselves once again as active subjects. Thus an emotional scene such as an exchange of insults has the participants "acting first on one and then on the other side of his or her own flesh" (Katz 1999, 342–343).

3. Nussbaum points out that the beliefs with which reason works can also be mistaken, inconsistent, or irrational and that these failings are no more a justification to dismiss beliefs than they are to dismiss emotions:

> Emotions can, of course, be unreliable—in much the same way that beliefs can. People get angry because of false beliefs about the facts, or their importance; the relevant beliefs might also be true but unjustified, or both false and unjustified . . .

But the fact that some beliefs are irrational has rarely led philosophers to dismiss all beliefs from practical reasoning. (1990, 42)

4. For an anthology including examples of different approaches to emotion, see Amelie Rorty (ed.), *Explaining Emotions* (1980). In "Emotions and Women's Capabilities" (1995) Nussbaum works through six different arguments against the legitimacy of including emotion in practical judgment and rational moral responses, arguing strongly for the place of emotions in moral life (see also Nussbaum 1990; 1993; 1996b, 2001). Justin Oakley (1992) demonstrates the limitations of a number of reductive theories of emotion that miss the richness and complexity of their contribution to ethics, as does Ronald de Sousa (1987).

5. See, for instance, de Sousa (1987, xv), Nussbaum (1990, 293), and Sherman (1989, 38).

6. In *The Sovereignty of Good* (1970), Iris Murdoch argues that emotions are morally significant even if they are *not* instrumental in motivating right action. Cultivating sensitivity to the difficulties faced by others can effect inner changes in attitude, perception, and disposition, enhancing the capacity to be sensitive and just. Murdoch suggests that without appropriate emotional responses we may suffer a form of ethical blindness.

7. Nussbaum's *Upheavals of Thought: The Intelligence of Emotions* expands the argument that emotions are "intelligent responses to the perception of value," by addressing how cultural norms and childhood experiences affect the development of emotional discernment, arguing that emotions relate to the ability to flourish and attain one's goals and play an important role in ethical judgment (Nussbaum 2001, 1).

8. Though these terms are related, each has a specific meaning and use, which it is not necessary to address in detail here. For useful discussions of the distinctions between objectivity, impersonality, and impartiality, see Friedman (1993) and for the relationship between detachment and impartiality in ethics, see Kyte (1996).

9. See Tress and Fulco (1995, 269). This view is attributed to "many feminists," though it is unclear who they may be referring to, or whether Tress and Fulco agree that narrative generally operates in this manner.

10. Michelle's narrow escape from Brett's assault in the laundry is also rendered in slow motion. As a cinematic technique, slow motion can enunciate the experience of being in a situation of extreme stress when every second and every movement through space holds magnified significance. Hence, although slow motion may look "unrealistic," it can carry a high modality and an experiential, emotive charge.

11. In an article entitled "Imagining from the Inside" which builds on his work in *Engaging Characters,* Smith clarifies the distinctions between the kind of "acentral imagining" or imagining "from the outside" involved in sympathy, and the affective, emotional dimensions of empathic responses to film texts. While the latter are not properly classed as forms of imagination, he suggests, "along with other aspects of the film, they may help us to imagine vividly, from the inside, some situation or experience" (1997, 417).

12. Following Aristotle, Sherman claims that the "mimetic enactment" of somebody else's feelings, as they are depicted in and evoked by a dramatic narrative "is a way of coming

to feel from the inside the relevant qualities of character and emotion. It is an emulative and empathic kind of identification" (1989, 182). This is similar to the phenomena de Sousa refers to as "vicarious resonance."

13. Paul Ekman's research shows that emotions can be triggered by forming certain facial expressions that generate the corresponding emotion (2003, 36). Ekman also details a variety of other emotional pathways including memory, imagination, learned responses, autoappraisal, talking about emotion, or witnessing someone else's emotion (2003, 33–35).

14. Autonomic reactions are related to autoappraisal, the core emotional pathway detailed in Paul Ekman's research (2003). Ekman argues that "emotions evolved to prepare us to deal quickly with the most vital events in our lives" by automatically appraising stimuli in the surrounding environment and enabling us to make swift, complex evaluations based on affective, desiderative, and cognitive action-responses (2003, 19–21). This autoappraisal occurs as emotions hook into narrative schemas, which Ekman describes as the bare bones of a scene or event stored in memory: a combination of behavioral scripts based on universal themes and specific individual variations (2003, 23–24). Further, Ekman claims that we interpret other people's emotions by locating them within an inferred cause and effect narrative sequence, as each emotion embodies a story regarding "what that person is going to do next or what made the person feel the emotion" (2003, 14).

15. Long shots can also invite empathy, even though they do not enable us to read a character's expression. For instance, when images of Nola isolated in the background of shots evoke empathy for her feelings of loneliness and insignificance.

16. The connection between narrative and emotion is widely recognized by theorists from many different disciplines. In addition to the philosophical studies of emotion undertaken by de Sousa (1987) and Nussbaum (2001), it is also pertinent to Ekman's empirical, functionalist study of emotion (2003), and to the sociologist Jack Katz's phenomenological approach to emotion (1999), and it is implicit in the explanations of emotion's causal structure advanced by cognitive film theorists such as Noel Carroll (2006).

17. Consider Gaspar Noé's *Irreversible (*2004), a rape revenge story told jerking backward in time. The first two-thirds of the film, which form its second and third act chronologically, exist at the outer limits of watchability. The camera moves to express extreme stress and rage with a red hued, relentless, frenzied, lurching motion accompanied by a sickening sonic pulse and looping music designed to induce nausea in the audience. In fact, the visceral impact of the film is so intense that it comes with an epilepsy warning.

18. There is an extensive body of literature about film music. Key texts include: Brown (1994), Dickinson (2003), Donnelly (2001), Gorbman (1987), and Prendergast (1977). Rather than considering sound bridges, the relationship between sonic and visual editing pace and rhythm, or musical themes that accompany certain characters, here I will focus on the way a film's music and sound design can facilitate identification with characters by articulating their subjective experience and eliciting an emotional reaction.

6

Imagination:
Inner Sight and Silent Voices

Imagination has a significant place in ethical understanding and ethical deliberation in terms of the construction of and engagement with narratives. We require a theory of imagination that is generous enough to encompass the term's rich and various uses. This necessitates expanding some of the narrowly defined conceptions of imagination that we work with to include the diversity of ways in which the term is applied. For instance, the term imagination can at times be used interchangeably with conception, fantasy, simulation, pretence, supposition, wondering, make-believe, illusion, delusion, conjecture, speculation, and even memory and understanding. This chapter attempts to develop a broad account of imagination that enables a productive exploration of its ethical dimensions through an examination of the nature of imagination at play in film texts.

The Piano, directed by Jane Campion (1992), and Michel Gondry's *Eternal Sunshine of the Spotless Mind* (2004) provide focal points around which various approaches to imagination are situated. These films will be used to explore the relationship between imaging and imagining in film, questioning how film represents imagination and evokes the inner lives of characters, and also how it elicits imaginative engagement from spectators. Within this exploration of representation and spectatorship, problematic issues are addressed regarding the power of the imagination to deceive, mislead, convince, and corrupt.

Jane Campion's film *The Piano* draws heavily on symbolism and intertextual references to fairytales as it invites its spectators to imagine the conditions shaping a mute woman's life as a new bride, involuntarily wed to a settler she has never met, and shipped off to live with him in the inhospitable, uncultivated countryside of New Zealand in 1847. The film commences with the arrival of Ada (Holly Hunter) and her small daughter, Flora (played by Anna Paquin), at an isolated trading settlement. The narrative follows her complicated struggle to express her desires as she is caught in the undercurrents of a world where sacred traditions, people, their bodies, and their feelings are all used as capital to bargain with.

The Piano is an interesting text in which to consider the relationship between imagination, narrative, and ethical understanding because the muteness of the heroine necessitates an unusual degree of imaginative interpretation by characters in the story world. As spectators we both observe and participate in the efforts of the screen characters to understand things that are not made explicit by means of dialogue. Ada's struggle to express herself is resolved when her husband, Stewart (played by Sam Neill) and her lover, Baines (Harvey Keitel) both eventually manage to imagine what Ada, in her resolute silence, is saying. When they come to perceive her as a person, rather than as part of a bargain, they can imagine what words might fill her silence. Only then, when she is perceived as a full human being, does she begin to find her outer voice and to connect with others.

Much of the narrative of *Eternal Sunshine of the Spotless Mind*, expertly scripted by Charlie Kauffman, unfolds inside the mind of its introverted protagonist Joel Barish (Jim Carrey), representing his decaying memories muddled up with things that he imagines as he desperately struggles to avoid having his relationship with the vibrant and volatile Clementine Kruczynski (Kate Winslett) erased in a memory-wipe procedure. Joel requests the procedure from a futuristic but low-tech organization called Lacuna, staffed by Dr Howard Mierzwiak (Tom Wilkinson), Mary (Kirsten Dunst), Stan (Mark Ruffalo), and Patrick (Elijah Wood), after discovering that Clementine has impulsively had him erased from her memory. When the procedure is underway and he is helpless in a dreamlike, drugged slumber Joel realizes he cherishes memories of the relationship and still cares for Clementine. Dimly aware that Patrick has appropriated his journal and mementos to woo Clementine, Joel frantically tries to hide her deep in his mind where she cannot be deleted. The circular storyline of the film shows the significance of emotional memory narratives to self-understanding, and it pushes the boundaries of cinematic representation using sound technology, lighting effects, and clever set design and editing techniques to represent Joel's subjective experience. The visual effects of *Eternal Sunshine of the Spotless Mind* (hereafter abbreviated as *Eternal Sunshine*) are astonishing and while some tricks like digital compositing are used, many of the techniques employed to represent the inner workings of Joel's mind are visionary in their cleverness and creativity. Working in a low-budget, low-tech manner like Lacuna itself, Ellen Kuras, the director of photography, uses a hand-held naturalistic style to communicate a sense of emotional realism and believability amidst the surreality of the science fiction romance's deeply subjective setting. Given that all representations of interiority in film require an act of imagination since we can never truly know the inner life of another mind, even the techniques used to evoke dreamlike moments and reminiscence warrant consideration here. This is particularly important for cinema studies since what we perceive to be Joel's memory is also evidence of the creative imaginations of Charlie Kaufman, Michel Gondry, and their cast and crew.

This chapter begins with a consideration of some of the ways in which imagination has been understood by philosophers, in an attempt to clarify the cloudy relationship of imagination with imagery, reality, and belief. In the process of contrasting commonly held beliefs about the nature of imaginative engagement in film and literature, the second section examines some common assumptions about film spectatorship that are linked to restrictive notions of imagination. Finally, building upon these ideas surrounding the role of imagination in engaging with narrative texts and the potential therein for corrupting or cultivating ethical sensibilities, the discussion turns to consider the ethical imagination more directly.

Defining Imagination

Imagination is part of a family of interconnected terms; hence, theoretical accounts of imagination are multiple, complex, and varied. Here I am interested primarily in those accounts that have a bearing on the kinds of spaces that film narratives open up for creative and ethically productive imaginative activity. Of course, imagination can also be implicated in unethical thought and action. Such might be the case when a villain tries to imagine the most heinous form of torture, or the most devious and deceitful crime, or when a particularly nasty screen character captures the imagination of an impressionable spectator, influencing their behavior and attitudes. However, such misuse of the faculty of imagination is not necessarily an indication that imaginative activity is itself dangerous or inappropriate for ethical thought. Like the misuse of intellect or the cultivation of destructive emotions, such misuse of imaginative ability is indicative of a weak sense of the value of human life or a poor grasp of the significance of our interrelatedness with one another and within the broader pattern of life. (As the famous line in Wes Craven's 1996 film *Scream* goes, "movies don't create psychos, they make psychos more creative.")

I will argue that imagination has an important place in ethical life in inductive reasoning, in structuring understanding, and as a faculty that enables us to connect the general to the particular, to form bridges of understanding between the sensible and the conceptual. I will also consider imagination as a creative process of constructing histories and projecting possibilities (into the future, and into the interstitial spaces of narrative texts and accounts of lived experience). But first, given the nature of film as a medium of communication working with audiovisual images, the connection between imagination and imaging, and the distinction between image and concept require elaboration.

The understanding of imagination as "seeing with the mind's eye" is one that is based in a long philosophical tradition. Influential thinkers from Plato through to Descartes theorized imagination in terms of imagery. As a cognitive faculty, the imaginative process was understood to be limited because it entailed copying, mimicking, or somehow reproducing or receiving pale images of concrete, original sensory experience. Following this line of thought, it would not be considered possible to imagine a never-ending story, or to visualize precisely 93,351,353 empty cinema seats, although we can certainly conceptualize such things. However, as Alan White points out in his book *The Language of Imagination* (1990), common language usage indicates that the term imagination encompasses much more than that which can be visualized, or for which a sensory image can be formed. We often speak of imagining a thing (such as another person's emotions or thoughts, or the feeling of freedom) that it is difficult or impossible to form a mental image of. Rather than suggesting that in such instances the term imagination is being misused or used imprecisely, it is more accurate to say that we are capable of exercising many different forms or aspects of imagination which work in conjunction with thought, feeling, and sensory perception to aid understanding.

The notion of imagination as *phantasia* and *mimesis* in Greek thought placed it in a problematic relationship to "reality" and established its reputation as potentially deceptive and subversive. One component of imagination for the ancient Greeks, *mimesis*, is associated with imitation, mimicry, and forgery. The other, *phantasia*, translates as "a state of being appeared to," which amounts to a state of being deceived or being subject to illusions, given the distinction between (false) appearances and the ultimate reality of the prototypical "forms" on which thinkers like Plato believed appearances to be based.

Indeed, Plato's "Allegory of the Cave" (*Republic*, vii.514), which has been likened to the description of a primitive cinema,[1] ironically begins by asking readers to "Imagine the condition of men living in a sort of cavernous chamber underground . . . prisoners so confined would have seen nothing of themselves or of one another, except the shadows thrown by the firelight on the wall of the Cave facing them." In this story Plato leads his readers along the path to enlightenment, away from the shadowy images in the cave and up toward the sun. However, despite the fact that it commences with this direct appeal to the imagination and requires for its comprehension an imaginative reach of understanding, the allegory is intended to reveal how images can deceive us and deflect our attention from the truth and reality of "ideal forms" to illusory "appearances" that mimic the real, impress themselves on the senses, and prey upon the imagination. This link between the reception of images and deception carries through into present day attitudes to visual media yet, as Alan White's work indicates, the claim that one can only imagine something for which it is possible to form a sensory image confuses imaging with imagining. Hence the role of imagination in the construction and interpretation of cinematic narratives requires reframing, as it so often remains ill defined in film theory.[2]

Like Plato, Aristotle[3] described an intimate association between imagery and imagining, saying, "Imagination is that in virtue of which an image arises for us" (Aristotle 1941a, *De Anima*, III.3, 428a, 1–2). Furthermore, he believed that the images inhabiting the imagination were necessarily derived from sensation:

> Imagination must be a movement resulting from an actual exercise of a power of sense. As sight is the most highly developed sense, the name *phantasia* (imagination) has been formed from *phaos* (light) because it is not possible to see without light and because imaginations remain in the organs of sense and resemble sensations. (Aristotle 1941a, *De Anima*, 429a: 1–5)

In this passage the complex relationship between imagination, conception, and empirical or material reality emerges. Following Aristotle, many philosophers[4] claim that it is only possible to imagine those things or concepts of which we are capable of forming sensory images (including visual, auditory, olfactory, tactile, and gustatory images). The term "concept" is often used to refer to ideas that are not necessarily representable in terms of imagery. Love, the nature of the soul, and various mathematical functions like *pi* or infinity are concepts for which it is not possible to form an image: we can conceptualize them and offer metaphors and examples of them from our experience, but they are "unimaginable," in the strict sense of the term imagination (as it has been distinguished from conception).

In Kant's work, too, imagination is linked to imagery as a copy or simulation of a sense impression. In the *Critique of Pure Reason* (hereafter abbreviated as CR) Kant maintains the distinction between image and concept, and asserts that imagination "belongs to sensibility . . . it is an operation of the understanding on sensibility . . . the faculty of representing an object even without its presence" (CR, 104). In the *Critique of Judgment* (CJ) Kant also holds that imagination is incapable of inventing or "producing a presentation of sense that was *never* before given to our power of sense" (CJ, 94; 243, n73). However, in detailing the convoluted relationships between imagination, conception, images, and sensory phenomena, Kant does credit the imagination with the creative capacity to extend understanding into new territory. Indeed, Kant's account of the faculty of imagination encompasses and distinguishes between a variety of imaginative forms and functions: the productive imagination, the reproductive imagination, and the transcendental imagination, or figurative synthesis.

Prior to Kant, imagination had been understood as an instrumental faculty, mediating between sense experience and reason by providing images of the former for the latter. Kant believed that though the imagination does perform this mediating function (imaging and representation), it is a function so crucial to understanding that it underpins the very possibility of conceptual thinking, of rendering sensory phenomena intelligible. The imagination, according to Kant, fulfils a synthesizing, schematizing role (CR 118). Thus the imagination actually *enables* conceptual understanding by means of synthesizing many particular sense impressions into a general rule that is representative of the multiplicity of individual instances that it encompasses.

Kant uses the example of seeing, or forming an image of an individual dog and being able to imagine dogs in general:

> The conception of a dog indicates a rule, according to which my imagination can delineate the figure of a four-footed animal in general, without being limited to any particular individual form which

experience presents to me, or indeed to any possible image that I can represent to myself *in concreto*. (CR 119)

This suggests that the imagination works with but is not limited to either the images derived from sensory experience or to concepts, since images are particular and determinate and the imagination moves (mediates) between particularity (images and sensations) and generality (concepts, rules, and understanding), relating (synthesizing) the two. The image of the dog Flynn licking Stewart's fingers as he spies on Ada's erotic liaison in *The Piano* is at once a "figure of a four-footed animal" that is understood to be a dog in relation to our general concept of "dog," and a concrete, particular image that proceeds to embellish our conception of "dogginess." Flynn's humorous role in the text is also the product of Campion's creative imagination.

Having established a general view of the importance of the imagination's work, Kant then refines the tasks of the imagination, distinguishing between productive and reproductive capacities of imagination. The imagination grasps the category or type that an object belongs to by forming analogies and associations between numerous individual instances or objects. The general concept or rule and the particular object or instance never map exactly onto one another. Kant uses the term the *reproductive imagination* (CR 105) to refer to a derivative, representational process (imaginings derived from empirical sensory experience), governed by associative relationships. Imagining is, however, more than just intellectual conjunction or thought analogies.

For Kant, imagination can also entail another process, working in a spontaneous way as a productive cognitive power:

In this process we feel our freedom from the law of association (which attaches to the empirical use of the imagination); for although it is under that law that nature lends us material, yet we can process that material into something quite different, namely into something that surpasses nature. Such presentations of the imagination we may call *ideas*. (CJ 182; 314)

The ideas Kant refers to are imaginative products that not only surpass particular instantiations in nature, they also surpass the ability of concepts to adequately capture and describe them (concepts cannot embrace the details unique to an individual). Kant says that in this capacity the creative, *productive imagination* can entertain us, educate us, and restructure experience

(CJ 182; 314). Its products are original in that they precede experience (we often imagine things that we have never and will never experience), though they are necessarily related to things we have sensed or experienced previously.

The Creative Imagination: Inductive Reasoning in Ethical Deliberation

If the imagination is involved (through synthesis and schematization) in relating particular, detailed instances and images to broader, more general conceptions, and (through extension and innovation) in relating actual experiences to possible experiences in ways that we can learn from and use to restructure experience, then imagination will be implicated in ethical thought, which often involves precisely that process. The link between ethical forms of thought and the faculty of imagination is reinforced in Kant's Third Critique, when he articulates the relationship between imagination and judgment.

Judgment, by Kant's definition, is "the ability to think the particular as contained under the universal" (CJ 18; 179). Though the synthesizing role of the imagination is crucial for forming general concepts, it is because the imagination also works with particular instances and images that it is able to extend the understanding, formulating, and expressing original ideas. Kant argues, in the theory of the transcendental imagination, that the ability to imagine (to synthesize and create, to exercise the productive imagination) "precedes *a priori* all experience" and "forms the basis for the possibility of other cognition" (CR 104). Thus the action of the transcendental imagination, which Kant refers to as "figurative synthesis," is distinguished from the mere representation of *a posteriori* knowledge as images, and distinguished also from purely conceptual thought (CR 104).

Here, where Kant develops the notion of figurative synthesis, similarities can be perceived between the processes involved in narration and imagination. The composition of a narrative is itself clearly a creative, imaginative act, but it is also a process that is central to the way human beings structure understanding. Although they are conceived as functioning on different levels, a distinctive parallel can be discerned between the process Kant refers to as "figurative synthesis" and the process of "configuration" that Ricoeur uses to define the creative acts of composition involved in narration and narrative interpretation. Both figurative synthesis and configuration are considered to be absolutely foundational in epistemological terms: Kant and Ricoeur argue that without cognitive capacities such as figurative synthesis and configuration we could not make sense of the world, in the way human beings characteristically make sense of things. In addition, both processes are also so fundamental to the way that human beings engage with the world that they operate continuously, without their conscious effort, as well as manifesting themselves in more overt, intentionally directed ways as part of deliberation, reflective thought, and creative projects. Figurative synthesis and configuration also both centrally involve the formation of relationships, mediation between the particular and the general, and the creation of a new understanding through the unification of particular details into a larger pattern or whole.

I don't necessarily want to embrace the metaphysical implications of Kant's move to the transcendental imagination, or to defend a position where imagination is "prior to and independent of both sensation and reason" (Kearney 1988, 111). However, I do want to work with Kant's epistemological point about imagination's ability to create and produce understanding and new ideas in the process of forming associations, metaphors, and analogies or effecting a dialectical synthesis of differing terms or elements, as well as being able to copy and rearrange existing knowledge or impressions of the world into coherent sequences, and to extend knowledge in new directions.

A Kantian understanding of imagination avoids some of the problems involved in restricting imagination to visualization (or to other forms of conjuring sensation). By describing the complex interconnection between concepts and images, Kant allows for the capacity of the imagination to deal with concepts and ideas that cannot be adequately defined in terms of sensory impressions, as well as referring to images representing or derived directly from sensation. Another theorist, Robert Nozick, offers a straightforward but extremely useful definition of imagination, stating that "By imagination I simply mean the ability to think up new and fruitful possibilities" (Nozick 1993, 172). Though this does not detail the many different functions of imagination, or distinguish between the various ways in which the term is used, it does provide a foundation for an exploration of the role imagination can play in ethical life, while at the same time suggesting connections to the creation of fictional narratives. Nozick goes on to outline an important connection between imagination and choice which, again, is applicable to the innovation or creative simulation of alternatives in both inductive ethical reasoning, and in the processes of narrative configuration:

> The generation of new alternatives plays an important role in action as well as belief. A choice of action is made among alternatives. Better

choosing among the existing alternatives is one way to improve the results. Another way is to widen the range of alternatives to include existing new ones. An imaginative construction of a new alternative, heretofore not thought of, might be what makes the greatest improvement possible. (Nozick 1993, 172)

It is easy to recognize the imaginative process of deliberating among alternatives as a universal feature of ethical life (represented in countless films) but Nozick's words are also relevant to film as a creative narrative art form in which imaginative possibilities for human life are constructed and explored. While this is clearest in the genre of science fiction, it applies to all fiction films whether they are set in the past, present, or future.

In the remainder of this chapter imagination is treated as creative and productive, with levels of complexity that often include, but certainly exceed image formation alone. In considering both film narratives and imagination to be centrally concerned with the creation and projection of possibilities, I'll be taking a closer look at how the narrative imagination is involved in ethical thought, and at some assumptions underlying the claim that literature exercises the imagination to a greater extent than film.

The Projection of Possibilities: Imaging and Imagining in Film and Literature

As noted above, narrow understandings of imagination have given rise to misguided assumptions about film spectatorship including metaphorical descriptions of consumers of audiovisual media as "couch potatoes" or "sponges" who passively and unreflectively absorb the "hypnotic" "illusions of reality" presented on the screen.[5] In order to speak of imaginative engagement with film narratives, and later to address what might be called the "ethical imagination" in relation to lived experience, as well as in relation to the creative process of narration and imaginative responses to narratives, it is necessary to examine how the faculty of imagination is activated in the practices and processes of film spectatorship.

Often when the topic of imaginative engagement with film arises, so does the claim that in visual texts much of the imagination's work is done for us. Those who would argue that the cinema presents few challenges for the imagination claim that in media where there is a greater degree of "perceptual approximation" of reality, as there is in the cinema, the "work of the imagination is lessened" (Turvey 1997, 435). For instance, when reading the imagination actively forms images mediating between understanding of the narrative content and knowledge of the sensory phenomena that the story refers to and describes. In projecting representations of narrative content, it has been suggested that the production of images in film performs this imaginative work for spectators. Since in film the "mental content" (that is, the material the imagination works with) is also *already* an image, the creative level of imagining where (in literature) mental images are evoked by linguistic signifiers, is bypassed.

Furthermore, critics of film claim that the images representing the narrative content constrain the possibilities for interpretation. Film spectators are able to imagine what Ada would look like *if* she had fair hair and a florid, freckly complexion, but it is difficult to imagine—as the reader of a novel might—that Ada *does* have those attributes when confronted with the image of a pale brunette; however, this is a constraint on image formation, not on imagination as such. While film provides us with vivid, detailed images of the narrative content, there is still much work for the imagination to perform. As film spectators our imaginations can manipulate and extend the narrative content (imagining, in *The Piano*, for example, what Ada and Flora's lives would have been like if Stewart had not finally allowed them to go away to Nelson with Baines) and fill in the empty spaces in the narrative (by imagining what the story of Flora's anonymous father might be, for instance). The imagination is nowhere nearly as reliant on or restricted to image formation as it is usually considered to be, and in consequence, the fact that film deals in imagery does not necessarily make the content of film narratives any easier or more difficult for the imagination to respond to.

Indeed, both Aristotle and Kant make it clear that the imagination conjures that which is not immediately present to the senses: *imagination works with absence*; it inhabits interstices and fills empty spaces. According to this account of imagination, we cannot imagine the content of a film narrative as we do when reading a literary narrative; we can only imagine things that do not actually appear on the screen. (Returning to the simple example given above, we *see* that Ada is a brunette, rather than being prompted by linguistic signifiers to imagine the color of her hair.) This suggests that even if we form images of the narrative content after it has passed from the screen, as we might in a discussion with other viewers after the film, such images are not the products of our imagination: they might be better termed recollections. The formation of inner images associated with imaginative activity can be stimulated by writing, speech, music, sculpture, performance and the visual arts, as much as they can be prompted by unmediated sensations and events. When images from films resurface in the mind and are reconstructed after the screening, their role

Figure 27 Eternal Sunshine of the Spotless Mind: *As the Lacuna spotlight searches for the emotional core of Joel's memories, the face of an anonymous woman in Dr Mierzwiak's office is obliterated.*

in furthering understanding of the narrative can legitimate their function as being genuinely imaginative.

The distinction between remembering and imaginatively representing something is subtle, since time is one of the spaces that the imagination bridges. Shadowy areas of screen space, gauzy scrims over lights, differential focus, and the disintegration or elision of peripheral details show the selectivity of memory in *Eternal Sunshine*. As patches of his memory begin to fade and he moves back further in time, Joel can only recall the fragments of his past that were immediately in front of him and formed the focus of his attention.[6] The context blurs away, a spotlight is used to show the Lacuna technicians searching for the emotional core of each memory, but also to show how the imagination reaches back through time to illuminate only the most salient details, therefore transforming the past.

Imagination often differs from remembering in terms of the nature and degree of deviation from the initial stimulus and the purpose of the imagery: imaginative activity produces new ideas or understandings as opposed to merely recalling or reproducing sensory experiences as mental images. This is particularly pertinent in *Eternal Sunshine*, when Joel has conversations that never happened with the figures populating his memory in the process of trying to create a way to save his past from destruction. In one imaginary conversation about trying to prevent his memories being erased

Figure 28 Eternal Sunshine of the Spotless Mind: *Book titles disappear from their spines.*

Clementine says, "Joel, I have another idea for this problem . . . What if you take me somewhere else, somewhere I don't belong and we hide there till morning?" When the tune "Row, row, row your boat" begins, it starts to rain inside their apartment and Joel scurries under the kitchen table in his childhood home, Clementine chortles, "It's working! I'm a genius!" but of course she is not really there. Joel has been conversing with himself, and the genius is entirely his, as the Clementine he remembers never had occasion to worry about being erased. Drawing on memories of Clementine seems to give his imagination license to come up with crazier ideas than Joel feels capable of inventing on his own.

The scenes in which Joel imagines Clementine inside memories of his childhood located "off the map" of their relationship and therefore hidden from the Lacuna technicians are illustrations of the creative interface of memory and imagination, especially as the film ingeniously utilizes techniques that replicate dream distortion and other mechanisms of the unconscious to represent Joel's subjective experience.[7] Instead of using chromakey to insert the actors inside a virtual set where scale could be manipulated, the art department created giant props, sloping floors, and warped perspectives in Joel's childhood kitchen so that Jim Carrey could literally experience and express what it would be like to be an adult suddenly thrown by memory back to age four when he wasn't tall enough to open the freezer door and reach the ice cream. This creates an odd sense of

Figure 29 Eternal Sunshine of the Spotless Mind: *Baby Joel in his childhood kitchen.*

verisimilitude for the audience as well as for the actors, which blue screen techniques lack.

As in a dream, the spatiotemporal relationships in the kitchen scene are distorted. Clementine appears in a stunning retro costume in Joel's mother's kitchen, beside a table that appears normal when she stands beside it, but is big enough at the other end for a tall man like Carry to seem dwarfed when he sits underneath. Suddenly both Joel and Clementine are being bathed by his mother in a gigantic kitchen sink, which could only have happened to a much younger Joel, well under age four.

One of my favorite moments in *Eternal Sunshine* barely relies on discernable images at all, yet it works to evoke a tangible sense of warmth, intimacy, and tactility through what Laura Marks terms haptic visuality (2000, 163).[8] The scene colors Joel and Clementine in soft amber light shining through the quilt covering their heads and it references objects so long buried in Clementine's past that the mind's eye can barely focus on them as she tells Joel the story of her loneliness as a little girl, and her desperate desire to look pretty so she would be noticed. As she talks about playing with her toys by herself, Joel's voice over begs to keep this memory, just this one. He tells her she is beautiful, leaning in to kiss her gently as the imagery softens and moments of time dissolve into each other again. This sequence, I believe, evokes the synaesthetic imagination, prompting the audience to translate sound and image into touch rather than concentrating on the plot of the story Clementine narrates.[9]

Figure 30 Eternal Sunshine of the Spotless Mind: *The warmth of a dissolving kiss.*

In light of clever scenes such as those in *Eternal Sunshine*, assertions that film does not challenge the viewer's imagination because the audience does not have to construct mental images seem absurd. Such claims conveniently overlook both the stimulus of the filmmakers' imaginations, and the fact that when those of us who are not blessed with creative genius imagine things we rarely form extended, detailed, clear images. As the scenes from Joel's imagination suggest, there can often be a trade-off between vividness and accuracy in mental imagery. Indeed, it is actually extremely difficult for most people to visualize color, motion, and detail in a way that even comes close to approximating the lucidity of life, of film images, or even of dreams. Imaginative activity does not usually engender *mimesis*, forging copies of sense impressions in the mind, instead it entails generating internal impressions that are more often half-formed or hazy than vivid and intricate. Few people, even those possessing extremely good imaginations, would claim to form distinct sensory images of all the detail that a film camera captures when they imagine, fantasize, or remember.

There is a scene in *The Piano* where young Flora is spinning a tale about her mysterious, absent father and viewers receive a glimpse of imagination at work. We already know (though her on-screen audience might not) that the story she tells is a fantasy because in it her mother, who we know to have been mute since the age of six, is singing a duet with Flora's father, a German composer. (Immediately prior to this Flora had also declared that fairies were attendant as bridesmaids at the couple's wedding.) At the climax of Flora's story, a fearsome storm thunders above the forest where her father and mother, oblivious to all else, are still raising their voices to the heavens. "Suddenly," Flora says, "a great bolt of lightning came out of the sky and struck my father so that he lit up like a torch." A rumble of thunder outside coincides with the bolt of lightning in Flora's story and the film cuts, for the space of a scant few frames, between close-up shots of Flora's dramatic little face to a subjective image of an august gentleman in a blue suit bursting into flame.

Interestingly, this subjective imagery, which represents the contents of the imaginations of both the storyteller and her rapt audience, is as sketchy as a young child's drawing. It is important to realize that this does not indicate a deficiency of imagination: that single, simple image captures sufficient information for the meaning and significance of the story to be grasped. Flora's father has vanished, traumatically, in the midst of his loving communion with Ada. Beyond signifying that the image is the product of a child's imagination, the crudity and brevity of the subjective image suggests that images derived from spoken or written stories are often briefly entertained and clumsily improvised. Their power, in many cases, lies in the contribution images make to understanding through their symbolic content and emotive impact, rather than their duration and detail.

Imaginative interpretation of narrative is more complex than creating a mental image of the scenes described, or of the sensory input they are derived from. Indeed, imagination may be as far removed from visualizing

Figure 31 The Piano: *Flora's father aflame, like a childish drawing illustrating her imaginative story.*

as it is from vision: it may not even be the image itself that is centrally important in either activating or deactivating the imagination, or in fostering understanding. The link between imagination and sensory perception as felt bodily responses is much more important: the association of imagination with sensation means that imaginative activity relates to body as well as mind. The mediating function of imagination as it *produces understanding* by bridging between sensory and cognitive responses has primacy over the *production of images* derived from sensation.

The example of Flora's fantasy about her father is suggestive of another way in which imaginative activity is often misunderstood, that is, in terms of its relation to belief.[10] Flora's story is situated squarely in the realm of "make-believe," but this term is misleading. Because she fantasizes about or imagines something does not necessarily mean that she believes it. This becomes evident when she amends the fabrication about fairy bridesmaids in response to a reproving glance from her babysitter. A similar distinction between believing and imagining is made in *Eternal Sunshine* when, in the midst of Joel beseeching Dr Mierzwiak to help stop the memory wipe, Joel acknowledges that he is actually in bed and the entire scene is playing out in his head. Dr Howard Mierzwiak tells Joel "I'm part of your imagination too Joel. How can I help you from there? I'm inside your head. I'm you." The surreality of the realization is underscored by the disorienting, sliding effect of sound moving through space when Joel appears mysteriously in different places within the same shot as he paces back and forth, roaming behind the camera.

Because imagination has traditionally been closely linked with illusion, it also has a strong association with the notion of "mistaken belief" (see the discussion of emotion, fiction, and belief in the previous chapter). A great deal of film theory has been based on the assumption that for the imagination to be engaged, the spectator has to suspend belief in the "real world" for the duration of the narrative, or suspend disbelief about the fictional world. This brings to mind the scene in *The Piano* where the community stages a production of *Bluebeard*[11] and the Maori members of the audience, who are unfamiliar with theatrical conventions, take it for reality and respond in a comical yet totally inappropriate manner by leaping to the defense of Bluebeard's young wife. As well as raising ethical and political questions about the representation of race, this example highlights the fact that in order to respond appropriately to a fictional narrative we must enter into the world of the text and engage with the characters depicted, but it is not necessary or usually desirable for us to take it to be real, to believe in its reality. To suspend disbelief in the story of *Bluebeard*, as the Maori

Figure 32 The Piano: *A shadow puppet play, showing Bluebeard axing his wife.*

Figure 33 The Piano: *Maori spectators watch the play in horror, ready to intervene.*

spectators depicted in *The Piano* do, is to evince of a *lack* of understanding of the text. We could say that as spectators, we do not rely on the belief that the story and the forms of representation within it correspond to facts about the world—though the text may bring to light certain truths about human experience.

Sometimes disbelief in response to the events in a narrative provides an important cue for interpretation, signaling that a move to a symbolic or metaphoric level of understanding is in order. The penultimate scene in *The Piano* in which Ada almost drowns after pushing her piano overboard provides an example of film footage that simply doesn't make sense if we try to read it according to the facts of the physical world that we abide by in our extratextual lives. No mortal woman could have risen to the surface of the sea wearing the layers of heavy clothing that dragged Ada down, tied as she was to her grand piano plunging to the bottom of the ocean. Though improbable in factual terms, through the use of symbolic imagery and visual metaphors this scene reveals something very true about the strong tie between the possibility of making a rational choice and the ability to articulate and account for one's choices and possibilities. At the moment of choice Ada was actually tied to the piano that had, throughout the film, represented her voice: her power of self-expression. "What a death," Ada muses, "What a choice. What a surprise. My will has chosen life . . . I am learning to speak."

Imaginative participation in a narrative allows for varying levels of activity and personal involvement (we always have the options of resistance and responsiveness). In the work of Murray Smith, a distinction is made between imaginative participation in a text that entails simulating an experience as though it happened to oneself (for example, putting oneself in the position of a fictional character), and imagining it from a more impersonal or objective standpoint.[12] Smith explains that we can imagine a situation or experience "from the inside" or "from the outside," and "when we imagine from the inside, either we ourselves or another person (or character) can be the 'protagonist' of our imaginative project" (1997, 413). I can, for example, imagine *Ada* plunging to the bottom of the sea, tied to her piano, or I can imagine *being Ada* in that situation, or I can imagine *myself* in that situation. On yet another level, I can imagine what significance, metaphoric meaning, or symbolism Ada's voyage to the bottom of the sea might have in terms of the narrative as a whole. These levels of imaginative participation and engagement and the range of interpretive possibilities they open up help to ensure that film spectators are not "hypnotized" by film, or passively assimilated into the various ideological or ethical dispositions and experiences we may be aligned with, at certain times, in any given text. Despite this, there is still a danger that narratives may appeal to a compelling, popular, but flawed moral vision which may pervert the spectator's view of reality.

Many theorists have taken up the possibilities of deception and moral corruption that convincing images are associated with. Susan Babbitt, whose work on narrative and moral imagination illustrates just how closely entwined the possibilities for ethically corruptive and constructive influences are, is very conscious of the central epistemological significance of narration. In *Impossible Dreams: Rationality, Integrity and the Moral Imagination*, Babbitt reminds us that a narrator's descriptive skill makes what might otherwise be unimaginable come to be understood, but this same power to be seductive or convincing can also potentially be used to make something that is ethically monstrous seem reasonable or attractive, in the manner of Leni Riefenstahl's *Triumph of the Will* (1935). The style in which a narrative is communicated is selective and evaluative as well as evocative, but often it may be unclear that the narrator is omitting certain details or describing an intentionally limited range of perspectives or experiences that may reinforce a moral or political agenda. Thus, the imaginative capacity to resist, contradict, and claim the possibility of alternative readings and interpretations is as important as the ability to be responsive to the evolving story (see Babbitt 1996, 194).

The ability to resist being seduced by a persuasive story which captures the imagination relies in part on the fact that imagination is not the same thing as make-believe. Films do evoke imaginative responses in us, rather than making us believe that they are real, or even requiring that we pretend we believe they are real for their duration. Plato believed that the imagination could lead to corruption by inflaming the passions and deceiving the intellect partly because he did not clearly distinguish imagination from pretence and make-believe. Pretence is performative; as White says, we can "pretend to do something" but not "imagine to do something" since "pretence shows an ability to perform, whereas imagination shows an ability to conceive" (1990, 152). Here the link to conception and thought emphasizes the role of judgment and evaluation in the active, dialogical imaginative process of spectatorship. So, although the imagination can be involved in mistaken belief, make-believe, and pretence, it is not able to be reduced to any of these and they are not an important part of the notion of moral imagination that will be developed in the final section of this chapter.

The Cinematic Imagination

In *The Piano*, the visual impression of Ada's appearance helps us to imagine the concrete details of her life and the field of social values in which she moves. We witness the strictures and confines of Victorian femininity evidenced in the tightly laced, heavy clothing over restrictive boned and ribbed undergarments every time a European woman appears on the screen. These images pervade the story with a sense of how such garments

Figure 34 The Piano: *Ada, constrained by the tight corset of Victorian femininity.*

encumber the lives of the women who wear them. Film is able to communicate a multitude of circumstantial details economically and powerfully through sustained visual imagery that can add to, rather than distract from, the flow of action in the narrative. In *The Piano* the constant sensory awareness of something as easily overlooked as costume correlates with our developing understanding of the gender roles and expectations of the time, and the correspondingly limited possibilities for Ada to exercise self-determination or personal expression. Even if it is not the focus of our attention, the difficulty associated with negotiating dense bush and deep mud in a long, heavy woolen dress with voluminous petticoats and hoops, with keeping such clothes clean and getting them dry after they are washed, with putting them on and taking them off unassisted is an integral part of the unfolding story. Costuming in *The Piano* represents just one small aspect of the life circumstances that constrain Ada's possibilities. Ada's clothing can be read as a metonym for her life in general: both are stifling and restrictive of movement and heavily encumbered with the dark weight of social expectations surrounding a woman's role and responsibilities.

As spectators (or, indeed, listeners or readers of narrative) our imagination works "behind the scenes," aided, rather than impeded in this effort, by the presence of vivid images whether they are communicated by means of visual, aural, or linguistic signifiers. Since different forms of narrative activate the imagination in differing ways, the audiovisual nature of film texts can neither be divorced from the particular ways in which film might engage the spectator's imagination, nor can it be disregarded on the basis of the Aristotelian claim that to perceive is not to imagine. Though the formal differences between novels, plays, and films do lead to differences in the interpretive processes each elicits, this is largely a difference in emphasis as both are acts of configuration. Like the chapters of a novel or acts of a play, film scenes (and, as I suggested earlier, editing techniques) can disrupt the narrative flow and provide apertures for the imagination to enter the world of the story, fabricating material to fill the spatiotemporal gaps that are opened up in the process of narrative composition. Bridging the intervals between scenes and stretching forward and backward in the narrative to pursue expectations or explanations and to explore possibilities or fill in missing information is one way that the narrative imagination is exercised in film. *Eternal Sunshine of the Spotless Mind* harnesses a wide range of strategies, mainly finessed by sound, to bridge the different narrative levels dividing the external reality of the present, and the different memory spaces and imaginings of Joel's inner world. The first time Joel loses a memory it slips away under incongruous music and the tinny jingle of keys as the neighbor Frank, asks about Joel and Clementine's plans for Valentine's Day. We hear the gurgly *glup, glup* sound of the memory sinking down into the waters of Joel's unconscious, then the muffled underwater sound distorts as Frank's face fades away. Joel's friend Carrie's voice leaks in from the next scene until, with an electronic blip, the memory is deleted and Joel is in Carrie and Rob's apartment. Sonic overlap and sound bridges frequently cue such slippages between scenes, and sometimes nonsimultaneous sound in the form of an aural flashback enables us to inhabit two times at once, as when Joel hears Clementine's laughter while holding a snow dome paperweight that reminds him of the time they frolicked together on the snowy Montauk beach. In other instances, sound plays in fast forward, images rewind, or speed ramping alters the frame rate, distressing the relationship between sound and image or throwing the sound out of synch and degrading it like a corrupted digital file. Such techniques express Joel's experience of traveling through time and lurching from memory to decaying memory in the circular, fragmented narrative. These devices, along with the entirety of the film and its dialogue, are products of the filmmakers' imaginations. The filmic imagination can also be expressed through the use of visual counterpoint and juxtaposition, or accumulation of images in montage, as well as the use of music and audiovisual metaphors.

The Piano often uses extradiegetic music to set the atmosphere for a particular scene, such as the melancholic violin piece that articulates Ada's

Figure 35 The Piano: *Flora's wings signify freedom.*

loneliness, accompanying a scene in which she dines alone in the evening gloom of Stewart's silent house. *The Piano* also contains many striking visual metaphors including the motif of angel's wings that symbolizes freedom. The wings are part of Flora's costume for the performance of *Bluebeard*, and for the majority of the film they remain strapped to her heavy, dark woolen pinafore, becoming progressively grubbier and increasingly bedraggled as time passes. When, after hearing her voice in his mind, Stewart releases Ada from the house in which he has imprisoned her, Flora unties the wings and rinses them clean in a stream of clear water. Ada then emerges, weak and pale, into the sunlight. The metaphor of the angel's wings is a striking example of the capacity of imagination to use imagery to express a concept that has little basis in sensation. Though we cannot see or touch or hear freedom we understand it in association with flight and liberation from bondage (here those bonds take several forms: ribbons binding wings to a young girl's dress; the legally and morally binding vows of marriage, and Ada's "housebound" or imprisoned state).

Similar visual metaphors occur throughout *Eternal Sunshine*, including the cracks in what Joel fears to be thin ice when the couple test the footing of their relationship on the icy Charles River, and the dramatic disintegration of the house literally falling to pieces around them as they revisit the site where they first imagined the possibility of being together.

In addition, film has the capacity to represent imagining as a subjective experience of its characters. When voice-over is used to convey the contents of an interior monologue to spectators it can be equated to reading

Figure 36 Eternal Sunshine of the Spotless Mind: *A relationship cracking whilst on thin ice.*

out a similar descriptive or explanatory passage from a novel (or a journal, in Joel's case), giving an account of the character's thoughts. Or, if the voice-over is of a speculative or poetic nature (or the journal contains drawings or fantasies), it can express the contents of the character's imagination. When Ada explains in the very beginning of the film, "The voice you hear is not my speaking voice, but my mind's voice" we understand that her *thoughts* are being expressed. When, in another instance near the end of the film, she says: "There is a silence where no sound may be, in the cold grave under the deep, deep sea"[13] the poetic voice-over makes the voice of her *imagination* audible, emphasizing the strength of the connection between voice and life.

The absence of sound is also used to powerful effect in *The Piano*, not only by forcing characters and spectators alike to imagine the words that Ada is unable to voice, but also in a scene near the conclusion of the narrative when George Baines, Ada, and Flora are departing for their new life in Nelson with the piano precariously balanced atop an impressive waka (a Maori canoe). We presume Ada wonders about what the piano has bought for her, and what its price has been, as she looks sadly from the instrument to the sea and trails her hand in the deep green water (another visual metaphor for entering the submarine territory of the imagination). At this point in the film the diegetic sound becomes muted, signaling a retreat within and a move away from the sensory impressions of the outer world to focus on inner sight and silent voices.

Subjective imagery is another technique often used in film to depict the inner life of film characters. As with interior monologues, the subjective imagery can represent the content of thought, memory, hallucination, dream, or imagination. At the end of the film Ada's inner voice tells us, "At night I think of my piano in its ocean grave, and sometimes of myself floating above it. Down there everything is so still and silent it lulls me to sleep. It is a strange lullaby. And so it is: it is mine." In the imagery accompanying these thoughts the massive body of Ada's sunken grand piano is seen in close-up, enshrouded with seaweed. With the camera we float slowly away, distancing ourselves from the piano and gradually enlarging the visual frame to include Ada herself tethered to the piano, silent and dead, floating above its corpse. We continue to move away from this vision of a lost possibility until it is completely hidden from us and the now quiet screen is filled only with watery blue light. In this instance the vision of the underwater scene that never eventuated represents an image formed in Ada's imagination, an image that helps her to understand and come to terms with the choices she has made in her life. She gave up her reliance on the piano, slipping from the noose that tied her to it.

Beyond giving expression to the imaginative activity of filmmakers and characters, film narratives also elicit or evoke an imaginative response from their audiences. Some of the ways in which this is achieved have already been mentioned, such as the invitation to fill in spaces in the narrative or wonder about the thoughts and feelings encoded in Ada's silence and expressed in her gestures and the nonverbal sounds she makes. Here the spectator's imagination may shape what the film leaves implicit into a more developed form, assisting our understanding of the narrative.

The spectator's inner eye also plays creatively in off-screen space, where the presence of an unseen person watching what is visible on the screen may become palpable in our imaginations, as when Ada walks home from a rendezvous with her lover through the blue shadows of the forest toward her husband, a menace at first concealed from her view and ours by the trees. As spectators, our expectations stretch anxiously toward the next shot because we are aware that Stewart shared our voyeuristic glimpse of Ada's earlier transgression. Again, the material expression of the film's (or filmmaker's) imagination becomes the substance with which the spectator's imagination works as we interpret the text. The tangled vines and branches in the bush between Baines' and Stewart's houses often fill the screen in the transition between scenes. This dense woodland represents the film's imaginative expression of the complexity and difficulty of the

Figure 37 The Piano: *Tangled vines and dense foliage obstruct the path between Ada and Baines' homes.*

territory that must be negotiated, and also the virtually insurmountable obstacles separating Ada from her lover. Here the spectator's imagination works backward, building a link from the image of the tightly tangled branches to the idea of the impediments and difficulties strewn across the path leading Ada to Baines.

Plainly, the images crowding together on a cinema screen leave plenty of space for the imagination and engage it in a variety of tasks that sometimes differ from, but are rarely "easier" than those set by a literary narrative. The productive imagination creates works of art, or contributes in other ways to expressing the ideas it generates and to restructuring experience, as Kant suggests. Imagination is also significant in traversing the boundary between fiction and life, and in predicting or visualizing consequences. In this respect imagination is similar to supposition[14] or speculation (we could say "imagine," or "suppose" that Ada were to return to Europe). In relation to speculative understanding and the investigation of possibilities, imagination is both instrumental and valuably creative in its own right. It mediates between the virtual and the actual, and between one thing and another, producing an understanding that differs from and is greater than an understanding of any of those things as such, whether singly or together. It is with respect to the inductive or inferential roles of imagination, and the relation between imagination and creativity, that imagination is closely linked to narrative.

Narrative Imagination

Narration and imagination have much more in common than the above analysis of film as a particular medium of creative expression has indicated. The production and interpretation of film and literature are constituted by what might be termed the narrative imagination. In terms of formal structure, film operates in accordance with narrative conventions that are similar to those of other story forms in many ways and that, therefore, evoke similar kinds of interpretive activities. As Murray Smith puts it, engaging with fiction is a variety of imaginative activity in two complex senses:

> First, in comprehending, interpreting, and otherwise appreciating fictional narratives, we make inferences, formulate hypotheses, categorise representations, and utilise many other cognitive skills and strategies which go well beyond a mere registration or mirroring of the narrative material. Secondly, fictions prompt and enrich our "quasi-experience," that is, our efforts to grasp, through mental hypotheses, situations, persons, and values which are alien to us. Our imaginative activity in the context of fiction is, however, both guided and constrained by the fiction's narration: the storytelling force that, in any given narrative film, presents causally linked events occurring in space across time. (Smith 1995, 74)

In the discussion of *Lost Highway* the importance of the moments of ellipsis or omission in stories became evident. I argued that such empty spaces are integral to narrative structure, claiming that they are as characteristic of, and as significant to the structure of narrative as the unifying relationships that weave the story together. Structurally, imaginative understanding is very similar to narrative understanding since the imagination is also as much constituted by "that which is not present" as it is concerned with bridging that absence using devices like metaphor. Narrative and imagination both necessarily work with spaces and gaps, forming relationships across them that unite the material on either side of the ellipsis in our understanding. Such narrative spaces include building expectations, guessing the outcome of the story, or speculating about the consequences of a character's action, questioning feelings and motivations not made explicit. All of these textual spaces are invitations for the narrative imagination to enter, whether to "bridge" the gap, to fill it, or to move through it and take us somewhere not previously understood.

One point of entry for imagination in *The Piano* was the lack of explanation for Ada's actions toward Stewart after he barricaded her within the house to prevent her seeing Baines. Why, one wonders, did she begin to caress her husband when she was supposedly in love with Baines? Her complicated relationships with these two men also invite questions about her past, about her history with other men, and about how whatever went on with Flora's papa and with her own father might have later caused her to act in ways that other people could find difficult to understand and relate to.

Ada's intentions in tantalizing Stewart and touching him seductively are difficult to discern, though possible motives are suggested in the succeeding and preceding scenes. The spectator's imagination must harvest information from these scenes in an attempt to build up an understanding of the thoughts and feelings that might have been driving Ada. The scene where she emerges from what was obviously a sensual dream to find herself snuggling up against her daughter suggests that the awakening of her physical appetites compelled her to turn to Stewart,[15] yet she will not allow him to touch her. Perhaps, then, she was attempting to make the best of her situation, hoping to eventually come to love him and build tenderness in her marriage by using techniques similar to those Baines had so successfully seduced her with. On the other hand, as the narrative develops, the consequences of Ada's overtures lead us back by a different path to her possible intentions. A later scene where Stewart decides to remove the physical constraints on Ada's liberty and replace them with bonds of trust and honor forbidding her to see Baines indicates that Ada's overtures toward her husband may have been part of a more manipulative bargain or bribe. A person in Ada's situation might, after all, do anything she could think of to make him trust her just so that she had an opportunity to escape.

Though we may never reach a definitive understanding of another person's intentions and actions, imagining possibilities is part of the process of achieving a narrative synthesis. In this manner spectators make sense of Ada's actions by incorporating new information into the pattern of the evolving story, and by reflecting back on past scenes, adjusting interpretations of their significance in terms of the overall narrative as they go. The imaginative extension of possibilities and patterns that engages the spectator in speculation and projection is crucial to narrative understanding. In order to fill out our understanding of things that are not made explicit in the narrative, we must investigate the possibilities alive in off-screen space, exploring things that lie implicit between the scenes, weaving material that we dredge up from the character's pasts and futures back into the pattern of the plot. The narrative imagination, like the exercise of practical reason in ethical deliberation, relates the particular to the general, the part to the developing whole, detail to context, past to present to future, cause to consequence.

Ethical Imagination: Envisioning Possibilities and Cultivating Insight

Susan Babbitt claims, "The work of moral imagination is in some manners like the work of the creative imagination, especially that of novelists" (1996, 182). It is equally true for both the ethical imagination and the narrative imagination that "imagination, or the capacity to go beyond interpretations and evidence that are readily available, is required to identify a particular *as* something and to link particulars together without disregarding their rich and vivid concreteness" (Babbitt 1996, 182). The imaginative capacity to go beyond that which is readily available, to construct inferences and associations, and to project possible consequences is central to ethical deliberation and to the cultivation of ethical insight associated with empathy.

In film, and all narratives, the imagination serves the understanding by connecting and linking parts, gradually completing the pattern of the whole narrative. Both the narrative and ethical imagination help to cultivate the ability to form relationships between concrete details and broader perspectives, between the conditions and experiences of one's own life and those of others. Imagining and narrating have ethical ramifications when, for instance, they foster an empathic disposition or metaphorical understanding, or link a particular situation to a more general understanding of human needs and vulnerabilities.

In *The Sovereignty of Good*, Iris Murdoch's thoughts regarding the role of imagination in ethics give rise to interesting questions about the perception of, or attention to details, and the ability to generalize, abstract, or alter the complexity of a situation by projecting oneself into or outside the immediate context to explore surrounding possibilities and consequences. Murdoch champions some uses of the imagination in relation to ethical life and narrative art, and warns against others. Murdoch writes "As moral agents we have to try to see justly, to overcome prejudice, to avoid temptation, to control and curb the imagination, to direct reflection" (1970, 40). Here she is cautioning against imaginative activity leading to illusion, or the tendency to simplify a situation by putting oneself in another person's position, instead of attending to the details of how it is *for them*.[16]

The imagination takes us outside the given, inviting our minds to wander through that which is not present. This can undermine or be advantageous to the process of ethical reflection. Murdoch seems to be caught in the tension between these two possibilities since (in contrast with the caution against imagination, above) she also defends imagination, saying that the "task of attention goes on all the time and at apparently empty and everyday moments we are 'looking,' making those little peering efforts of imagination which have such important cumulative results" (1970, 43). It seems that for Murdoch, the chief danger of imaginative activity in ethics is that it will take the ethical agent, the one who is attending to the particular situation at hand, outside and beyond the reality of the specific context in ways that allow the ego to intrude, or cause salient ethical details to be overlooked.

As Baudrillard (1984) suggests, imagination can be instrumental in building up "false pictures" of the world. These pictures may be misleading, biased, egocentric, or lacking in detail. Ethical attention, or "moral vision" as Murdoch terms it, involves "the effort to counteract such states of illusion" (1970, 37). However, Murdoch does reserve a positive role for the imagination in ethics, a role of clarification rather than obfuscation or falsification. In a discussion of ethical agency and choice, she says, "I can only choose within the world I can *see*, in the moral sense of see which implies that clear vision is a result of moral imagination and moral effort" (1970, 37). Developing this same metaphor of vision or insight, Murdoch later says that imagination can also help us build up a picture of the world formed by "realistic vision with compassion" (Murdoch 1970, 87). It is evident in this tension between advocating and admonishing against the use of the imagination in ethical reflection and perception that, although Murdoch is aware of the ethically productive possibilities of imagination, she is wary of the term's associations with illusion, deception, make-believe, or fantasy and false belief. The experience of a productive form of imaginative engagement with stories and their characters is the foundation for a way of knowing the world that takes a narrative form and that enriches possibilities for ethical understanding. It is imagination that enables us to see beyond that which is before us, to think beyond the ethical concepts, principles, and experiences we are already familiar with, to see things from an unfamiliar perspective.

A number of the evocative cinematic techniques that invite us to engage with "that which is not present" are also intrinsic to the role of imagination in ethical reflection. It is difficult to fully grasp what is going on in a film narrative without traveling imaginatively beyond the detail present on the screen in each shot. Thus imagination extends understanding beyond the concrete experiences or images manifest before us, either in our own lives or on the screen. In traversing the spaces within the screen text and also in traveling between the screen and the spectator's realities, between 1847 and the present day, or between Joel's subjectivity and his outer world, we extend understanding outward from the sphere of our immediate experiences and attachments, potentially developing compassion, concern, and understanding for others whose lives differ from our own.

The term "moral imagination" as it is employed by writers such as Martha Nussbaum, Iris Murdoch, and Susan Babbitt, and as I want to utilize it here, has very little to do with visualizing images. The links between imagination and visualization have little bearing on the ethical imagination, which relies on evoking empathic and sympathetic responses, and on discerning, reflective processes of deliberation. When we say that someone has an active or good imagination we most often mean that they are adept at vividly projecting certain possibilities, at placing themselves in a position they do not actually occupy, as though they were, in various ways, enacting that possibility, or "feeling it from the inside" as Smith would phrase it.

Though the metaphors of moral vision, insight, and envisioning are often used by moral philosophers, such metaphors reflect the association between vision and knowledge or understanding, instead of articulating a necessary link between imaging and imagining. The term "moral imagination" is commonly used to refer to a "vision" of a better world, or an image that reveals problems in our own world. In this view, the author's moral vision may convey to the reader another way of seeing the world. Susan Babbitt's work explores the "role of moral imagination—the capacity to envision alternative social arrangements—in defining both individual reasonableness and the objective interests upon which judgments of reasonableness depend" (Babbitt 1996, 7) where moral imagination is "an appeal to moral vision of how a society *ought* to be" (1996, 37, original emphasis). Thus for Babbitt, as for Nussbaum, a "vision of a better world," as it is imagined by a storyteller and expressed in a description of the lives of particular characters in a narrative, is a vision that can be shared with and entered into by readers and viewers. Narrative engages both the reader and the writer in particular kinds of interpretive and constructive activities that, in themselves, constitute the function of the ethical imagination. Nussbaum says, "The experience of readership is a moral activity in its own right, a cultivation of imagination for moral activity in life and a test for correctness of real-life judgment and response" (Nussbaum 1990, 339). The ethical imagination is, in this constructive sense, the evaluative, configurative process of narrating and interpreting narratives, in ways that help make sense of ethical life.

The arts play a vital role in cultivating imaginative capabilities that are essential for understanding others. An ability to imagine how differences in culture, religion, class, disposition, and physiology might influence "the practical choices people face, but also their 'insides,' their desires, thoughts, and ways of looking at the world" (Nussbaum 1997, 85) is a very important part of ethical understanding. These "practical choices" and the circumstances and forces that influence and give shape to them often hinge on ethical values, on fine discriminations about good and evil and the possibilities for human flourishing. Consequently, Nussbaum argues that in order to foster ethical understanding, we must:

> Cultivate in ourselves a capacity for sympathetic imagination that will enable us to comprehend the motives and choices of people different from ourselves, seeing them not as forbiddingly alien and other, but as sharing many problems and possibilities with us. (Nussbaum 1997, 85)

The Piano illustrates how difficult the task of understanding another person's feelings and actions can be, even with the benefit of vivid narrative detail. Imagining the story of her life, and wondering why Ada might have acted as she did when she made physical overtures to her husband while she was in love with Baines, may help us to make an informed evaluation of moral issues such as deceit, adultery, and the deprivation of liberty as they are inscribed in her particular narrative. Again, the imagination negotiates for the understanding a relation between ethical norms or values and the particular instances in which they are lived out.

Correspondingly, in *Eternal Sunshine* we are led to see the necessity of confronting painful memories, emotions, mistakes, and unpleasant aspects of ourselves if we are to heal and grow and to imagine a better world, for as Jason Sperb writes "to forget is to repeat" (Sperb 2005). As Howard's erasure of his secretary Mary's memory of their affair demonstrates, locking off the past curtails an individual's agency, preventing them from accessing the experiences that enable them to imagine a better future and, therefore, preventing the possibility of change. Mary's gift at the end of the film is to return files of lost memories to Lacuna clients, because she imagines this to be the ethical and responsible course of action (just as Joel's friends do when they show him evidence that Clementine erased him). When Joel goes back in memory and really listens to Clementine when she says he's acting out of insecurity, then imagines telling her he didn't mean the hurtful things he said; when, in short, he imagines trying to do things differently, he makes that possible in a way that it was not when he refused to face (or even recall) his mistakes.

Some critics interpret *Eternal Sunshine's* cyclical narrative to indicate that love is somehow hopeless and Joel and Clementine are destined to eternal recurrence of their relationship problems (Sperb 2005). I think such readings fail to recognize the transformative significance of the imagination in deepening self-knowledge and facilitating understanding of others.[17] There is incredible intimacy evident in Joel and Clementine's ability to listen to each other's desires as she whispers "meet me at Montauk." Though these words were spoken by the Clementine of Joel's imagination, we know that through his imaginative efforts to hold her and to understand what derailed their relationship he finally tunes in to *her* rather than projecting onto her his own insecurities, or making assumptions based on her image or his desire to be saved, as she knows he is prone to do.[18] We believe Joel comes to see the real Clementine and to imagine her true feelings "from the inside," because she does, quite independently, turn up at Montauk on Valentine's Day on a whim she never actually expressed, prompted by a memory she no longer has. The depth of this intimacy and understanding was created by traveling back through the memory narrative of the relationship, and imaginatively renarrating it, searching for insight into himself and his lover, finally opening up in the disintegrating beach house to share his own feelings, and envisioning possibilities for a new ending. This mutual understanding is never more evident than when Joel and Clementine take responsibility for their cruel words, forgive one another, and express a touching willingness to fully acknowledge the possibility of failure and yet to embrace each other, flaws and all. With a shrug, and a brave, sweet smile from Joel and delighted, relieved laughter from Clementine, the last line of dialogue in the film is a single word of acceptance: "okay."

In "The Narrative Imagination," Nussbaum claims that because storytelling cultivates habits of conjecture, empathy, and wonder about the lives of other people, the narrative imagination is "an essential preparation for moral interaction" (1997, 90). This, she says, is all the more important because we cannot actually experience what it is like to be another person, nor can most of us ever hope to travel widely enough to cultivate an expansion of our sympathies through actual involvement in the lives of people very different from ourselves in a way that is comparable to being transported into other lives via narrative. The vicarious experience offered to our imaginations by narrative art may assist us to extend compassion to others and to notice "differences in the inner world, seeing the delicate interplay between common human goals and the foreignness that can be created by circumstances. Differences of class, race, ethnicity, gender, and national origin all shape people's possibilities, and their psychology with them" (Nussbaum 1997, 95). As I have said, Ada seems most alien when she wordlessly begins to caress Stewart, but, as Nussbaum might claim (1997, 91), my failure to identify with her or to be able to imagine her motives is itself a source of understanding about what life can do to people. Her possibilities for expressing herself, for making herself understood were so restricted by her circumstances that she behaved in ways that might not be readily understood by a modern viewer not bound by those constraints.

In one sense the ethical imagination is evaluative by definition: it is an interpretive activity akin to drawing a moral from a story. Yet it is also (and often simultaneously) a creative and constructive activity; the capacity to envision a better world. Finally, the ethical imagination includes the active formation of associations and contrasts, mediating between previously unrelated things. The ethical imagination involves processes that are also integral to narration and narrative interpretation: the ability to project and recollect, to play with and create imaginary scenes and conversations, to draw together information and emotion relevant to the lives of others, and to bring all this into a relationship with one's own life. It is here, in the imaginative activity through which a text's producers and interpreters relate the story to their own lives, that the ethical imagination becomes capable of restructuring reality, of overcoming discrimination and valuing difference.

****

While the formation of mental images may not be of central importance to the ethical imagination activated by film narratives, the presence of sensory images can stimulate rather than retard imaginative activity because they make the concrete details of unique situations and surroundings present to the embodied understanding of film spectators. An appreciation of the significance of contextual specificity as well as more general (or generalizable) moral values and guidelines are both crucial to ethical understanding. As the discussion of *The Piano* and *Eternal Sunshine* revealed, audiovisual representation of such things as subjective sound and imagery; the nuances of gesture, expression and tone, innovative uses of sonic and visual effects, and the ways in which the camera, the spectator, and the characters are positioned in screen space often indirectly inflect the interpretation and application of the ethical standards and guidelines that pertain to a given situation.

Imagination includes, but cannot be reduced to, the ability to form images in the mind, and it can be an active and creative process that produces the possibility for certain forms of understanding. Recognition of the active, productive aspects of imagination (as well as its more receptive, reproductive elements) avoids collapsing the distinctions between imagination and false belief that the term imagery has traditionally been associated with. This, in turn, allows for the possibility of a more dynamic, dialogical understanding of spectatorship as the imaginative interpretation of fictional narratives. Contrary to the taken-for-granted association between imagination and imagery, the moral imagination has little to do with eyesight or other sensory capacities, and a great deal to do with insight, perceptiveness, and careful attention to details and contexts requiring imaginative extension beyond immediate appearances or spoken words. In particular, imagination is very important in furthering ethical understanding by means of inductive reasoning and the projection or exploration of possibilities, forming or constructing a story from plot points, forging new understandings metaphorically, metonymically, symbolically, allegorically drawing associations and relationships between terms to create a whole greater than the sum of its parts. Imagination mediates or bridges spheres of experience, between the worlds of the text and its interpreters, between sensation and understanding, and between subjectivity and external reality. Narrative also has a role in ethical understanding developed in the practice of attentive engagement. This will be discussed in the next chapter which draws the emotive, imaginative, and conceptual dimensions of the configuring acts involved in constructing, interpreting, and engaging with narratives together into a picture of film spectatorship and ethical attention.

Notes

1. Like the people in Plato's allegory who are prisoners of their senses, Baudry's film spectators are also thought to be "captivated" and deceived by the powerful sensory impact of flickering images (1992, 310). The experience of film spectatorship is often described as "hypnotic," as a state in which cinema patrons are seduced by illusions, their eyes are glued or "chained" to the representation of reality that causes them to "lose touch with reality," and become more susceptible to influence and open to suggestion. It may well be the strong link between imagination and image that has caused the faculty of imagination to be understood as linked to sensory illusion and deceit. Baudrillard's work *The Evil Demon of Images* (1984) refers to Cartesian paranoia about the deceptive nature of appearances and images, which can also be traced to Plato's cave analogy and which rests on an understanding of

imagination as *phantasia*, a state of being appeared to. Imagination is, in this view, the reception of a mimetic image, a fake that appears before us—just like film images. If the fake is too good, if the image appears too real, we might be deceived, as the prisoners in Plato's cave were deceived by photophobic puppeteers, and as Descartes narrowly escaped being deceived by the evil demon manipulating appearances in his "First Meditation" (Descartes 1984, 12–15).

2. The largest body of work on imagination in film studies is found in cognitive film theory, primarily using Gregory Currie's influential book *Image and Mind* (1995) as a springboard for elaborating the process of mental simulation. Key points from this literature were dealt with in the previous chapter due to the interrelatedness of emotion and imagination. Currie argues that imagination can be understood in terms of mental simulation whereby film viewers run their normal beliefs and desires "off-line" when engaging with screen characters (1995, 144–145). While I am sympathetic to aspects of Currie's account, I share some of the reservations expressed by authors such as Karen Bardsley (2002) and Deborah Knight (2006), and the account of imagination offered here is not restricted to mental simulation.

3. Although Aristotle may have worked with a restrictive definition of the term imagination, unlike Plato, he does not discredit the products of the creative imagination. Indeed, he places high importance on the philosophical and social value of the creative arts (see Aristotle 1941c, *Poetics* Chapter 9, 1451b).

4. See, for instance, David Hume's thoughts on "ideas" in *Essays Concerning Human Understanding*, section II (1975).

5. With reference to the theories of classical film scholars such as Andre Bazin, Gregory Currie states that "The classical illusionist theory of cinema claims that the viewer is made to believe that he or she is a spectator at a real action, watching from within the space of the action, situated where the camera is" (1995, 165). In *Mystifying the Movies: Fads and Fallacies in Contemporary Film Theory* (1988), Noel Carroll works through examples of misconceptions about cinema and the "illusion of reality." The illusory nature of the cinematic image is created by "techniques of visual verisimilitude," which supposedly lead to delusions, false beliefs, and the dangerous, distracting phenomenon of identification with screen characters (Carroll 1988, 92).

6. Jason Sperb (2005) plays on the title of *Eternal Sunshine of the Spotless Mind* as he interprets the use of natural sunshine and artificial spotlights, revealing that natural light and dense shadow represent the absence of memory, and the searching spotlight represents the limitations of perception and recollection.

7. Displacement is also used, as when Patrick's eyes appear to be upside down when Joel catches a glimpse of him in Howard's office, or when Joel and Clementine are in bed together and with a subtle shift in lighting, they suddenly find their cozy bed is wondrously misplaced on the snowy Montauk beach.

8. In an essay in *Carnal Thoughts*, "What my Fingers Knew: The Cinesthetic Subject, or Vision in the Flesh," (2004) Vivian Sobchack discusses such a moment in *The Piano*, when the first two shots show an unfocused pattern of indeterminate red and pink forms as light shines through the fingers covering Ada's eyes. Discussing the tactile apprehension of this

haptic image, Sobchack writes, "We do not experience any movie only through our eyes. We see and comprehend and feel films with our entire bodily being, informed by the full history and carnal knowledge of our acculturated sensorium" (2004, 63).

9. Sobchack terms such moments in film an "involuntary, cross-modal sensory exchange" and terms the film viewer a "kinesthetic subject" for this reason (2004, 69).

10. Christopher Fahy distinguishes between "making things up" and imagination. Fahy argues that although objective processes like interviews and conversations, and subjective processes like remembering help to create knowledge of another person's situation, there are always missing pieces of the story that must be fleshed out by imaginative vision, which can include acts of reflection, interrogation, intuition, and memory (2002, 45).

11. The inclusion of this and other references to *Bluebeard* in the film is not the only reference to Angela Carter. Carter's tale *The Magic Toyshop* (1967) also prominently features a mute heroine, and in her rendition of *Bluebeard* as *The Bloody Chamber* (1979), the protagonist is a pianist. This particular tale has other striking similarities to *The Piano* in that it includes a new bride traveling to live with a previously unknown husband in a lonely land, imprisonment in the husband's domain, a blind piano tuner who listens with reverence to the pianist and thus falls in love with her (and with whom she eventually betrays her husband), and another nasty incident with an axe after certain prohibitions are breached. Campion's intertextual allusions to the fairytale, *Bluebeard,* are intentional and richly symbolic as they set the imagination to work with certain expectations produced by the parallel stories.

12. For other relevant discussions of the levels of personal involvement in imaginative simulation see Currie (1995; 1997), Novitz (1987), Walton (1990), Williams (1973), and Wollheim (1987). For instance, Wollheim distinguishes between central and acentral imagining, while Currie differentiates personal imagining (which is associated with empathic simulation and pretence; imagining being someone or somewhere, or sharing an experience) from impersonal imagining (a secondary level of imagination wherein we imagine things of the characters, not of ourselves) in ways that closely parallel Smith's "imagining from the inside" and "imagining from the outside," as Smith himself notes (1997, 413).

13. Here Ada is reciting a stanza from Thomas Hood's poetry (see Campion, 1993).

14. As White notes, "suppose" is grammatically similar to "expect;" to putting forward a hypothetical possibility and "imagine" is grammatically similar to "think;" to exercise an ability (1990, 147).

15. Campion's intention was to shift the erotic focus of the film to Stewart by having Ada objectify him, in an amoral way (Campion 1993, 138–139). This is so far from my own interpretation that it provides a good example of how performance can join with audience perceptions, opening up ambiguous spaces in a text, through which unintended meanings and imaginings may creep.

16. Murdoch advocates a practice of "unselfing," an attempt to clarify one's ethical vision of others by "altering consciousness in the direction of objectivity, unselfishness and realism" without losing sight of the special and specific details (1970). She cautions that "fantasies and reveries" and selfish egos can get in the way of moral insight: "By opening our eyes we do not necessarily see what confronts us. Our minds are continually active,

fabricating an anxious, usually self-preoccupied, often falsifying *veil* which partially conceals the world" (original emphasis 1970, 84).

17. The feeling that Joel and Clementine are doomed to repeat past failures also misses the positive message about change and love in the song playing over the film's closing images.

18. When Joel first asks her out in the bookstore, Clementine makes a speech that she reprises in abbreviated form when he later asks her to give their relationship another chance at the end of the film. Clementine says, "I'm telling you right off the bat that I'm high maintenance. Too many guys think I'm a concept, or that I complete them, or I'm gonna make them alive. But I'm just a fucked up girl who's looking for my own peace of mind. Don't assign me yours." "I still thought you were going to save my life, even after that," Joel admits.

7

Seeing in the Dark:
Attentive Engagement

This chapter proposes a way of approaching ethical understanding through sensitive, intentionally directed perception. In order to establish the value of attentive engagement in the cinema, the discussion moves from arguing for the ethical importance of attention, through examining how it is inscribed in film texts, to exploring how it is practiced by film spectators. The perceptual capacity referred to as ethical attention, or (in a sense that suggests more intense personal involvement) as attentive engagement, is characterized by concern for the specific needs and vulnerabilities of a unique individual or situation, within a concrete and particular ethical context. Ethical attention is a practice that involves the resources, faculties, and forms of responsiveness, resistance, and perceptiveness explored in the preceding chapters. It requires emotional, imaginative, and perceptual engagement, as well as acts of narration and narrative interpretation.

The objective of ethical attention is to progressively build up layers of understanding[1] comprised of different perspectives, situational detail, and an awareness of the interwoven influences of personal history, significant relationships, and other cultural and contextual factors that have bearing on questions of ethical choice. Ideally, such a perceptive practice produces a detailed, just, and caring awareness that enables an ethical agent to respond more appropriately to the unique requirements of a situation than the application of general ethical rules, guidelines, values, or principles would, on their own, allow.

Attentive engagement is an ethical process that contrasts with and can be seen as complementary to deductive or inductive reasoning based on the application of moral principles. Since the very concept of ethical attention diverts emphasis from such moral standards (though it might be balanced or guided by them), it is open to criticisms about the lack of criteria for moral deliberation, evaluation, and response and, consequently, to charges of moral relativism. Because attention is both contextually specific and a skill or disposition attributable to an individual, it is often thought to be as weak and indefensible a justification for an ethical action or judgment as intuition or "gut feelings." The responses arising from a practice of ethical attention are difficult to generalize or extend to other situations. Because of this it is hard to see how the moral insights and values which come to light through attention and which govern the ensuing ethical response might be based on understandings shared amongst a community in the manner that makes ethical life coherent.

More specifically, without reliance on principles or rules of conduct prescribing moral duties and obligations, clarity of ethical insight could be in danger of being clouded by ego, or personal and cultural bias. In practice, in each conception of ethical attention taken up in this chapter, the direction of attention extends outward from the self toward others rather than being primarily an act of introspection or reflection, though at the same time ethical attention may include and often necessitate self-scrutiny. Though these altruistic and self-reflexive characteristics of attention ameliorate concerns about self-centered perception, they raise equally disturbing questions about practitioners of ethical attention becoming self-sacrificing. If the ego does not assert itself and the act of attending is directed toward the needs of others then, in extreme cases, an unhealthy form of selfless servitude to others[2] may be enacted.

In this chapter, three different theoretical approaches to attention are considered, addressing the ways in which this central complex of difficulties surrounding relativism, moral criteria, and the ego's attachments is negotiated in each. The descriptive frameworks of these approaches center on philosophical accounts by Simone Weil and Martha Nussbaum of "moral vision" in narrative fiction and within lived ethical situations; on Maurice Merleau-Ponty's theory of attention in *Phenomenology of Perception* and Vivian Sobchack's phenomenological discussion of "the inscription of vision as movement" in film texts; and on attentive engagement as a cinema spectator. In film spectatorship, perception in the cinema is necessarily related to and partially directed by the expression and inscription of the film's own visible, visual activity. Consideration of the forms in which attention is enacted helps to illustrate and extend philosophical accounts of what ethical attention is and ought to be.

Examples from the films *Once Were Warriors* (directed by Lee Tamahori in 1994), and *Nil by Mouth* (Gary Oldman, 1997) are used throughout the chapter to illuminate how acts of attention are instantiated in film texts and in our engagement with them. In addition to treating filmic style as the expression or practice of a form of ethical attention (which in turn engages the attention of spectators), I contrast the styles of these two films, using them as metaphors for the different forms of ethical attention theorized by Weil and by Nussbaum.

After detailing the ethical significance of different modes of perception and ethical attention, the chapter explores the inscription of attention in film texts. Once again Sobchack's work provides a theoretical perspective and an analytical vocabulary to describe movements of attention in screen texts as films give visible expression to acts of perception. Here the possibilities for entwining an awareness of the ethics of attention with Sobchack's phenomenological film analysis are elaborated. As well as gaining opportunities to access and reflect upon examples of various modes of perception made visible in the visual style of the films we watch, as spectators we also participate in and practice the form of perception expressed by the film and by its characters. In the final section of the chapter the conjunction of the film's visual activity and the attentive engagement of spectators with film texts is explored, concluding by suggesting that film spectatorship itself is an attentive practice that provides a model for ethical attention.

Perception and Attention

In a metaphor reminiscent of the spotlight that focuses on the emotional core of memories in *Eternal Sunshine of the Spotless Mind*, Merleau-Ponty compares acts of attention to a searchlight's beam that illuminates hidden aspects of a dark landscape, exploring the possibility that "perception awakens attention" and attention subsequently "develops and enriches" the life of consciousness (Merleau-Ponty 2002, 31). As any cinematographer knows, intensity of illumination or clarity of focus affects the ability of viewers to perceive detail and to understand what we see. By acting as a filter or a focus puller for the chaos of sensory impressions and by delineating a perceptual or mental field of clarity and concentration, attention "presupposes a transformation of the mental field, a new way for consciousness to be present to its objects" (Merleau-Ponty 2002, 33). Thus, Merleau-Ponty concludes, "To pay attention is not merely further to elucidate pre-existing data, it is to bring about a new articulation of them" through "the active constitution of a new object which makes explicit and articulate what was until then presented as no more than an indeterminate horizon" (2002, 35).

According to Sobchack, perception itself is an evaluative, intentional act, not simply a passive, receptive, and uninterpretive physiological process. Perception makes intentionality manifest, that is: intention points or extends toward significant things in the visual field, picking them out from their surroundings. Sobchack claims that perception is a fundamental mode of engagement with the world, and a structuring activity of consciousness (1992, 72). In order for sense perceptions to have meaning or conscious significance, perception must involve the exercise of something like categorization and evaluation: perception, then, can be thought of as the reception and identification of something through sensory engagement with it. The process of evaluative perception, however, often occurs on what might be called an automatic or subconscious level (hence the value of phenomenological analysis, which brings to light such "naturalized" aspects of experience by delving into the processes of recognition and categorization). Perception, though we may rarely notice this, is inseparable from recognition and understanding: "It works on us without us; it hides itself in making the object visible" (Merleau-Ponty 1964, 167).

With Merleau-Ponty, Sobchack links perception with judgment, deliberation, and evaluation: "Perception is the diacritical emergence of judgment in existence . . . the empirically formal link between embodied consciousness and any significance the world might have for it" (Sobchack 1992, 71–72). This suggests that the perception of phenomena is inherently qualitative and selective, and that it entails value judgments (often of a covert nature). Noticing, overlooking, and ignoring, like more discerning and deliberative evaluations that recognize something as important or as devoid of interest and value, are acts that can have ethical ramifications. For instance, it is often easier to allow people like the Sprague brothers, or Nola, in *The Boys,* or Matthew Poncelet in *Dead Man Walking* to remain outside the zone of our attention, than to focus on them and their difficulties. Once an injustice has been acknowledged, it can exert an ethical claim.

As a precursor to a more systematic working through of modes of attending, an example from Gary Oldman's film *Nil by Mouth* details how perception can have ethical consequences if we shift the context of our perception slightly to include particular and relevant details. *Nil by Mouth* takes a close look at abuse and dependence in the lives of Val (Kathy Burke) and Ray (Ray Winstone), a dysfunctional couple living in council flats in South London.[3] Val's appearance throughout the film is unattractive: she looks dowdy and never fixes her hair or wears anything remotely presentable. In perceiving Val's image on the screen, we not only see her physical appearance, but we also unavoidably see her appearance *as* something good or bad, important or insignificant. We evaluate her appearance, perhaps without consciously realizing it, by comparing her with others and by interpreting our perceptions within the context of her life and our own range of experiences. "Dowdy" is not a term of appreciation. Such an observation and the accompanying evaluation merely seem derogatory if we stop at the level of sense-perception or aesthetic judgment. To stop there would constitute a failure of ethical attention, a failure to discern the relevant details and to deepen understanding of another person's situation. As ethical attention, the act of perception must reach further, moving through successive levels of insight and accumulating layers of narrative detail and context.

As distinct from ordinary perception, ethical attention may extend to the recognition that Val's unkempt state is indicative of her inability to adequately care for herself or receive care from others. This point might remain unnoticed if the attender does not care about Val, or if her image is frozen and abstracted from its context (as in still photography, a description in a news article, or a note in a case record), but it reveals itself when her appearance is set against the circumstances of her life and read as symptomatic of depression, poverty, a lack of support and care through pregnancy, and debased self-esteem.

Figure 38 Nil by Mouth: *Val's dowdy appearance.*

For a different individual, or even for the same individual in a situation that differed in some significant way, the same "symptom" (a dowdy appearance) might stem from completely different causes. Val's appearance could be a matter of practicality and economy, or a positive choice expressing her personal preferences or political convictions; equally, it could indicate a lack of time or inclination to focus on something considered trivial, or a means of resisting dominant ideological positions relating physical appearance to personal-worth. While our attention to Val is, in this instance, reliant on vision, it is also inseparable from evaluations related to an imaginative and conceptual grasp of her situation. This example brings to light the link between ethical attention and contextually specific details, as well as demonstrating how the qualitative dimension of embodied, sensory perception constitutes a fundamental practice of engaging with the world on an ethical level.

Although the terms perception and attention are often used interchangeably, or in senses that overlap with one another, a variety of philosophical distinctions have been drawn between the two, and different philosophers often use the same term in disparate ways. For instance, Martha Nussbaum counts perception[4] as central to the nature of practical reason. Following Aristotle, she claims that discerning the correct decision in an ethical situation rests on perception, understood as "complex responsiveness to the salient features of one's concrete situation" (1990, 55). Nussbaum's conception of the nature of perception is not incompatible with Sobchack's; however, the two theorists emphasize differing objectives in their descriptions of the same capacity. Nussbaum investigates the ethical implications of the involvement of attender and attendee; she considers the significance of responsibility and responsiveness, and attitudes of care and concern. In *Address of the Eye*, Sobchack's concern lies principally with the embodied, hermeneutic, and mediated nature of perception in film. However, she has taken up the ethical implications of cinematic vision in relation to documentary film in "Inscribing Ethical Space" (1984), an article which I draw upon below because it details a number of different ways of encoding an ethical gaze on film.

In Simone Weil's moral philosophy a very different distinction is drawn between the terms perception and attention. Weil classes attention as an active form of looking, yet she believes its ethical value lies in the activity remaining rigorously noninterpretive. Since, for Weil, just and truthful vision incorporates the revelation of reality,[5] subjective acts of evaluation are unnecessary and the attender must actively abstain from interpretation and from engaging in the kinds of implicit evaluations with which personal involvements, attachments, and experiences may be laden.

Nussbaum, in contrast, understands moral attention as necessitating deep involvement: intensity of emotion, reflection, and responsiveness of the physical senses (1990, 207) and a caring engagement with actual individuals (1990, 189). The form of attentive engagement that Nussbaum advocates is very like that of a reader engrossed in a literary work, feeling themselves drawn deeply into the lives of the characters therein. This is an analogy she develops in various ways throughout many of the essays in *Love's Knowledge: Essays on Philosophy and Literature* (1990) an analogy that Wayne Booth also takes up in *The Company We Keep: An Ethics of Fiction* (1988).

In the following analysis, the term attention will be used to describe a deliberately directed, differential awareness or perception, which delineates one element or figure from another and places it in a meaningful relation to background and circumstance. Thus attention is understood as an active, purposeful form of perceiving that entails evaluation on a more conscious level than the naturalized process of identification and categorization that is involved in the phenomenological understanding of ordinary perception discussed above, or in the truthful revelations resulting from Weil's ideal of attention.

Moral Vision

One important sense in which ethical attention has been taken up within philosophy is that of moral vision. As derived from the work of Nussbaum and Weil, moral vision[6] requires a sensitive attunement to the particular situation that allows points of ethical salience to come to light. This ability to see what counts and what is at stake entails an open and receptive disposition. Later, I will examine how this disposition may be cultivated by the process or practice of film spectatorship.

As with a phenomenological approach, Simone Weil's attitude to understanding experience requires a certain "bracketing away" or dislocation of those aspects of the self that generate assumptions, preconceptions, personal involvement, and other complications that might interfere with pure, impartial, objective knowledge. Weil's conception of ethical attention (which differs from the notion of attentive engagement I will develop in this chapter, but balances and informs it in significant ways) implicitly situates the attender outside the space in which the moral action unfurls, rather than as an integral part of it. In a sense the structural features of cinematic spectatorship (as distinct from the practices and processes of spectator-ship) provide the ultimate manifestation of Weil's ideal of ethical atten-tion. Not only are the will and the ego, and all personal relationships de-emphasized in the context of cinematic spectatorship, but the physical body is also excluded from the arena in which attention is focused. Though this may be appropriate for a spectator, it is not necessarily appropriate for an agent participating in ethical life.

Once Were Warriors, a film which deals with domestic violence in a con-temporary Maori family, is interesting because the way in which it is filmed has remarkable parallels with the form of attention that Weil describes as being fully and appropriately ethical. With the exception of the opening sequence, the film is shot almost entirely from middle distance, rather than using close-ups or long-shots, and the camera is usually static with few zooms, pans, or tracking shots (and when these are utilized, the motion is slow and smooth). Editing also moves at a measured pace and each shot tends to be held for some time, rather than being cut rapidly. This film utilizes the transparent, naturalized editing conventions of "seamless suture" rather than using arty, obvious, or jarring techniques that draw attention away from the narrative to the means, mode, and medium of production and elicit a more self-conscious form of engagement. Similarly, the soundtrack and lighting are unobtrusive. Apart from half a dozen instances where conventional techniques (such as the extradiegetic siren of an ambulance that segues into a human scream, the halo effect of back-lighting, or extreme high and low angle shots) are used to highlight a significant element of the narrative, the contrivances of the film recede into the background. In consequence, the film is like a hidden observer, allow-ing the story and the characters to reveal themselves to its patient eyes, and thus also to the spectators. While these well established realist conventions certainly don't preclude emotive engagement with characters in the narra-tive, I will argue that they implicitly position the spectator in a particular ethical relation to the story world.

The judicious use of medium-close-ups and forward zooms, and the complete absence of extreme close-ups in *Once Were Warriors* maintains a distance between the viewing subject and the characters which might be associated with a desire to be unobtrusive or to maintain a degree of detach-ment.[7] In many cases, close-ups invite a certain intensity of engagement with the viewed subject, perhaps because the perceptual proximity afforded by close-ups position the viewer inside the personal space boundary that is usual in Western culture; such framing is often associated with an intimate gaze. Of course, intimacy is not the only function that close shot-scale can

fulfill. Like any other cinematic technique, the effects of perceptual proximity are largely contextual. Tight framing that brings us right up against
Ray, or Val's bruises, or Brett Sprague in *The Boys* can be confronting, disturbing, or oppressive rather than intimate, and wide shots can also evoke
empathy with characters, by conveying feelings of insignificance or alienation as the view of ugly, impersonal council flats in *Nil by Mouth* does.
Furthermore, in *Lost Highway*, the opening close-ups of Fred Madison
are enigmatic rather than empathic whereas the extreme close-ups of
Alice's scarlet lips whispering into the phone have an undeniably fetishistic
quality to them. In the latter context, fragmentation of the body transforms
Alice into a viewed object, rather than a subject, and objectification sits
uneasily alongside intimacy.

Although it is clear that cinematographic devices need to be interpreted
in relation to the narrative they feature in, consistent avoidance of close-
ups does work to maintain a perceptual distance between the film and the
characters and, in doing so, between the audience and the characters. *Once
Were Warriors* seems to do this, to an extent.[8] However, this too needs
qualification in relation to the phenomenological description of cinematic
vision. As we have already established, while the audience's gaze is mediated by the gaze of the filmic body, spectators can also look away, we can
use our imaginations to explore beyond the fringes of screen space, or we
can focus in and look more closely and attentively at details that are embedded in the context of the frame. This means that the viewing distance
determined by shot-scale can be described as a mode of perception that
keeps us at arm's length from the characters, but it doesn't necessarily
follow that the audience will maintain an emotional distance. As much as
Once Were Warriors holds the ethical situation it perceives and narrates in
perspective for us, it also offers an invitation to wonder, to wander further
into the story world and to think beyond its boundaries to its implications
for social reality. Thus this "detached" form of moral vision is not practiced
at the expense of attending to details or engaging with character and
context.

Once Were Warriors' filmic style enunciates a mode of attending to the
story that seems to allow information to be disclosed, rather than using
attention as a tool to extract or define meaning, or to share knowledge as
part of a close relationship with the subjects of attention.[9] This attitude of
detachment and "bearing witness" parallels the attitude that Weil advocates as appropriate for an ethical agent when attending to another, for
Weil believes "attention should be a looking and not an attachment" (Weil
1978, 174). The driving force behind this idea is that the distance that

detachment offers allows the observer to keep the ethical situation in perspective, and thus to remain "objective" about it. The mode of attention inscribed in the visual style of *Once Were Warriors* is not coded as a subjective gaze, but rather as a universal perspective and thus as a more just viewpoint. In a discussion of the ethical implications of different ways of looking at death (or at moral atrocities) via film, Sobchack characterizes the "humane stare" as one in which:

> [T]he image is inscribed by the mark of a steady camera, placed in a generally measured distance from its visual object, and by smooth technical and physical activity. When zooms occur, they are controlled and steady. Vision is purposefully framed and clearly focused. (Sobchack 1984, 297)

Although it is not the only possible form of ethical vision, the nonjudgmental, nonintrusive, objective "humane stare" about which Sobchack writes perfectly describes the mode of vision enacted by *Once Were Warriors'* filmic body. Such a gaze can be a way of attending to the ethical agents whose lives are being documented by the film with respect, depending on the nature of the scene we view. Attending in a detached manner allows disclosure and opens up a valuable space for the unexpected to reveal itself in the absence of the personal projections and expectations that can arise if one is too deeply immersed.

My main concerns with the description of moral vision Weil has developed are that the ideal of detachment implies that ethical truths are revealed to the mind at the cost of emotional intimacy and embodied involvement, and that perception itself can be innocent or devoid of evaluation. Like filmic perception and attention, human vision is an act of composition, of framing what we see within a context in order to narrate its place in life and understand it. While I believe that Weil's notion of attention is an unattainable ideal due to the intersubjective, embodied, and evaluative nature of perception, her insight into the importance of a form of moral vision that is neither invasive, nor judgmental is valuable. It changes the character of ethical insight from something that can be extracted from or applied to a situation, to a valuable gift of understanding that arises from the experience of attending and that is offered freely to the attentive observer.

The primary objectives of ethical attention are similar for Nussbaum and Weil, but the strategies each theorist offers are very different. In direct contrast with Weil, Nussbaum defends the view that ethical perception ought to involve active engagement of the whole person, without restricting the ethical resources and faculties that one might otherwise productively draw upon. Again, supporting an Aristotelian approach to ethics, Nussbaum says that:

> With respect to any complex matter of deep human importance there is no "innocent eye," no way of seeing the world that is entirely neutral and free of cultural shaping . . . Even where sense perception is concerned, the human mind is an active and interpretative instrument, and that its interpretations are a function of its history and its concepts as well as of its innate structure. [Furthermore] the nature of human world interpretations is holistic. (Nussbaum 1993, 260)

For Nussbaum, Weil's ideals of perception and attention are impossible, in that it is never possible to fully rise above or stand outside of one's own point of view. A practice of attending and engaging at close range, being involved in emotional and empathic contact can lead to perception of the extent and depth and impact of the relevant details of a situation, and may even prevent unethical actions:

> If you really vividly experience a concrete human life, imagine what it's like to live that life, and at the same time permit yourself the full range of emotional responses to that concrete life, you will (if you have at all a good moral start) be unable to do certain things to that person. Vividness leads to tenderness, imagination to compassion. (Nussbaum 1990, 209)

Such vivid insights into other lives may be blurred by a quest for ethical understanding that was practiced in more general or more abstract ways. Nussbaum makes this point when she suggests that sometimes maintaining a calculated, impartial distance and refraining from feeling a sense of attachment and emotional responsiveness constitutes an ethical oversight or failure. Indeed, voyeurism and objectification, two problematic forms of cinematic vision, are reliant on distanciation, which suggests a requirement for another way of seeing.[10] In "Perceptive Equilibrium" Nussbaum critiques perception devoid of strong, affective, emotional involvement, suggesting that in a "perceiver's impartiality, the equipoise of the body drawn strongly to no extreme—there is an almost voyeuristic 'curiosity,' the curiosity of the uninvolved gaze" (1990, 187). According to Nussbaum's argument, which I took up earlier when discussing Stevie's insensitivity in *The Boys*, such a form of perception can lead to becoming distanced from others, seeing them in an abstract way, and consequently it can prevent us from perceiving crucial facts about the ethical situation.

Nil by Mouth can be seen to exemplify a practice of attending that differs substantially from Weil's ideal of ethical attention as detached, receptive observation. *Nil by Mouth* is shot almost entirely in close-up: it infiltrates the lives of the characters in a very intimate way, zooming in close in its efforts to focus on subtle shifts of expression.[11] This close, confronting view of human beings is in no way a fetishistic fascination. Cinematic vision in *Nil by Mouth* eludes ready classification as either voyeurism or fetishistic scopophilia. On the contrary, it is more aptly likened to an ethical mode of cinematic vision that Sobchack describes as an "endangered gaze," which is encoded with markers of subjective proximity of the viewer to the violent events being viewed. In this form of attention, "The representation is marked by the relative instability of its framing . . . vision is frequently obstructed, inscribing its fragile yet concerned relation to the horrors of mortality it grasps" (Sobchack 1984, 295). Often the film will pull focus to follow a change in the balance of power, or shift in the locus of interest when several characters are engaged in conversation. The presence of the film's body is tangible throughout *Nil by Mouth*, not least because the camera is almost always hand-held. This gives the impression that the film is, indeed, a living body, in a way that is not as apparent in *Once Were Warriors*, where the camera is stable and often motionless, seemingly calm and certainly uninvolved in the action. Even in the midst of the most tumultuous and chaotic fight scenes in *Once Were Warriors*, the tempo of the editing alters minimally and the camera remains like a dispassionate observer, resting safely in the middle distance.

The spectator gets a very different sense of perceptual participation when the film's body occupies the narrative space like a participant, closely aligned with the experiential, intentional, and attentional movements of the characters. In *Nil by Mouth*, the picture we see is constantly reframed or visibly and visually readjusted in response to new information. The use of whip pans makes it seem as though the film turns its head, darting glances toward the action as it moves in close proximity with those it attends to. In this style of filmmaking the film attends to its subject matter in a way that emphasizes the value of getting close, engaging with the characters on an intimate, emotional level, empathizing and feeling involved in their lives.[12] This is not to say that *Once Were Warriors* lacks a sensitive engagement with its subject matter, or fails to induce an empathic reaction in its spectators. On the contrary, it succeeds in engaging its audience on many different levels. Different ways of seeing are instantiated in the two films, which parallel two different approaches to attention. Since we can never fully set aside our own embodied viewing position or transcend our personal histories and commitments, Weil's account of attention seems to be more useful as a theoretical ideal[13] than it is in practice. However, both forms of attention have ethical possibilities. It is a movement between these two extremes that best represents the form of attentive engagement for which I will argue.

In *Once Were Warriors* the filmic body stands back and bears witness to the unfolding story, allowing the elements of ethical salience to reveal themselves and be received by a patiently waiting, attentive entity.[14] *Nil by Mouth*, on the other hand, establishes a more dynamic relationship between the film's body and the characters; it engages in active participation with the story in order to be better placed to see a change of mood. An early scene from *Nil by Mouth* illustrates this active movement of attention when Ray and his mates are sitting around the lounge room chatting, telling stories about their sexual conquests and drug experiences. The flat is tiny and the camera is very close to the characters in the confined space, watching as they smoke cigarettes and talk and laugh. The camera moves from one face to another as the conversation flows, transferring attention by pulling focus if two characters are in the same frame and interest shifts from one to the other. For instance, when Ray's friend Mark is telling a story in this scene, his face takes up over half the screen. Ray is just visible, out of focus beside and behind Mark until he interrupts his friend, at which point the film racks focus, clarifying its vision of Ray and blurring the image of Mark. Unlike *Once Were Warriors, Nil by Mouth* has a characteristically shallow depth of field, instead of maintaining an equitable clarity of focus across everything in the visual frame. This film often looks closely at one thing at a time, rather than holding everything in focus.

Another thing that is significant about this scene is its length. The conversation dribbles on incessantly, without driving the plot. Ordinarily for a scene in which the temporal span of the film's attention is so extended, the content of the conversation upon which we dwell would contribute crucial information to the story-line. In *Nil by Mouth* the longest scenes are the ones that must seem interminable in the life of the protagonist, Val, and that are a repetitive and integral part of her everyday existence. The length of these scenes helps spectators to feel what her life must be like. They are not there to make a point; they *are* the point, and the film attends to them at length for this reason. Close aural attention to the content of the dialogue divulges little of significance. Any "point" contained by verbal content of the long scenes could have been made in less than a minute of screen time, but we can observe where the power rests among the speakers, and such interactions illustrate Val's disempowerment.

Another very long scene in the film shows Ray in a drunken rage after Val leaves him. We watch as he becomes progressively incoherent, alternately repentant and violent over what must be a period of about six or eight hours of his life. We see him on the phone to Val several times, slurring and sobbing out his confusion, pleading his love and need. The length of this scene is a torment. Like Ray, it just goes on and on and on, stumbling over the same ground until it is almost as familiar to us as it must be to his wife.

This aspect of *Nil by Mouth*, where the camera stays with a particular scene or shot for reasons that are not immediately apparent or that do not serve the narrative in an obvious way, tends to involve the spectator in the process of attention and interpretation on a different level than the tactics used in *Once Were Warriors*. *Once Were Warriors* articulates ethically salient details primarily by including them in the narrative content, focusing only on significant moments. As I suggested earlier, because the process of deciding which events and conversations are significant is not itself foregrounded, it implies that those particular scenes *revealed themselves* to the patient gaze of the film, and that attentive observation is best practiced discretely, with minimal active engagement in the unfolding picture of an ethical situation. While the selective, evaluative process of narrative composition also occurs in Val and Ray's story, the style and structure of *Nil by Mouth* complements and underwrites the narrative content, directing attention to *the way* of experiencing, seeing, sensing, and framing a situation, as well as to *what* is seen, sensed, or experienced in the frame.

The gritty detail and narrow focus allows us to see a fuller picture in a different way. Here the claim that the form in which the story is told is inseparable from its content is once again substantiated. To see or show the content of an ethical situation from a distance, or to capture it calmly with the sense of being uninvolved is to know a different world and tell a different story. There is a sense in which the inclusion of more detail in *Nil by Mouth* makes the spectator attend more carefully because we know that we must piece it together ourselves and search for or construct its relevance. Furthermore, and importantly, the mode of attention each film practices is appropriately responsive to the particularity of the situation into which it endeavors to gain insight and which, as a screen text expressing the process of its own perception, it illuminates for us. From a more detached or distant vantage point it may not be apparent why Val is unable to see beyond and escape her abusive relationship. Conversely, the attentive practices of the filmic body in *Once Were Warriors* express, and allow spectators to experience the sense of perspective Beth has on her own life and possibilities, and thus to better understand how she, but not Val, is capable of changing her situation.

One of the most striking aspects revealed by the style of cinematography employed in *Nil by Mouth* (as well as by the film's content) was just how painful it was for the characters to even attempt to look at their own lives outside the present moment. They looked back on a history of disadvantage and abuse and looked forward to much of the same, or to loneliness and half-way houses, prison, poverty, and unemployment. They were so enmeshed that they could not face the bigger picture; they could only struggle on from day to day. Coming to terms with the past and looking into the future or attempting to envision change was too frighteningly difficult. Val's past and her heritage are as miserable as her present: she continues a long line of suffering. When Val's Nan asks her mum, Janet, "Why doesn't she leave him?" Janet replies, "Where's she gonna go? To a half-way house with a five year old and another one on the way? Leave off Mum!"

The film offers only brief, stark glimpses of the "bigger picture" within which the lives explored in *Nil by Mouth* are situated, showing a depressing view of massive blocks of concrete council flats set against the dismal backdrop of a desolate section of London. This is significant precisely because a fundamental part of their lives, and one that determines their actions and attitudes to a large extent, is that the characters cannot see outside their own lives. They are not able to see a way out; they don't have access to a bigger picture including better possibilities, a picture that might place things in context and identify avenues of escape. What they can see, beyond their immediate problems, is an unbearable view of more of the same. In attention to gritty detail and the restricted glimpses of unpromising surroundings, we sense the presence of a bigger social picture, an ethical problem extending beyond the borders of the frame.

Once Were Warriors is startlingly different in this respect, in terms of its visual style and its narrative. In it we are shown the broader perspective because the film practices a nonintrusive form of attention that values cultivating an awareness of the wider cultural contexts influencing a particular situation. Regarding the film's content, Beth is able to invoke a positive sense of strength and stability from her past, and reach out to access social support; she is intelligent and confident enough to see a way forward and to see herself as something other than a victim. Beth's pride as a member of a long line of brave people who fought with honor for their land, livelihood, and culture is what gives the film its title and the narrative of Maori heritage gives the film social significance by problematizing the present and future of indigenous communities in New Zealand. Everything in *Once were Warriors* locates the individual within a larger discourse, framing their particularity in a sociocultural narrative, rather than zeroing in on its detail. Even as the detail is disclosed it is given importance as part of a broader picture. The detail attracts the film's attention, but never fills it—even the closest shots in this film are medium-close-ups, characterized by their brevity and rarity.

A mode of ethical attention in which the balance between detail and context is woven together into an intelligible whole so that detail finds its place within a broader context often entails a narrative form of understanding. If perception or attention is a fundamental organizing structure of intentional consciousness, then narrative form is fundamental to the placement of phenomena that we attend to within meaningful contexts. Tracing the pathways of attention through a film in the above examples reveals how narration and interpretation can structure the practice of ethical attention.

Filmic Attention

In Sobchack's understanding, attention in film texts has to do with things being "noticed" (by both the film and the spectators who are a constituent part of it) to a greater or lesser extent: "That is, in their relative importance as the destination of our attention, certain figures dominate other figures. Less dominant figures are still figures and visible as such, but they are less present in their visible presence in our vision" (Sobchack 1992, 240). Here the word "dominant" (and other terms such as "submissive" or "subordinate" with which it is implicitly associated) foregrounds one way in which the practice of attending can be taken up as an ethical concern, enmeshed with the power relations or hierarchies of significance that permeate the perceptual field.

In a discussion of the extensions and contractions of attention made possible by the "phenomenological frame" the cinema screen offers to the viewer, Stanley Cavell claims that "the altering frame is the image of perfect attention" (1996, 163). Cavell distinguishes between the attentive possibilities offered by different cinematographic techniques. There are, he suggests, cinematic means of expressing perception that actively direct attention (such as racking focus), and there are those (such as deep focus) that give the viewer's vision more freedom to wander within the frame and to respond to the objects in our field of vision:

> Early in its history the cinema discovered the possibility of calling attention to persons and parts of persons and objects; but it is equally a possibility of the medium not to call attention to them but, rather, to let the world happen, to let its parts draw attention to themselves according to their natural weight. (Cavell 1996, 163)

Certainly, the later form of attention is still inescapably selective, evaluative, and focused, but it is a qualitatively different form of cinematic vision, and of ethical attention. Having already drawn the distinction between the ways of seeing enacted in *Nil by Mouth* and *Once Were Warriors*, I would like to explore this qualitative difference further and apply it to cinema and ethical life in a broader sense.

Although literature allows us to explore other perspectives imaginatively, emotively, and conceptually, it cannot *physically* make the actual movement of other eyes and bodies, and thus the passage of their attention, visible to its readers. There is something practically useful in such a physical demonstration of attention in action. In a unique manner, the cinema grants us access to a space of shared vision, allowing us inside the world of someone else's outlook. The intersubjective quality of film, in which spectators are offered insight into other perspectives, is one of the medium's great strengths. We see so much more on the cinema screen than the images of characters looking at one another: we see the representation of an aspect or interpretation of their perceptual experience. As Sobchack remarks, "What is so unique about the cinema's 'viewing view' . . . is that it presents and represents the activity of vision not merely as it is objectively seen by us, but also as it is introceptively lived by another" (1990, 25).

Since the mode in which one views the world frames it in a certain way, capturing some aspects in the centre, marginalizing, excluding or obscuring others, the way in which each individual sees, views, or attends to a situation is qualitative. The quality of attention affects interpretations and responses to a given situation, hence tracing the process and passage of attention and investigating the qualitative dimensions of perception through focusing on our own and others' perspectives can be a valuable part of developing ethical understanding.

Differentiating between various forms of perception is important within film theory because, though film expresses and describes perception, filmic perception also differs from ordinary perception due to the fact that it is a technologically mediated representation. As Singer observes, the value of cinema "rests precisely in its distance and difference from natural vision. [. . .] as a supplementary discourse which amplifies and enhances the breadth, range and depth of our perception" (Singer 1990, 65). The film renders the structured, selective aspects of perception evident, providing a visible record of the latent bias that may distort the process of ethical attention. As spectators, we are able to see who the film (and its characters) overlooks, who is listened to and concentrated on, whether the focus is clear, whether the whole person is seen or certain parts of them are objectified, and so on. Although we may not always fulfill the potential, the medium of film gives spectators the opportunity to see and analyze how ways of looking reveal evaluations that are usually concealed in the subjective nature of vision.

The distinctive opening shot in *Once Were Warriors* illustrates the material differences between human and filmic perception, and demonstrates the ethical and communicative value of these differences from ordinary perception. In this shot, which is complemented by soft, melodious extradiegetic music, we see nothing but a tranquil, pastoral scene in the New Zealand countryside for the first moments of the film. Slowly the camera begins to move backward including more and more of the picture, and finally, with the intrusive blare of diegetic sound, moving to the left and revealing that we were looking at an advertising billboard for ENZ Power in the middle of a dirty, depressing industrial area.

This wider view still stops short of adequately grasping the scene, but then we perceive further layers of information: as the camera moves back and cranes down to take in the streetscape, the sound of cars speeding by overwhelms us[15] and involves us even more intensely in the scene. The billboard

Figure 39 Once Were Warriors: *An idyllic, pastoral opening shot.*

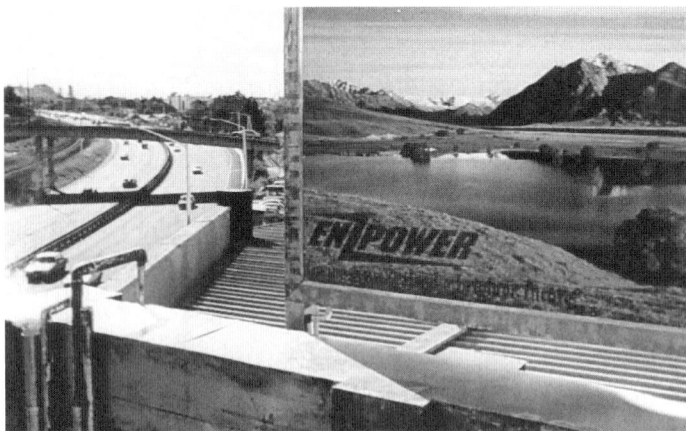

Figure 40 Once Were Warriors: *The camera pulls back to reveal urban reality.*

represents a prevalent, if superficial impression publicized in the postcard image of itself that New Zealand expresses and exports, but the film exercises what can be interpreted as a form of ethical attention committed to filling out the picture and allowing more details to reveal themselves. With camera movement, the film gives a sense of coming down to earth, descending from illusion into reality.

The human eye doesn't have access to exclusive framing or zoom lenses: though we can notice one detail to the exclusion of its surroundings, we cannot see *only* that upon which we focus our attention. Nor can we actually turn the volume of the traffic down momentarily (we can only tune it out, withdrawing attention from it). However, conceptually, we can achieve precisely the same effect that the camera and microphone express perceptually: we view something one way and then, with a shift in perception (like changing the framing or the volume) we realize it to have been illusory or incomplete. By changing perspective, we perceive that something was missing or excluded from the position we had previously occupied. Techniques like altering camera position, pulling focus, and reframing function metaphorically to represent the subtle shifts in perspective and attention, and to cue a particular way of viewing and interpreting the subject matter. The opening shot in *Once Were Warriors* suggests that film's intent is to *inform* the audience (utilizing the visual metaphor) that it will divulge to us a sense of "the bigger picture," placing the issue of domestic violence into a cultural context.

Sobchack explores the experiential differences between zooming in and forward tracking shots, speaking in terms of the film's body inhabiting space and directing (its own and our) attention. Cutting between close-ups and long-shots, or the use of Steadicam, dollies and tracking shots in which the camera actually moves around, toward or away from its subject are experienced, in Sobchack's terms, as movements of the film's body. Such bodily movement is similar to the movement of subjects in the frame, in that it increases or decreases proximity to the viewing subject. Either of these forms of physical movement alters the nature of the material depicted within the frame—they represent a shift in the proximal relationship of the viewed subject to both the camera and the spectators. In cinematographic techniques such as shifting focus, zooming in or out, or changing the lens (to a wide angle, for instance), the picture also "moves," but different changes in the nature of perception are traced on the screen. Spectators notice this visual movement, but it is experienced only as a movement of attention, rather than physical movement of the film's body:

> Attention, then, is a lived-body movement which does not involve movement of the material body through space . . . Attention is a creative act, an alteration of the subject's relation with the world . . . Always contingent and motivated, always situated as the concrete relation of the body-subject living its changing projects (its autobiographical narrative) in the world. (Sobchack 1990, 27)

There are important distinctions between and within pictures of motion (*Once Were Warriors* classical tripod-mounted cinematography) and moving pictures (exemplified by *Nil by Mouth's* inquisitive and restless hand-held camera). As Sobchack suggests, if the picture or frame itself moves, rather than the subjects within it, this represents a change of the frame of reference of the attender, the viewer. This is ethically significant because it represents a change in understanding and value, an active, actual shift in perspective and, especially in the case of pulling focus, a qualitative difference in the way the subject of perception is interpreted.

In similar ways to the optical movement of the film camera, the movement of ethical attention of human beings is also a "lived-body movement" which, though it can be expressed by actually moving closer to someone, can also be unrelated to physical movement toward or away from the attendee. Moving closer to an object (either with our actual bodies, or by increasing the intimacy and intensity of our attention) alters our awareness of it, effecting a change in the way the object appears and is meaningful for us in terms of its contextual location, framing, or focus. With such a perceptual movement, the object swells or diminishes in importance in relation to the viewing subject and we access more or less of the fine detail or the surrounding context.

The understanding of perception as active and mobile in ways that are not limited to, or by, physical movement indicates that although perception (and with it, ethical attention) is embodied, and clearly bound in important ways to particular contexts, situations, and unique individuals, it is not necessarily tied to relations of physical proximity. This point adds strength to Nussbaum's argument that ethical attention is not only instructively exemplified in certain works of art, but can also be cultivated and practiced by those who engage with such art.

Cultivating an awareness of what is included in our visual field is far from being the only way in which we are able to attune our attention to a situation. Movements of attention can also be experienced as imaginative leaps, as the tightening or loosening of emotional ties, and as varying intensities of reflection and self-reflection. (Consider, for instance, the scene from *Dead Man Walking* depicting the intersubjective nature of understanding with the metaphoric use of actual reflections in the glass.) Nondiegetic material and gaps in the narrative can also be of considerable significance, just as the things that are not said sometimes lie at the heart of a story. This brings to mind the point in *Nil by Mouth* when Val was severely beaten by her husband because of his unfounded jealousy, and deep-seated rage and insecurity. In the treatment of Val and her daughter Michelle, this scene highlights two of the ways in which off-screen space can be used as part of the sphere of attention addressed by the film.

In this scene attention was concentrated outside the frame as Val was beaten—her body is not present in the frame itself. The camera certainly does not ignore Val (though its eye, and ours, are averted); it is more as though it cannot bear to look or is unable to do so. The inability to see Val's body also links the spectator across off-screen space to the couple's small daughter Michelle who we later see cringing out of Ray's sight on the stairwell. Like us, she is also following the action but unable to see all that is going on.

Throughout the film Michelle is mostly out of frame and silent to the extent that it might appear that the film overlooks her, as the characters within it often do. However, on closer inspection it is evident that the film's perception of Michelle is keen and sympathetic. The single most beautiful shot in the film shows Michelle's delicate, serious little face in profile as she spells her own name to her Nan, who carefully writes it on a bright red helium balloon, which seems to represent all the freedom, vibrancy, and buoyancy lacking in her life. In other scenes we see that Michelle is too good and too quiet and obedient for a five year old child, suggesting that her unobtrusive demeanor articulates her fear as well as her desire to do anything required to be loved and accepted. She is not rendered invisible by the film so much as perceived by the film as attempting to avoid drawing attention to herself. The film *does* notice Michelle as it repeatedly shows how she makes herself invisible. Like her mother, she desperately wants Ray's attention, but knows she is often safer without attracting it.

As with the treatment of Michelle, the fact that the film refrains from looking directly at Val's beating does not constitute a failure to attend to her. Despite the lack of graphic detail the beating is felt acutely, imagined vividly and heard with clarity. In the closing shots of this scene we are separated from Val by a partition in the kitchen that prevents us from seeing her body and we are only able to see Ray's absorption in his own irrational rage, however, our attention is engaged below the screen and to the right, where Val lies bleeding at Ray's feet.

As the scene concludes we encounter a moment of ellipsis in the narrative, unlike *Once Were Warriors*, where we see Jake, the male protagonist's callous response to his wife's wounds, and we see Beth's reaction and her attempts to clean herself up and deal with the situation, listening as she is sick in the toilet, watching as she confronts her own reflection and winces in the mirror.

Figure 41 Once Were Warriors: *Beth faces her injuries in the bathroom mirror.*

In *Nil by Mouth*, our concern stays with Val, focused on her injuries and her pain for some time before the camera finally visibly discloses the detail of her wounds. We never see her look at herself, and we never see Ray look directly at what he has done to her. When eventually the camera moves in close, we see Val show her lacerations and bruises to her mother while she describes being hit by a car in the parking lot at the local shopping center (the make-up artist worked her over with convincing skill, so when we finally do see, we perceive the full extent of her injuries).

We feel Val's inability to face the reality of her own situation in this scene as we hear her tell a desperately reassuring lie about the doctors at the hospital informing her that her unborn baby is mercifully unharmed. Because of the blank interval of time between the beating and this next scene, the viewer is at first uncertain whether Val has indeed sought medical attention. Then, as we listen to the lie unfold it becomes evident that this woman is unable to face up to her situation, even to the extent of confronting her image in the mirror, looking after herself and seeking the most basic level of help: physical care.

Both *Nil by Mouth* and *Once Were Warriors* address the subject of domestic violence directly as a matter of moral and political concern. In a sense the creation of a film narrative (and other forms of art), can be understood as a "project of envisioning" (Singer 1990, 65) which is projected toward an audience who will participate in that vision. Some films create

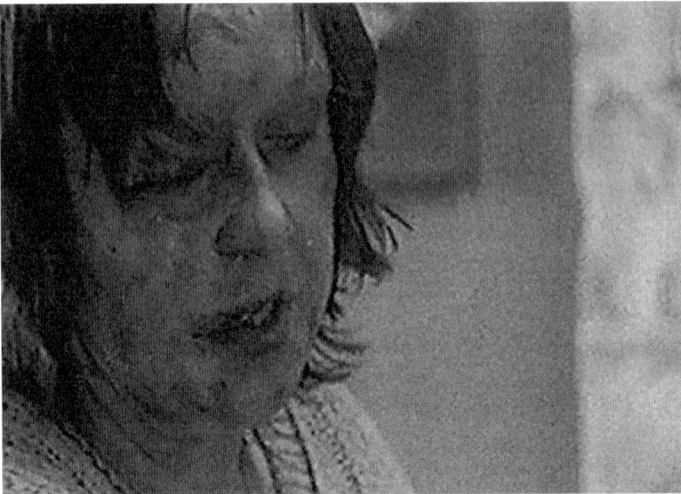

Figure 42 Nil by Mouth: *Val is unable to face up to the gravity of her situation.*

and project a "moral vision" involving the depiction of ethical practices and role models. However, as Nussbaum rightly points out, even if the subject matter is not specifically of an ethical nature, both the form and the content of a text express a "view of life" and convey a sense of what information is important to know, and what faculties are important for knowing (1990, 7).

Not only do the films *Once Were Warriors* and *Nil by Mouth* attend to similar subject matter of an explicitly ethical nature and make a social comment on the actions of their characters and the cultural contexts in which they are implicated, but they share a sensitive approach which aims to enrich understanding of the characters without vilification or polarization of their positions. In addition, they share claims about "what matters" intrinsic to the form of film production and reception that are dealt with in the concluding section of this chapter. However, in demonstrating through visual movement their individual "views of life" the two films exhibit stylistic differences expressing variations in ethical values and practices. These stylistic differences articulate differing practices of ethical attention and disparate attitudes regarding the degree and type of involvement an ethical agent ought to experience in relation to the subject of his or her attention.

Spectatorship

When viewing a film we are often "present" in a way that we might not be when watching television, reading, or even listening to a friend relate a personal story because of the specific ways in which we are drawn, bodily, into the narrative space. Our attentive, perceptual presence is incorporated into the story as an active part of the technologically mediated filmic perception, and many of the distractions of the external world are removed in the dimly lit, quiet cinema. While we do come to the cinema with our personal history, beliefs, values, and relationships intact, at the same time we step away from the claims that these elements exert upon us in everyday life.

Often, life's competing demands distract and disperse attention, but in the cinema attention can be more sustained and focused for the duration of the film. Though the process of interpretation is ongoing, our responses, along with the possibility for interruptions and interjections, are suspended until the entire story has been told. As Singer so aptly puts it, "The situation exacts an investment of attention" (1990, 55). Singer suggests that the "zone of inattention" that is created by the dark space surrounding the bright

screen and the silence of the audience facilitates fascination and engagement by clearly delineating the parameters of attention (1990, 57). There is
a significant difference between the investment of attention described here
and the idea of a sponge-like spectator who passively absorbs the contents
of the cinema screen. As Sobchack points out in a discussion of the dialogic
experience of cinematic spectatorship:

> Certainly, a form of absorption can and does occur in the film experi-
> ence. But it is not a concrete absorption into the *body* of the other or
> the *consciousness* of the other. Rather, it is a mutual absorption in the
> world, a mutually directed interest that converges in the visible and
> its significance. (Sobchack 1992, 273, original emphasis)

The cinema gives us the luxury of a more contemplative space, and in doing
so it actually diverts the focus from the ego's interests, channeling it toward
the narrative. Thus, in the model of cinematic spectatorship the problem of
"unselfing"[16] (or, alternatively, the tension between evading the distractions
of the ego and its desires, and recognizing the significance of partiality,
emotion, and one's personal investment in the process of interpreting and
responding) is resolved, at least in part, by the contextual conditions in
which the narrative is received. We do, and we don't, "lose ourselves" in the
practice of attentive engagement. We are present in the act of attending in
an unsteady oscillation between personal involvement and immersion
in someone else's story. The self, in this understanding, does not distract us
from the story, rather, it is through the self (and its intersubjective incorporation into the larger body of the film) that we are able to engage with and
understand the story and form connections with the characters within it.
The importance of the sense of connection to others that the cinema can
offer need not exist at the expense of, or diminish the value of more
detached forms of discernment and the role they play in ethical deliberation. Just as physical distance is essential if the picture is to be comprehensible
(if one is too close to the action, perspective is lost and one only sees
blotches of color moving on the screen) a kind of distance is also essential
to obtain "breadth and clarity" of understanding.

In order to illustrate further the ethical implications of film spectatorship, consider one final sequence from *Nil by Mouth*: a scene in which Billy
has appropriated some drugs belonging to Ray, his brother in law.
Ray discovers the theft and assaults Billy, despite Val's attempts to intervene. As the scene begins, Billy passes in front of the camera and sits down

on the couch in such close proximity to the "film's body" that our vision is disturbed. Short panning movements, as though the film is turning its head to follow Billy's motions, trace the passage of Billy's attention to the illicit "gear" in his hands, and to the threat of being approached from behind and caught in the act. The film uses the evocative *mise-en-scene* and the nondiegetic sound track to describe its perception of Billy's experience. The dull, melancholic blue light and the blues guitar work in conjunction with the unsettled camera movement to articulate a sense of despair and distress surrounding the subject we (film and spectators) are viewing.

In two of only five extreme long shots in a film dominated by close-ups of the human figure, the film moves its attention briefly to the context in which Billy is surreptitiously indulging in an interlude of drug-assisted escapism. We see for a moment the bleak bulk of endless blocks of council flats in the chilly, grey light of a windy dawn. With this interstitial image the film reflects on the alienating social conditions of the urban environment that contains, and to a certain extent gives rise to the problems of the dysfunctional family whose story we are involved in. It is important to note that this shot, and the other extreme long shots are not taken from the visual perspective of any of the screen characters. The oppressively close visual style of the film is, as I have already suggested, indicative of the inability of the characters themselves to step back and look beyond their immediate problems to other possibilities. When we do see a glimpse of what lies beyond the immediate scenario, it seems that there is no escape in sight.

In the remainder of the scene whip pans, short, fast zooms, and unsteady hand-held shots locate us inside the confined space in which the conflict erupts and focus our attention on Ray's aggression and those to whom it is directed in a confronting dialectic of repulsion and fascination. As much as spectators might get the sense of being so close to the action that they may well need to duck or dodge the next assault, there are also times when, with the film's body, spectators experience the scene from behind a barrier that obstructs vision and effects a partial separation from the characters. The lounge room in which the conflict takes place is separated from the kitchen by low wainscoting and a glass partition. At times (particularly when there is no "innocent" perspective to occupy and one is most reluctant to be implicated in the action) the film's body moves behind this, and we see a confused view of the action through reflections on the glass. Filmic techniques such as these, which leave spectators with a sense that the action is difficult to follow, are appropriate to convey a sense of the complex nature of the ethical situation the film is describing. Thus the film engages spectators in the ethical practices involved in the different levels of narrative configuration: composition, attention, and interpretation.

As a pregnant woman with an abusive and drug-dependent spouse Val may attract sympathy; however, the film does not allow a straightforward identification with her as an innocent victim. One of the most uncomfortable moments in the film occurs when we witness Val lash out at her brother for causing trouble, after he has just been beaten by Ray.[17] At this point we are confronted with the pervasive impact violence has on the lives of those involved. The complexity inherent in the situation thus portrayed highlights the inadequacy of reductive moral principles which, by labeling actions as right or wrong in isolation from the surrounding causal influences, often fail to further ethical understanding.

As spectators we experience an intersubjective involvement in this scene: we engage with the film's subjective perception of the situation as it articulates its own point of view, and we literally have our sensory experience aligned with that of Ray, Val, and Billy momentarily. The transition between shots exclusive to the film's subjective vantage point, and those also associated with the viewing positions of the characters makes us, as spectators, feel their sense of entrapment in circumstance, and sense the way in which this perpetuates the victim-victimizer dynamic.

In order to trace or tune into shifts in perspective and disentangle from one another the levels of vision that are experienced in film spectatorship, I am going to return to and enlarge upon the understanding of technologically mediated vision proposed by Sobchack. As Sobchack states, the film's vision is experienced "as our own vision, in our own vision, and in addition to our own vision" (1992, 271). While the film's optical movement explores the horizons of its world, our own vision merges with the film's, overlapping with what the film sees: the image framed by the screen. Thus, as spectators, we actively participate in the film's vision and practice seeing *as* another, and from another's perspective inside the screen space. Our attention traverses the gap between our bodies and the screen, entering into the story world and exploring it in fusion with the film, practicing the very movements of attention that the film is expressing through its own bodily engagement with the narrative. (There may also be another layer of vision hidden here: when the film "borrows" a character's point of view, spectators also adopt that perspective.) Since our sensory experience of the narrative is enabled by our own bodily perceptual capacities and mediated by the filmic technology (to which we are joined as active, integral parts of the film's body), cinematic spectatorship is a practical exercise in the cultivation of the modes of embodied, attentive engagement demonstrated and enacted on the screen.

At the same time, the cinema screen itself is an object situated *in* the spectator's visual field. We are not actually situated inside the screen space; we are seated in the dark cinema looking at a screen text. The spectator is not totally subject to or immersed in another's vision (we also see the cinema, the edges of the screen etc.), additionally, the filmmaker or camera's viewing position often really does change, whereas ours is actually static (however mobile our attention may be). Superimposed on the film's vision of its subject is the spectator's vision of it and, as Sobchack states: "In so far as the visual space I see before me is not completely isomorphic with the bodily space from which I see, there will be a pressure from, an echo of, the machine that mediates my perception" (1992, 172).

Here Sobchack is suggesting that, as a result of the differences between human perception alone and the humanlike, instrument mediated perception visibly expressed on the cinema screen, the audience is constantly reminded of the mediated and intersubjective nature of the visual experience. On this level we can see the film in more conceptual terms as the inscription and description of attention: the articulation of attentive-perceptive practices (its own and those of the characters). This awareness may not always be at the forefront of our consciousness (centered in our attention), however, it indicates that although spectators are drawn into the screen space and the subjective outlooks rendered visible there, we are not seduced into collapsing their own perspectives into the perspectives represented on the screen.

Finally, film spectatorship is an attentive practice in its own right, a practice that involves the vision of the spectator *in addition to* the vision of the film. As attentive spectators we experience moments of resistance and rapport as we draw from off-screen perspectives informed by our own lived experience and mediated by our own abilities. As such, spectatorship is an intersubjective dialogue of vision and interpretation that transcends the individual (but indivisible) units of text and viewer, and incorporates the external world of the spectators' lived experience, to which narrative films refer.

When Sobchack describes these three levels on which the film's vision is experienced, she does not explicitly address a fourth dimension of visual experience associated with film, but elsewhere in her work she refers to ways in which film sometimes offers us what might be understood as a view *of* our own vision, referring to "those moments in which we grasp ourselves in the recognition that our vision differs from that of the other" (Sobchack 1992, 276). In such moments the focus shifts back to the self, to the attender and her or his personal responses to the text.

Occasionally our own view becomes clearer when we recognize how it differs from the vision expressed on the screen. For example, the striptease sequence in *Nil by Mouth* might reinforce spectators' perspectives on the objectification of women by differentiating their views from those of Ray and his friend Mark. Occasionally we also recognize our own biases for what they are when we see them represented in some way on the screen. For instance, perhaps our concern for Michelle's well-being in *Nil by Mouth* might cause us to admit to the limitations of a previously unexamined perspective or opinion, if we recognize ourselves in the view that associates quiet children with good children.

Teasing out the various layers of attention in the cinema generates a better sense of how and why we can come away from a film that moves us with a more developed sense of understanding our own and other's stories, perspectives, and values. This is partly because the film engineers in us or elicits from us a process of discernment and interpretation as it structures information, puts things in perspective, changes frame and focus, shifts, and borrows viewpoints. As attentive spectators we find engaging with and exploring other people's narratives a pleasure or a fascinating challenge, rather than a grueling discipline as Weil believes ethical attention must be. In part this is due to the fact that the physical viewing context provided by the cinema does for us the work of focusing attention on the narrative rather than on the extraneous distractions of the ego and its attachments. Ironically, though the practice of attention Weil describes has much in common with the methods of transcendental phenomenology, and though phenomenology itself aims to describe experience or consciousness, it is Nussbaum's account that more accurately describes the embodied, self-conscious experience of attending on an interpersonal level. In any actual or cinematic context we can no more divorce ourselves from our ego, will, and emotional attachments or relationships than we can amputate our physical body from the process of perception.

✶✶✶✶✶✶✶✶✶✶✶✶✶✶✶✶✶✶✶✶✶✶✶✶✶✶✶✶

I have demonstrated how films (in Sobchack's understanding of the filmic body as a viewing subject) can at once practice modes of ethical attention, provide visible examples of attentive practices for critical reflection, and evoke ethical responses from the spectators who participate in the modes of attention exemplified in the filmic style and structure. The filmic expression of perception is simultaneously an act of representation and a redescription of the object of vision, in which changes (in perspective and value) can be brought about by swelling or diminishing the importance of the viewed object in relation to the attender. Since the spectators' attention is closely linked to the film's, the attentive practices of both film and spectators contribute to the production of a "new" object (an object that is experienced and understood in a different way, a way that can enhance possibilities for ethical insight). The act of viewing a film also produces "new subjects" to the extent that the instrumental mediation of perception and participation in the technologically mediated filmic body effects a transformation of the spectator's subjectivity, rendering it an intersubjective state. Viewed in this way, the cinema might be seen as a richly attentive way of engaging with others and with the world in search of narratively understood ethical insight, through all the confusion of detail and the multiplicity of perspectives that complicate moral vision. Though the vision of a "new object" offered to us in the cinema is ethically limited in that it lacks the possibilities for responsiveness that are present in life, practicing attentive engagement in the cinema can still advance our self-understanding and alter the way in which we relate to others, making the dimensions of our care and understanding keener and more inclusive.

As Laura Marks writes, "Attentive recognition is a participatory notion of spectatorship, whose political potential shouldn't be ignored" (2000, 48). This political potential necessarily broadens the scope of attentive engagement, opening it out beyond interpersonal ethics, or individual responses to particular films. It highlights the necessity of buttressing the ideal of attentive engagement and the particularist responses of care, with compensating ethical structures that balance the partiality of emotion, failures of imagination, the arbitrariness of attention, or the limitations of compassion with some reference to general principles of justice. We need, on principle, and not on the chance that the story of an individual moves us, to counteract the economic imperatives of media production by paying attention to those whose stories are not told, who are underrepresented and who cannot manage to call attention to themselves as individuals or as social groups. Attentive engagement with film can do no more than identify structuring absences and systematic misrepresentation—spectatorship alone cannot redress such injustices. The conclusion of this book considers some of the possibilities and limitations surrounding the transfiguration of ethical experience and understanding resulting from practices of attentive engagement with film narratives, practices that draw deeply on a broad range of ethical resources.

Notes

1. Peta Bowden describes this clarification of moral situations and values through ethical attention as a process of "accumulating understandings" (1998, 60).

2. Bowden addresses the problems that can arise when the flow of care and attention is continuously unidirectional, arguing that the character of moral attention must "focus explicitly on the shared and communal aspects of attenders and the potential for collaboration and mutual support that such connections hold" (1998, 71) in order to avoid falling prey to imbalances in relationships.

3. Samantha Lay's book *British Social Realism: From Documentary to Brit-Grit* (2002) contextualizes Brit-Grit within contemporary developments in the media industry and notes current trends in style, characterization, theme, and reception, including a good case study of *Nil by Mouth* in final chapter "1990s and Beyond: Contemporary Social Realism." She writes:

> All the features and conventions of British social realism can be found in *Nil by Mouth*: "loose" episodic narrative structure with a cyclical resolution and ambiguity defying the closure demanded by mainstream cinema; the use of location shooting; the use of non-professional actors and well-respected "small picture" actors like Ray Winstone and Kathy Burke (surely the Albert Finney and Carol White of our times), in an ensemble cast; the use of naturalistic light, sound and dialogue; high angled shots of depressed urban environments, along with the "gritty" sights and sounds of a certain way of London life. (Lay 2002, 111)

These features of the British social realist style have clearly influenced the work of Australian director Rowan Woods, and have themselves been influenced by earlier film movements like Italian Neo-Realism and *Cinéma Vérité*, and by parallel developments like the Danish Dogme95 movement. In each instance, there is an important relationship between style, story, politics, and a particular vision of what is ethically important in life that is distinct from much mainstream cinema.

4. Nussbaum uses the terms perception, discernment, moral vision, and moral attention in closely related ways throughout her work on moral insight. Of these terms, discernment is the most actively deliberative. See especially two essays in *Love's Knowledge*: "Finely Aware and Richly Responsible" (Nussbaum 1990, 148–149) and "The Discernment of Perception" (Nussbaum 1990, 54–55).

5. Weil says that while practicing ethical attention, "what is real becomes evident . . . in the end illusions are scattered and the real becomes visible" (1952, 174). This has similarities with the phenomenological project of bracketing away preconceptions to perceive the "essence" of a thing.

6. "Moral vision" is also discussed by Iris Murdoch (1970, 35–43) in relation to the moral imagination.

7. In "Inscribing Ethical Space," Sobchack suggests that a distanced mode of vision can connote the helplessness of the viewer in relation to the moral atrocity that is being viewed. From a distance, one cannot be expected to intervene (1984, 295).

8. Alan Duff's book (1990), on which the film *Once Were Warriors* is based, was considered radical at the time of its publication and it raised strong sentiments in New Zealand. Perhaps to avoid alienating the prospective audience, in the adaptation to film some of the more disturbing and confrontational elements were omitted, such as the intimation that Jake Heke, Grace's father, may have been her rapist. A more subjective, confronting form of visual storytelling in the film may have been considered inflammatory, implying value judgments that the filmmakers wished to avoid.

9. A willingness to see and an ability to wait for revelation are two attributes that Cavell places great emphasis upon in documentary filmmaking because, he says, "the only thing that really matters [is] that the subject be allowed to reveal itself" (1979, 127).

10. Within the framework of feminist psychoanalytic film theory, Mary-Ann Doane (1992) and Gaylyn Studlar (1990b) suggest the immersive, masochistic gaze of fetishistic scopophilia as one such alternative to the sadistic aspects of voyeurism described by Laura Mulvey (1992).

11. Samantha Lay argues that the Griersonian legacy of naturalism and social realism that informs *Nil by Mouth* is best suited to small screen, which helps to explain the predominance of close-ups in the film as tight framings work better on television (2002, 101–102).

12. As Samantha Lay writes in her analysis of *Nil by Mouth*, "The criticism of this focus on the personal and the private argues that the concentration on the family's problems undermines any sense of the social and economic reasons that might lie behind alcoholism and domestic violence" (2002, 111–112). However, I would counter that understanding Ray and Val's family helps us to understand the broader social problems in which their story is enmeshed.

13. By this I do not mean that the way of seeing Weil advocates *is ideal*, but rather that as a theoretical ideal it shows that we tend to see what we look for, and therefore we must guard against interpreting everything we see in ways that merely reinforce our existing presuppositions. In practice, I think that the greatest lesson that might be derived from Weil's account of attention would involve acknowledging the necessity of examining what we see in terms of what we look for, and thereby developing self-understanding and critically evaluating our own viewing positions.

14. The emotional response of spectators to a film that maintains reflective distance on a stylistic or formal level will not necessarily mirror the film's own attitude of detached observation, nor will we necessarily engage more thoroughly with a film that is shot in close-up. The film's attitude to the subject of its attention and the spectators' responses to the expression or articulation of that attitude are not the same issue, and this is further complicated by the spectators' own attitudes to the narrative content.

15. In some films, such as those directed by David Lynch, the film's body expresses itself and demonstrates its attention with heightened aural/oral sensitivity. For example, the

musical lyrics and the nondiegetic sound in Lynch's work often articulate the attitude the film takes to its subject and at the same time suggest a position or attitude that spectators might adopt. Consider, for instance, how the "various ominous drones" in *Lost Highway* both *express* and *instill* a sense of uneasiness, which is compounded by the vocal cues of the opening track, "I'm Deranged" (by David Bowie).

16. "Unselfing" involves directing one's attention and moral imagination away from one's own interests, toward the needs of others (Murdoch 1970, 84).

17. In a striking parallel, *Once Were Warriors* unsettles viewers with a similar realization when a drunken Beth slaps her son Nig across the face, immediately before she herself is beaten by Jake.

Conclusion:
Ethical Transformation

As Stanley Cavell's work attests, the most powerful aspect of cinematic experience is what we take with us when we walk out of the movies: the enduring memories, ideas, and insights that we draw from film, which go on to figure in our own lives. Throughout the previous chapters, work substantiating the significance of narrative and narrative engagement in ethical life has suggested that affective, imaginative, and conceptual involvement in narrative has the capacity to transfigure experience in many different ways. Narrative film can, therefore, be more than a privileged site of analysis for the content of stories: it has the capacity to transform us as we learn from it.

The work of Maria Lugones suggests ways to explore possibilities for refiguring ethical understanding by engaging with and extending oneself into other people's stories. "Playfulness, 'World'–Traveling, and Loving Perception" (1987) is an article by Lugones in which the concepts of identification, perception, and ethical inclusiveness are explored within the context of a personal narrative. Lugones' work describes the skills and attitudes involved in ethical attention to others, and reveals how such a practice can be transformative and enriching.

I have not adopted the term "loving perception" for a number of reasons, the first being that Lugones' interest is specifically in interpersonal relationships where love is often an extension and an important dimension of care, whereas my interests are broader. Second, as the "aspectual" account of identification developed in earlier chapters on emotion and identification suggest, I want to retain the sense in which knowledge of another person's subjectivity and values need not necessarily mean that we sympathize with or embrace perspectives that we find repellent or unethical. In film, as in life, we sometimes encounter people who live in "worlds" that are morally repugnant. Although at the end of *Dead Man Walking* Helen tells Matthew, a rapist and a murderer, that she will be "the face of love for him" as the lethal injection is administered, in many contexts this extraordinary act of "loving perception" will not be the most appropriate form of response when traveling into a world as dark as the one he inhabits. Lugones' work has much to teach us, but my interest in it requires qualification from the outset as love is not the only path to keen perception and depth of understanding.

Lugones makes the intuitively self-evident claim that the world at large would be a better place if we were all prepared to focus on one another with a more loving perceptiveness, and if we were to attempt to enter into and take into account the specific nature of other people's circumstances with sensitivity, care, concern, and a desire to understand how life is for them (1987, 18). She refers to this reach of understanding (which is at once a movement toward others and a means of understanding ourselves in relation to other people and situations) as identification. Lugones uses the term identification partly because she is interested in drawing out the implications for personal and ethical identity that the attitudes and practices she advocates entail.

The argument that Lugones presents suggests that identification is necessary to ethical understanding and care, and that there is a close connection between identifying with another person, and really knowing them through understanding their circumstances, through inhabiting their world. When we travel into another person's world, we know and understand them more fully. We become able to relate to them and this understanding and feeling for the other person alters us in the process of what Lugones terms "identification" (and what I have referred to as attentive engagement with narratives and their characters).

Lugones' description of the transformation of insight that immersion in another person's subjective experience can have is relevant to phenomenological claims about the intersubjective nature of perception in film spectatorship. Lugones tells the story of "coming to consciousness as a daughter" and "coming to consciousness as a woman of color":

> Loving my mother also required that I see with her eyes, that I go into my mother's world, that I see both of us as we are constructed in her world, that I witness her own sense of herself from within her world. Only through traveling to her "world" could I identify with her because only then could I cease to ignore her and to be excluded and separate from her. Only then could I see her as a subject, even if one subjected. (Lugones 1987, 8)

The reversibility of seeing and being seen, of being simultaneously and self-reflexively a subject and an object of perception is of crucial importance to the concept of "world"–traveling that Lugones elucidates. "The reason," she says, "why I think that traveling to someone's "world" is a way of identifying with them is because by traveling to their "world" we can understand what it is to be them and what it is to be ourselves in their eyes" (1987, 17). In other words, identification is only partly constituted by "seeing myself in" another person (1987, 5), it is also to do with aligning ourselves with someone else's perspective so that we are able to see ourselves differently and, potentially, reflect critically on our own perspectives, attitudes, and values.

Failure to identify with others is, according to Lugones, a failure to connect with them and enter "their world" (seeing from within their circumstances, habitat, and world view, their field of social construction). Lugones suggests that "traveling" is entering these worlds in a way that entails changes to oneself, one's orientation, and attitude rather than one's location. Traveling also involves the ability to inhabit a number of different "worlds," not in the guise of various personas or different aspects of the same self, or by donning different costumes and customs—but as a significantly different person[1] or character in each (1987, 10–11). "World"–traveling is, therefore, predominantly an inner journey.

Mapping the pathways of "world"–travel can lead to revelations about oneself as well as insight into and connections with others. Peta Bowden points out, "It is a form of this connection between self-knowledge and attention that Weil detects when she claims that the movement of attention into the 'centre of thought from which another person reads values,' reveals the contingency and circumstantial nature of our own position" (1998, 68). Ethical attention unquestionably involves self-understanding, but I have placed the emphasis on a kind of narrative understanding of self, based on the argument developed in relation to *Lost Highway* that ethical identity is reliant on notions of accountability closely associated with narrative.

Ricoeur's work on narrative provides further insights into the issue of accountability in ethics and self-understanding. Ricoeur says, "by evaluating our actions, we contribute in a specific way to the interpretation of our own selves in ethical terms" (1989, 99). This means that, potentially, the process of evaluation (which entails accounting for and thus narrating our actions and intentions) contributes to the constitution of the person as a self. We come to know ourselves indirectly through the narratives of everyday life, our own life stories and those of others, and as we construct narratives in the process of justifying our actions and decisions. We also come to know ourselves as we appropriate our identity from the roles offered up in stories: thus our identities are narratively constituted.

Lugones maintains that throughout these travels and the transformations they entail, there is no underlying "I" and she means this in the strong sense that there are logically distinct selves with different attributes that inhabit different worlds, rather than one constant self who alters slightly in different contexts. Although it is true that one person can be many things—that many stories can be cut from the same cloth—and to this extent identity is flexible, complex, and contingent; it is equally true that there are limits on this instability and plurality. As the analysis of *Lost Highway* demonstrated, human identity is limited by our physicality, by the fact that we have just one body that lives in and extends through time and space in particular, predictable ways. Contrary to Lugones' suggestion, it is not necessary to exclude the possibility of an underlying "I" or a unifying life story in order to retain the sense of radical personal and ethical transformation that "world"–traveling makes possible. Ricoeur's narrative model of identity can incorporate the nature of a nomadic identity with all its instability and plurality within an interconnected self, linked through a web of relationships to different people and groups because it is possible to tell a coherent story about the travels of one body through time. This is true even when the one body contains two or more selves in the same situation or context.[2] Lugones herself accounts for (narrates) the relation between the different identities that she experiences, which suggests that if there is no underlying "I," no unitary self, there is at least the possibility for a unifying story of selfhood.

The fluidity of identity or the changeful nature of selfhood as one's identity shifts and develops over time and in response to alterations in circumstance and outlook is explained in Ricoeur's model of narrative identity. Ricoeur's work, in turn, is enhanced by Lugones' willingness to speak in concrete, experiential terms of real, sensitive human beings and our living relationships. Identity and narrative, as we have learned from Ricoeur, have similar forms of unity and meaningfulness: the coherence of an emplotted story. Narrative and identity both involve the "synthesis of the heterogeneous" in sense that for personal identity, sameness (*idem*) provides temporal synthesis and selfhood (*ipse*) incorporates multiple, particular, and changing characteristics and circumstances. In interpreting stories, then, we practice the same skills that we turn upon ourselves to make sense of our own lives, and that we use to connect with and understand other people. As Ricoeur says, "Self-understanding is an interpretation;

interpretation of the self, in turn, finds in narrative among other signs and symbols, a privileged form of mediation" (Ricoeur 1992, 114).

When viewing films we are honing skills of interpretation, imaginative projection, discernment of salience, empathic connection, and engagement with others, developing a certain mobility of perception (rather than a rigid, restricted, unitary point of view) and, with this, a sense of intersubjectivity. All of these things are central to the practice of "world"–traveling, but "world"–traveling is not an exercise in textual interpretation: it is an experience that involves relating to actual human beings. Traveling into the story-worlds the screen invites us to enter gives practice in developing the skills we need to take with us as we travel in the outer world, and within our selves.

We not only perceive ourselves as being different by looking through the eyes of other people when we travel to their "world," we actually *become different* as a result of our immersion in their situation. Upon returning to the world in which we are film spectators at the cinema, we might be changed by the experience of the travel and by the relationships or connections to others formed during the journey. In the practice of attentive engagement or "world"–traveling, we become immersed, but not submerged in the circumstances, situation, and identity of another.

Traveling Between the World of the Text and the World of the Audience

As Bowden says, "Lugones' traveling suggests possibilities for the movement of attention that rely on an inner connection between persons: a shift between rich and multidimensional selves that is at once a part of the journey that affirms their complex connections and differences" (Bowden 1998, 74). Lugones shows that as a practice and a disposition, ethically attentive engagement with self and others can involve traveling between the "worlds" of our own inner plurality, and also traveling into the worlds of other living people. Ricoeur's work on narrative identity, narrative ethics, and also on narrative interpretation (hermeneutics) reveals how the "configuring acts" (the practices of composition and interpretation of meaning) involved in ethical attention can involve traveling into the textual worlds of characters in narratives. Ricoeur speaks of narratives possessing the capacity to reveal new worlds of possible experiences.[3]

Drawing together the insights of Lugones and Ricoeur, ethical attention and the narrative understanding this entails (according to the model of attention as active, evaluative, embodied perception) involves engaging in acts of configuration, in processes of narrating and interpreting. During this process, we travel between the world of the text, our inner "worlds" of imagination and felt personal experience, and the outer world(s) we inhabit wherein we relate to living human beings.

Ricoeur claims that as a result of engaging with or appropriating a text in the act of interpreting it, the reader is able to occupy a dual position inside the experience of the text and outside it as its audience (1991e, 26). Ricoeur's suggestion that we travel between the world of the text and the world of the audience, experiencing a sense of leading a double life as we occupy both worlds at once is similar to, but also quite a different way of understanding "world"–traveling to that proposed by Lugones. Both theorists attempt to account for the lack of a sense of a unitary identity and both suggest a model of identity that incorporates the actual experience of duality or plurality that arises in response to changes over time, and changes in context and relationships and roles.

Instead of becoming a different person in each "world" or context or textual construction, we hold onto both (or, perhaps, many) aspects of ourselves at once, though some parts of the self recede into the background as others emerge through our involvement with the narrative and its characters. The practice of engaging with others, of traveling into their stories and into their worlds is, in itself, part of the traveler's story and it contributes to the development of the traveler's identity. In this way, both fictional narratives (for instance, the poetic and metaphoric imagery of narrative film), and the stories of everyday life (the story of our own developing selves, and the stories of those we relate to), "contribute to the redescription of reality" (Ricoeur 1995, 29). In drawing our attention to focus on certain aspects of life rather than others, narratives may sensitize us to previously overlooked contours of value, leading us to notice, engage with, understand, and represent the "worlds" around us in different ways.

Ricoeur reminds us that "stories are recounted, but they are also lived in the mode of the imaginary" (1991e, 27), in other words, as spectators, readers, or listeners we project ourselves imaginatively into the world of the text. Viewing films, reading novels, listening to and interpreting stories in all the different ways we do involves entering into and involving oneself in the fictive universe of the text on an experiential level. Narrative fiction leads its interpreters into the vivid imagery of other worlds, and it involves us in the experiences of joy and suffering along with that world's inhabitants. A certain kind of knowing and understanding arises from this felt involvement in the textual world; from living alongside the characters, accompanying them through their decisions, dilemmas, and delights.

Interpretation of the narrative also entails participation in it: participation in the act of narrating and in the experience of discerning, deliberating, and feeling the way through the ethical situations and problems that arise in the story world.[4] To varying degrees (dependent on many factors, including the style, content, and context of the story, and the extent to which it resonates with or challenges our preconceptions) we internalize the text as we experience it, thus as it becomes part of us, we "know" it on a level that differs from a purely conceptual or objective knowledge.

The views of life offered in *Nil by Mouth* and *Once Were Warriors* enable an understanding of the effects of domestic violence that spectators may not otherwise grasp. The form of felt understanding that can arise from immersion in these narratives reveals how a woman who knows only too well what it feels like to be beaten could still lash out in anger and hit her child, or her badly hurt brother. It shows why she could fail to turn up at a court hearing in which she might have prevented her son from being sent to a juvenile detention centre. How awful would you feel about yourself if you did such things? How difficult would it be to imagine that you deserved a better life? Spending time in the worlds that Val and Beth inhabit reveals how profoundly living conditions and life stories shape character development and possibilities for making choices and envisioning alternatives. Being the son of an abusive alcoholic did not make Ray an abstemious pacifist: it taught him to live just such a life and to hate himself for it, but it showed him no way out. By five years of age, being Ray and Val's daughter had already taught Michelle the art of subtracting herself from life, rendering herself invisible, becoming a nonperson already beaten by circumstance. Sadly, we can see an image of her in the character of Grace from *Once Were Warriors*, and perhaps even in Nola, in *The Boys*. Twelve years down the track another sweet and timid girl is hidden just outside the frame, or blurred in the background of a household churning with violence. Again the alternatives seem to be taking refuge in a half-way house, or taking her own life.

Genuinely paying attention to a story like Val's or Beth's means transforming the ways we think and act when we face such issues in our own worlds. It is not enough for an author to compose a story and for an audience to receive it; we haven't finished our part in making the story mean something until we live out that understanding in some way. Regarding the process of attending to, interpreting, or as he terms it, "reading" stories, and the importance of narrative in ethical life, Ricoeur says:

> My thesis here is that the process of composition, of configuration, is not completed in the text but in the reader, and under this condition, makes possible the reconfiguration of life by narrative . . . The act of reading thus becomes the critical moment of the entire analysis. On it rests narrative's capacity to transfigure the experience of the reader. (Ricoeur 1991e, 26)

Since the configuring act is a creative process of narration completed in the reader or interpreter of a text, the interpreter (rather than the author) is the one who is finally empowered to transfigure reality, according to Ricoeur (1991a). Thus, the role of narrative fiction in shaping or configuring reality has several components. The first act is the formal creation of the story; the second involves the imaginative activity and the affective and conceptual engagement of those who interpret the story; third is the self-creation of personal and ethical identity through developing self-knowledge and knowledge of other people and perspectives. Finally, configuration involves the experiential creation of ethical action, cultivated and practiced when engaged with the text and potentially extended into the outer world. The story-world influences and contributes to creating new possibilities for ethical agency and identity both in its content (the role models and examples it provides and the information it imparts about other lives) and its structure (narrative necessitates an interpretive, evaluative endeavor, it makes us practice trying out different perspectives as we attempt to answer the questions posed by the text and the moments of ellipsis in the text).[5]

The role of narrative in the transfiguration or transformation of "moral vision" or ethical understanding encompasses the ability of stories to catalyze or effect change by restructuring understanding, and their capacity to extend across and influence diverse forms or aspects of life. Narrative film has the ability to reveal aspects of life that may otherwise remain unrecognized or outside personal experience. In addition, by rendering the structures of narration and perception visible (and thus by pointing backward to the intentions, motives, contexts, and consequences surrounding the practice of configuration) film reveals the restructuring that occurs when fragmentary happenings and ideas are composed as a narrative. Form and content, style and structure, composition and interpretation contribute to giving narratives explanatory and transformative abilities that may enhance understanding of the ethical issues arising within the story in ways that extend to alter attitudes and perceptions of such issues in other areas of life.

In an interview about the ambiguity of his work, David Lynch once said that he loves films that leave room to wonder (Lynch and Rodley 1997). I've argued that narrative characteristically includes spaces for the imagination to fill, spaces opened up by metaphor, lost in lacunae, extending behind, above, and beyond every border of the screen, and reaching outward into the lives of the audience; spaces that can not be fully contained by narrative closure. In a sense attentive engagement with film invites us to occupy the seventh dimension of screen space, inhabiting the intersubjective spaces of the film itself and the characters living on the surface of the screen. Given that so much of contemporary life is lived inside screen space of one kind or another, particularly for those of us working in the field, we might do well to live out the best possibilities screen texts offer, infiltrating the spaces they create for the imagination and making a little more room in our own lives for wonder.

Notes

1. Note here that, in Sobchack's phenomenological understanding of film spectatorship as an intersubjective, cybernetic symbiosis or synthesis with the filmic body, spectatorial engagement with each individual film (if not each of the characters within a film) entails becoming a different self because the spectator's own embodied locus is extended technologically. As spectators, we are literally *incorporated* into the body of each film we watch, our vision of the story world is enabled by, and at least partially fused to, the perceptive and attentive practices of the film as a viewing, experiencing, narrating subject. We are still ourselves (we relinquish nothing of ourselves), but we are also distinctively "other" in a phenomenological interpretation of filmic experience.

2. It is still possible to narrate the relationship of, for instance, Lugones' stereotypically "intense" Latino "self" to her authentically intense (Latino) self (1987, 11–13). These two "selves" relate to the people surrounding Lugones and they come to life (are animated) by the "worlds" those people inhabit when a character trait such as intensity is perceived in her, and drawn out from her, or projected onto her.

3. In a commentary of Ricoeur's work on narrative, Vanhoozer explains: "Fictions 'remake' human reality by projecting a possible world which can intersect and transform the world of the reader . . . The world projected by the work allows one to explore possibilities for action and so have 'fictive experiences' [thus fictional narrative offers] a new world, a new way of perceiving things or possibilities" (Vanhoozer 1991, 48–49).

4. The hermeneutic interpretation of textually represented experience is significant here, as a text mediates understanding through referentiality, communicability, and

self-understanding, between the interpreter and the world, between narrators and narratees, and between the interpreter of the text and herself or himself (see Ricoeur 1991e, 27). Narratives "make sense" when, in the case of film, they are "sensed" by the audience. They become significant due to the intersection of the "world of the text" and the "world of the interpreter" during the processes of seeing, hearing, feeling, projecting, responding, and reflecting.

5. "Metaphorical and narrative statements, taken in hand by reading, aim at refiguring reality, in the twofold sense of uncovering the concealed dimensions of human experience and of transforming our vision of the world" (Ricoeur 1995, 47).

REFERENCES

American Academy of Pediatrics, Committee on Public Education. 2001. "Media Violence." The full text of the report of the committee comprising Miriam Baron, Daniel Broughton, Susan Buttross, Suzanne Corrigan Alberto Gedissman, M. Rosario Gonzales de Rivas, Michael O. Rich and Donals L. Shifrin. In *Pediatrics* 108.5: 1222–1227.

Arendt, Hannah. 1958. *The Human Condition.* Chicago: University of Chicago Press.

Aristotle. 1941a. "*De Anima*". In *The Basic Works of Aristotle.* Ed. and trans. R. McKeon. New York: Random House.

Aristotle. 1941b. *Nicomachean Ethics.* In *The Basic Works of Aristotle.* Ed. and trans. R. McKeon. New York: Random House.

Aristotle. 1941c. *Poetics.* In *The Basic Works of Aristotle.* Ed. and trans. R. McKeon. New York: Random House.

Aristotle. 1941d. *Politics.* In *The Basic Works of Aristotle.* Ed. and trans. R. McKeon. New York: Random House.

Armstrong, Edward G. 2004. Eminem's Construction of Authenticity. *Popular Music and Society* 27.3: 335–356.

Babbitt, Susan. 1996. *Impossible Dreams: Rationality, Integrity and the Moral Imagination.* Boulder, CO: Westview Press.

Bandura, Albert. 1994. "Social Cognitive Theory of Mass Communication." In *Media Effects: Advances in Theory and Research*, ed. J. Bryant and D. Zillmann, 61–90. Hillsdale, NJ: Lawrence Erlbaum Associates, Inc.

Bandura, Albert. 2006. "Imitation of Film-Mediated Aggressive Models." In *Critical Readings: Violence and the Media*, ed. Kay Weaver and Cynthia Carter, 30–44. Maidenhead: Open University Press.

Bardsley, Karen. 2002. "Is It All in Our Imagination? Questioning the Use of the Concept of Imagination in Cognitive Film Theory." In *Film and*

Knowledge: Essays on the Integration of Images and Ideas, ed. Kevin Stoehr, 157–173. Jefferson, NC: McFarland.

Baudrillard, Jean. 1984. *The Evil Demon of Images*, 80–97. Sydney: Power Institute Publications.

Baudry, Jean-Louis. 1986. "Ideological Effects of the Basic Cinematographic Apparatus." In *Narrative, Apparatus, Ideology: A Film Theory Reader*, ed. P. Rosen, 286–298. New York: Columbia University Press.

Baudry, Jean-Louis. 1992. "The Apparatus: Metapsychological Approaches to the Impression of Reality in Cinema." In *Film Theory and Criticism: Introductory Readings* (Fourth Edition), eds. Gerald Mast, Marshall Cohen, and Leo Braudy, 690–724. New York: Oxford University Press.

Bennett, William J. 1992. *Devaluing of America: The Fight for Our Culture and Our Children*. New York: Simon and Schuster.

Berry, Gordon and Joy Asamen. 2001. "Television, Children and Multicultural Awareness: Comprehending the Medium in a Complex Multimedia Society." In *Handbook of Children and the Media*, ed. Dorothy Singer and Jerome Singer, 359–374. Thousand Oaks, CA: Sage.

Bettelheim, Bruno. 1975. *The Uses of Enchantment*. London: Thames and Hudson.

Bickham David, John Wright, and Aletha Huston. 2001. "Attention, Comprehension, and the Educational Influences of Television." In *Handbook of Children and the Media*, ed. Dorothy Singer and Jerome Singer, 101–120. Thousand Oaks, CA: Sage.

Booth, Wayne. 1988. *The Company We Keep: An Ethics of Fiction*. Berkeley, CA: University of California Press.

Bordwell, David. 1985. "Believing and Seeing." In *Narration and the Fiction Film*, 40–70. London: Methuen.

Bordwell, David, Janet Staiger, and Kristin Thompson. 1985. *The Classical Hollywood Cinema*. New York: Columbia University Press.

Bordwell, David and Kristen Thompson. 2004. *Film Art: An Introduction*, Seventh Edition. Boston: McGraw Hill.

Bowden, Peta. 1998. "Ethical Attention: Accumulating Understandings." *European Journal of Philosophy*, 6.1: 59–77.

Brooker, Will. 2001. "Readings of Racism: Interpretation, Stereotyping and *The Phantom Menace*." *Continuum: Journal of Media and Cultural Studies*, 15.1: 15–32.

Brown, Royal S. 1994. *Overtones and Undertones: Reading Film Music.* Berkeley, CA: University of California Press.

Brown, William and Benson Fraser. 2004. "Celebrity Identification in Entertainment-Education." In *Entertainment Education and Social Change: History, Research and Practice*, eds. Arvind Singhal, Michael J. Cody, Everett M. Rogers, and Michael Sabido, 98–111. Mahwah, NJ: Lawrence Erlbaum Associates.

Browne, Nick. 1992. "The Spectator-in-the-Text: The Rhetoric of Stagecoach." In *Film Theory and Criticism: Introductory Readings* (Fourth Edition), eds. Gerald Mast, Marshall Cohen, and Leo Braudy, 210–225. New York: Oxford University Press.

Buckingham, David. 2006. "Children Viewing Violence." In *Critical Readings: Violence and the Media*, ed. C. Kay Weaver and Cynthia Carter, 279–288. Maidenhead: Open University Press.

Bushman, Brad and Craig Anderson. 2001. "Media Violence and the American Public: Scientific Facts Versus Media Misinformation." *American Psychologist* 56.6/7: 477–489.

Bushman, Brad and L. Rowell Huesmann. 2001. "Effects of Televised Violence on Aggression." In *Handbook of Children and the Media*, ed. Dorothy Singer and Jerome Singer, 223–254. Thousand Oaks, CA: Sage.

Butterss, Philip. 1998. "When Being a Man Is All You've Got: Masculinity in *Romper Stomper, Idiot Box, Blackrock,* and *The Boys.*" *Metro Magazine* 117: 40–46.

Campion, Jane. 1993. *The Piano*. New York: Miramax Books.

Cantor, Joanne. 1994. "Confronting Children's Fright Responses to Mass Media." In *Media, Children and the Family: Social Scientific, Psychodynamic, and Clinical Perspectives*, ed. Dolf Zillman, Jennings Bryant, and Aletha Huston, 139–149. Hillsdale, NJ: Lawrence Erlbaum and Associates.

Cantor, Joanne. 1996. "Television and Children's Fear." In *Tuning in to Young Viewers*, ed. Tannis M. MacBeth, 87–116. Thousand Oaks, CA: Sage.

Cantor, Joanne. 2001. "The Media and Children's Fears, Anxieties, and Perceptions of Danger." In *Handbook of Children and the Media*, ed. Dorothy Singer and Jerome Singer, 207–221. Thousand Oaks, CA: Sage.

Carr, David. 1986. *Time, Narrative and History*. Bloomington, IN: Indiana University Press.

Carr, David. 1991. "Discussion: Ricoeur on Narrative." In *On Paul Ricoeur*, ed. David Wood, 160–187. London: Routledge.

Carroll, Noel. 1988. *Mystifying the Movies: Fads and Fallacies in Contemporary Film Theory*. New York: Columbia University Press.

Carroll, Noel. 2006. "Film, Emotion and Genre." In *Philosophy of Film and Motion Pictures: An Anthology*, ed. Noel Carroll and Jinhee Choi, 217–233. Boston, MA: Blackwell Publishing.

Carter, Angela. 1967. *The Magic Toyshop*. London: Heinmann.

Carter, Angela. 1979. *The Bloody Chamber and Other Stories*. London: Gollancz.

Casebier, Allan. 1991. *Film and Phenomenology: Towards a Realist Theory of Cinematic Representation*. Cambridge: Cambridge University Press.

Cavell, Stanley. 1979. *The World Viewed: Reflections on the Ontology of Film*, enlarged edition. Cambridge, MA: Harvard University Press.

Cavell, Stanley. 1996. "The Same and Different: The Awful Truth." In *The Cavell Reader*, ed. S. Mulhall, 167–196. Cambridge, MA: Blackwell Publishers.

Code, Lorraine. 1991. *What Can She Know? Feminist Theory and the Construction of Knowledge*. Ithaca, NY: Cornell University Press.

Cohen, Jonathan and G. Weimann. 2000. "Cultivation Revisited: Some Genres Have Some Effects on Some Viewers." *Communication Reports* 13.2: 99–114.

Creed, Barbara. 1993. *The Monstrous Feminine: Film, Feminism, Psychoanalysis*. New York: Routledge.

Currie, Gregory. 1990. *The Nature of Fiction*. Cambridge: Cambridge University Press.

Currie, Gregory. 1995. *Image and Mind: Film, Philosophy and Cognitive Science*. New York: Cambridge University Press.

Currie, Gregory. 1997. "The Film Theory That Never Was: A Nervous Manifesto." In *Film Theory and Philosophy*, ed. Murray Smith and Richard Allen, 42–60. Oxford: Clarendon Press.

Day, James M. 1991. "Role-taking Revisited: Narrative and Cognitive-Developmental Interpretations of Moral Growth." *Journal of Moral Education* 20.3: 305–315.

Deleuze, Gilles and Felix Guattari. 1987. *A Thousand Plateaus: Capitalism and Schizophrenia*, trans. B. Massumi. Minneapolis, MN: University of Minnesota Press.

Descartes, Rene. 1984. "First Meditation from Meditations on First Philosophy." In *The Philosophical Writings of Descartes*, vol. 2, trans. J. Cottingham, R. Stoothoff and D. Murdoch. Cambridge: Cambridge University Press.

de Sousa, Ronald. 1987. *The Rationality of Emotion*. Cambridge, MA: Massachusetts Institute of Technology Press.

Dickinson, Kay, ed. 2003. *Movie Music: The Film Reader*. London: Routledge.

Doane, Mary-Ann. 1992. "Film and the Masquerade: Theorizing the Female Spectator." In *Film Theory and Criticism: Introductory Readings* (Fourth Edition), ed. Gerald Mast, Marshall Cohen, and Leo Braudy, 248–256. New York: Oxford University Press.

Donald, James. 1989. *Fantasy and the Cinema*. London: British Film Institute.

Donnelly, K. J. 2001. *Film Music: Critical Approaches*. New York: Continuum.

Dubow, E. and L. Miller. 1996. "Television Violence Viewing and Aggressive Behavior." In *Tuning in to Young Viewers*, ed. Tannis M. MacBeth, 117–148. Thousand Oaks, CA: Sage.

Duff, Alan. 1990. *Once Were Warriors*. Auckland, New Zealand: Tandem Press.

Eby, Lloyd. 2003. "Why Eminem is a Problem." *World and I* 18.3: 288–298.

Ekman, Paul. 2003. *Emotions Revealed: Understanding Faces and Feelings*. London: Weidenfeld and Nicholson.

Eliade, Mircea. 1963. *Myth and Reality*. New York: Harper and Row.

Elsaesser, Thomas and Warren Buckland. 2002. "Cognitive Theories of Narration: *Lost Highway*." In *Studying Contemporary American Film*, 168–194. London: Arnold.

Fahy, Christopher. 2002. "The Order of Rage: Epistemology and the Need for Knowledge in Paul Schrader's *Affliction*." In *Film and Knowledge: Essays on the Integration of Images and Ideas*, ed. Kevin Stoehr, 37–49. Jefferson, NC: McFarland.

Fay, Brian. 1996. "Do we Live Stories or Just Tell Them?" In *Contemporary Philosophy of Social Science*, 178–198. Oxford: Blackwell.

Frank, Arthur. 1995. *The Wounded Storyteller: Body, Illness, and Ethics*. Chicago, IL: Chicago University Press.

Freud, Sigmund. 1985. "The 'Uncanny.'" In *Pelican Freud Library, vol. 14: Art and Literature*, 339–376. Ringwood, Victoria: Penguin Books Australia.

Friedman, Marilyn. 1987. "Care and Context in Moral Reasoning." In *Women and Moral Theory*, ed. Eva Kittay and Dianna Meyers, 190–204. Totowa, NJ: Rowman and Littlefield.

Friedman, Marilyn. 1993. *What Are Friends For? Feminist Perspectives on Personal Relationships and Moral Theory*. Ithaca, NY: Cornell University Press.

Funk, J., G. Flores, D. Buchman and J. Germann. 1999. "Rating Electronic Games: Violence is in the Eye of the Beholder." *Youth and Society* 30.3: 283–312.

Fuss, Diana. 1995. *Identification Papers*. New York: Routledge.

Gauntlett, David. 1998. "Ten Things Wrong With the 'Effects Model.'" In *Approaches to Audiences: A Reader*, ed. Roger Dickinson, Ramaswami Harindranath, and Olga Linne. London: Arnold.

Gaut, Berys. 2006. "Identification and Emotion in Narrative Film." In *Philosophy of Film and Motion Pictures: An Anthology*, 260–270. Boston, MA: Blackwell Publishing.

Geen, R. 1994. "Television and Aggression: Recent Developments in Research and Theory." In *Media, Children and the Family: Social Scientific, Psychodynamic, and Clinical Perspectives*, ed. Dolf Zillman, Jennings Bryant, and Aletha Huston. Hillsdale, NJ: Lawrence Erlbaum and Assoc.

Gerbner, George. 2006. "Television Violence: At a Time of Turmoil and Terror." In *Critical Readings: Violence and the Media*, ed. C. Kay Weaver and Cynthia Carter, 45–53. Maidenhead: Open University Press.

Gilligan, Carol. 1982. *In a Different Voice*. Cambridge, MA.: Harvard University Press.

Gorbman, Claudia. 1987. *Unheard Melodies: Narrative Film Music*. London: British Film Institute.

Grundmann, Roy. 2003. "White Man's Burden: Eminem's Movie Debut in *8 Mile*." *Cineaste* 28.2: 30–37.

Heins, Marjorie. 2006. "Media Effects." In *Censoring Culture: Contemporary Threats to Free Expression*, ed. Robert Atkins and Svetlana Mintcheva, 173–184. New York: The New Press.

Hilton, Rod. 2003. *8 Mile: The Abridged Script*. http://www.the-editing-room.com/8mile.html (accessed October 29, 2007).

Hodge, Bob and David Tripp. 1986. *Children and Television*. Cambridge, UK: Polity Press.

Hoijer, Birgitta. 2006. "Global Discourses of Compassion." In *Critical Readings: Violence and the Media*, ed. C. Kay Weaver and Cynthia Carter, 346–360. Maidenhead: Open University Press.

Hudson Jones, Anne. 1996. "Darren's Case: Narrative Ethics." In Perri Kalss's *Other Women's Children. The Journal of Medicine and Philosophy* 21.3: 267–287.

Hudson Jones, Anne. 1999. "Narrative in Medical Ethics." *British Medical Journal* 318.7178: 253–256.

Hume, David. 1939a. "Of Personal Identity." In *A Treatise of Human Nature*, vol. 1, sect. 6, part 4, 238–249. London: J. M. Dent and Sons Ltd.

Hume, David. 1939b. "Of Scepticism With Regard to the Senses." In *A Treatise of Human Nature*, vol. 1, sect. 2, 182–210. London: J. M. Dent and Sons.

Hume, David. 1975. *Essays Concerning Human Understanding: Enquiries Concerning Human Understanding and Concerning the Principles of Morals* (Third Edition). Oxford: Clarendon Press.

Huntemann, Nina and Michael Morgan. 2001. "Mass Media and Identity Development." In *Handbook of Children and the Media*, eds. Dorothy Singer and Jerome Singer, 309–321. Thousand Oaks, CA: Sage.

Hunter, Kathryn Montgomery. 1996. "Narrative, Literature and the Clinical Exercise of Practical Reason." *The Journal of Medicine and Philosophy* 21: 303–320.

Huston, Aletha and J. C. Wright. 1996. "Television and the Socialization of Young Children." In *Tuning in to Young Viewers*, ed. Tannis M. MacBeth, 37–60. Thousand Oaks, CA: Sage.

Jardine, Murray. 1998. *Speech and Political Practice: Recovering the Place of Human Responsibility*. Albany, NY: State University of New York Press.

Kant, Immanuel. 1934. (CR) *Critique of Pure Reason* (Second Edition), trans. J. Meiklejohn. London: J. M. Dent and Sons Limited.

Kant, Immanuel. 1987. (CJ) *Critique of Judgment*, trans. W. Pluhar. Indianapolis, IN: Hackett Publishing Company.

Kassabian, Anahid. 2001. *Hearing Film: Tracking Identifications in Contemporary Hollywood Film Music*. New York: Routledge.

Katz, Jack. 1999. *How Emotions Work*. Chicago, IL: University of Chicago Press.

Kaye, Barbara K. and Barry S. Sapolsky. 2004. "Offensive Language in Prime-time Television: Four Years after Television Age and Content Ratings." *Journal of Broadcasting & Electronic Media* 48.4: 554–560.

Kearney, Richard. 1988. *The Wake of Imagination: Ideas of Creativity in Western Culture*. Melbourne: Hutchinson.

Kemp, T. Peter. 1989. "Towards a Narrative Ethics: A Bridge Between Ethics and the Narrative Reflection of Ricoeur." In *The Narrative Path*, ed. Peter Kemp and D. Rasmussen, 65–89. London: MIT Press.

Kemp, T. Peter. 1995. "Ethics and Narrativity." In *The Philosophy of Paul Ricoeur*, ed. L. Hanh, 371–394. Chicago, IL: Open Court.

Knight, Deborah. 2006. "In Fictional Shoes: Mental Simulation and Fiction." In *Philosophy of Film and Motion Pictures: An Anthology*, ed. Noel Carroll and Jinhee Choi, 271–280. Boston, MA: Blackwell Publishing.

Krcmar, M. and P. Valkenburg. 1999. "A Scale to Assess Children's Moral Interpretations of Justified and Unjustified Violence and its Relationship to Television Viewing." *Communication Research* 26.5: 608–634.

Kristeva, Julia. 1982. *Powers of Horror: An Essay on Abjection*, trans. L. Roudiez. New York: Columbia University Press.

Kyte, Richard. 1996. "Moral Reasoning as Perception: a Reading of Carol Gilligan." *Hypatia* 11.3: 97–113.

Larrabee, Richard, ed. 1993. *An Ethic of Care: Feminist and Interdisciplinary Perspectives*. New York: Routledge.

Lay, Samantha. 2002. *British Social Realism: From Documentary to Brit-Grit*. London: Wallflower Press.

Locke, John. 1961. "Of Identity and Diversity." In *An Essay Concerning Human Understanding*, vol. 1, book 2, chap. 27, 274–293. London: J. M. Dent and Sons Ltd.

Lugones, Maria. 1987. "Playfulness, "World"–Traveling and Loving Perception." *Hypatia* 2.2: 3–19.

Lynch, David and Chris Rodley. 1997. *Lynch on Lynch*, ed. Chris Rodley. London: Faber and Faber.

MacIntyre, Alasdair. 1977. "Epistemological Crisis, Dramatic Narrative and the Philosophy of Science." *Monist* 60: 453–472.

MacIntyre, Alasdair. 1981. *After Virtue: A Study in Moral Theory*. London: Duckworth.

Malina, Debra. 2002. *Breaking the Frame: Metalepsis and the Construction of the Subject*. Columbus, OH: Ohio State University Press.

Malinowski, Bronislaw. 1926. *Myth and Primitive Psychology*. New York: Norton.

Mares, Marie-Louise and Emory Woodard. 2001. "Prosocial Effects on Children's Social Interactions." In *Handbook of Children and the Media*, ed. Dorothy Singer and Jerome Singer, 183–207. Thousand Oaks, CA: Sage.

Marks, Laura U. 2000. *The Skin of the Film: Intercultural Cinema, Embodiment and the Senses*. Durham and London: Duke.

Marks, Laura U. 2002. *Touch: Sensuous Theory and Multisensory Media*. Minneapolis, MN: University of Minnesota Press.

McCrillis, M.P. 2003. "Why Eminem is Important." *World and I* 18.3: 274–287.

McMahan, Alison. 1999. "The Effect of Multiform Narrative on Subjectivity." *Screen* 40.2: 146–157.

Merleau-Ponty, Maurice. 1964. *The Primacy of Perception and Other Essays on Phenomenological Psychology, the Philosophy of Art, History and Politics*, ed. James M. Edie, trans. C. Dallery. Evanston, IL: Northwestern University Press.

Merleau-Ponty, Maurice. 2002. *Phenomenology of Perception*. London: Routledge.

Metz, Christian. 1977. "Identification, Mirror." In *Psychoanalysis and the Cinema: The Imaginary Signifier*, 42–52. Basingstoke: Macmillan.

Metz, Christian. 1992. "Aural Objects." In *Film Theory and Criticism: Introductory Readings* (Fourth Edition), ed. Gerald Mast, Marshall Cohen, and Leo Braudy, 313–316. New York: Oxford University Press.

Milavsky, J. R., R. Kessler, H. Stipp, and W. Rubens. 1982. *Television and Aggression: A Panel Study*. New York: Academic Press.

Mink, Louis O. 1970. *Mind, History and Dialectic*. Bloomington, IN: Indiana University Press.

Mintcheva, Svetlana. 2006. "Protection or Politics? The Use and Abuse of Children." In *Censoring Culture: Contemporary Threats to Free Expression*, ed. Robert Atkins and Svetlana Mintcheva, 167–172. New York: The New Press.

Moeller, Susan. 1999. *Compassion Fatigue: How the Media Sells Disease, Famine, War and Death*. New York: Routledge.

Mulvey, Laura. 1992. "Visual Pleasure and Narrative Cinema." In *Film Theory and Criticism: Introductory Readings* (Fourth Edition), ed. Gerald Mast, Marshall Cohen, and Leo Braudy, 746–757. New York: Oxford University Press.

Murdoch, Iris. 1970. *The Sovereignty of the Good*. London: Routledge and Kegan Paul.

Murray, Janet H. 1997. *Hamlet on the Holodeck: The Future of Narrative in Cyberspace*. New York: The Free Press.

Naigles, Letitia and Lara Mayeux. 2001. "Television as Incidental Language Teacher." In *Handbook of Children and the Media*, ed. Dorothy Singer and Jerome Singer, 135–152. Thousand Oaks, CA: Sage.

Nathanson, A. and Joanne Cantor. 2000. "Reducing the Aggression-promoting Effect of Violent Cartoons by Increasing Children's Fictional Involvement with the Victim: A Study of Active Mediation." *Journal of Broadcasting & Electronic Media* 44.1: 125–142.

Neill, Alex. 2006. "Empathy and (Film) Fiction." In *Philosophy of Film and Motion Pictures: An Anthology*, ed. Noel Carroll and Jinhee Choi, 247–259. Boston, MA: Blackwell Publishing.

Newton, Adam Z. 1997. *Narrative Ethics*. Cambridge, MA: Harvard University Press.

Novitz, David. 1987. *Knowledge, Fiction and Imagination*. Philadelphia, PA: Temple University Press.

Noyce, Philip. 2001. "Director's Speak: Noyce on Sound." *IF (Independent Filmmakers) Magazine* (now renamed *Inside Film Magazine*) http://www.if.com.au/index.html p. 20 (accessed May 18, 2006).

Nozick, Robert. 1993. *The Nature of Rationality*. Princeton, NJ: Princeton University Press.

Nussbaum, Martha. 1990. *Love's Knowledge: Essays on Philosophy and Literature*. New York: Oxford University Press.

Nussbaum, Martha. 1993. "Non-Relative Virtues: An Aristotelian Approach." In *The Quality of Life*, ed. Martha Nussbaum and Amartya Sen, 242–269. New York: Oxford University Press.

Nussbaum, Martha. 1995. *Poetic Justice: The Literary Imagination and Public Life*. Boston, MA: Beacon Press.

Nussbaum, Martha. 1996a. "Compassion: The Basic Social Emotion." *Social Philosophy and Policy Foundation* 13.1: 27–59.

Nussbaum, Martha. 1996b. "Love and Vision: Iris Murdoch on Eros and the Individual." In *Iris Murdoch and the Search for Human Goodness*, ed. M. Antonaccio and W. Schweiker, 29–53. Chicago, IL: University of Chicago Press.

Nussbaum, Martha. 1997. "The Narrative Imagination." In *Cultivating Humanity: A Classical Defense of Reform in Liberal Education*, 86–111. Cambridge, MA: Harvard University Press.

Nussbaum, Martha. 2001. *Upheavals of Thought: The Intelligence of Emotions*. Cambridge: Cambridge University Press.

Oakley, Justin. 1992. *Morality and the Emotions*. London: Routledge.

Parfit, Derek. 1984. *Reasons and Persons*. Melbourne: Clarendon Press.

Plato. 1941. "The Allegory of the Cave." In Chapter XXV (vii. 541a–521b) of *The Republic of Plato*, trans. Cornford F. Macdonald. Oxford: Clarendon.

Porter, Elisabeth. 1991. *Women and Moral Identity*. Sydney: Allen and Unwin.

Prejean, Helen. 1993. *Dead Man Walking: An Eyewitness Account of the Death Penalty in the United States*. New York: Random House.

Prendergast, Roy. 1977. *Film Music: A Neglected Art*. New York: Norton.

Propp, Vladimir. 1975. *Morphology of the Folktale*. Austin, TX: University of Texas Press.

Propp, Vladimir. 1984. *Theory and History of Folklore*. Ed. A. Liberman, trans. A. Martin and R. Martin. Minneapolis: University of Minnesota Press.

Rascaroli, Laura. 1997. "Steel in the Gaze: On POV and the Discourse of Vision in Kathryn Bigelow's Cinema." *Screen* 38.3: 232–246.

Ree, Jonathon. 1987. *Philosophical Tales*. London: Methuen.

Ree, Jonathon. 1991. "Narrative and Philosophical Experience." In *On Paul Ricoeur: Narrative and Interpretation*, ed. David Wood, 74–83. London: Routledge.

Richardson, Jeanita and Kim Scott. 2002. "Rap Music and its Violent Progeny: America's Culture of Violence in Context." *The Journal of Negro Education* 71.3: 175–192.

Ricoeur, Paul. 1989. "The Human Being as the Subject Matter of Philosophy." In *The Narrative Path*, ed. Peter Kemp and David Rasmussen, 89–101. London: MIT Press.

Ricoeur, Paul. 1991a. "The Function of Fiction in Shaping Reality." In *A Ricoeur Reader: Reflection and Imagination*, ed. Mario Valdes, 117–136. Toronto: University of Toronto Press.

Ricoeur, Paul. 1991b. "Narrated Time." In *A Ricoeur Reader: Reflection and Imagination*, ed. Mario Valdes, 338–354. Toronto: University of Toronto Press.

Ricoeur, Paul. 1991c. "Life: A Story in Search of a Narrator." In *A Ricoeur Reader: Reflection and Imagination*, ed. Mario Valdes, 425–437. Toronto: University of Toronto Press.

Ricoeur, Paul. 1991d. "Discussion: Ricoeur on Narrative." In *On Paul Ricoeur: Narrative and Interpretation*, ed. David Wood, 160–187. London: Routledge.

Ricoeur, Paul. 1991e. "Life in Quest of Narrative." In *On Paul Ricoeur: Narrative and Interpretation*, ed. David Wood, 20–34. London: Routledge.

Ricoeur, Paul. 1991f. "Narrative Identity." In *On Paul Ricoeur: Narrative and Interpretation*, ed. David Wood, 188–199. London: Routledge.

Ricoeur, Paul. 1992. *Oneself as Another*. Chicago, IL: University of Chicago Press.

Ricoeur, Paul. 1995. "Intellectual Autobiography of Paul Ricoeur." In *The Philosophy of Paul Ricoeur*, ed. L. Hanh, 1–54. Chicago, IL: Open Court.

Rorty, Amelie, ed. 1980. *Explaining Emotions*. Berkeley, CA: University of California Press.

Ryan, Marie-Laure. 2004. "Metaleptic Machines." *Semiotica* 150.1/4: 439–469.

Sarbin, Theodore. 1986. *Narrative Psychology: The Storied Nature of Human Conduct*. New York: Praeger.

Sherman, Nancy. 1989. *The Fabric of Character: Aristotle's Theory of Virtue*. Oxford: Clarendon Press.

Singer, Linda. 1990. "Eye / Mind / Screen: Toward a Phenomenology of Cinematic Scopophilia." *Quarterly Review of Film and Video* 12.3: 51–67.

Singhal, Arvind, Michael Cody, Everett Rogers and Miguel Sabido, ed. 2004. *Entertainment-Education and Social Change: History, Research and Practice*. Mahwah, NJ: Lawrence Erlbaum Associates.

Smith, Murray. 1995. *Engaging Characters: Fiction, Emotion and the Cinema*. Oxford: Clarendon Press.

Smith, Murray. 1997. "Imagining from the Inside." In *Film Theory and Philosophy*, ed. Murray Smith and Richard Allen, 412–430. Oxford: Clarendon Press.

Sobchack, Vivian. 1984. "Inscribing Ethical Space: Ten Propositions on Death, Representation and Documentary." *Quarterly Review of Film Studies* 9.4: 283–300.

Sobchack, Vivian. 1990. "Active Eye: Optical Movement: Transformations of Attention." *Quarterly Review of Film and Video* 12.3: 21–36.

Sobchack, Vivian. 1992. *Address of the Eye*. Princeton, NJ: Princeton University Press.

Sobchack, Vivian. 1999. "Is Any Body Home? Embodied Imagination and Visible Evictions." In *Home, Exile, Homeland: Film, Media, and the Politics of Place*, ed. Hamid Naficy, 45–62. New York: Routledge.

Sobchack, Vivian. 2004. *Carnal Thoughts: Embodiment and Moving Image Culture*. Berkeley, CA: University of California Press.

Sontag, Susan. 2003. *Regarding the Pain of Others*. New York: Farrar, Straus and Giroux.

Spacks, Patricia Meyer. 1985. *Gossip*. New York: Knopf.

Sperb, Jason. 2005. "Internal Sunshine: Illuminating Being-Memory." In *Eternal Sunshine of the Spotless Mind. Kritikos*, vol. 2: np. http://garnet.acns.fsu.edu/~nr03/Internal%20Sunshine.htm (accessed March 25, 2008).

Stadler, Harald. 1990. "Film as Experience: Phenomenological Concepts in Film and Television Studies." *Quarterly Review of Film and Video* 12.3: 37–50.

Stam, Robert and Louise Spence. 1983. "Colonialism, Racism and Representation: An Introduction." *Screen* 24.2: 3–20.

Studlar, Gaylyn. 1990a. "Reconciling Feminism and Phenomenology: Notes on Problems and Possibilities, Texts and Contexts." *Quarterly Review of Film and Video* 12.3: 69–78.

Studlar, Gaylyn. 1990b. "Masochism, Masquerade and the Erotic Metamorphosis of Marlene Dietrich." In *Fabrications: Costume and the Female Body*, ed. Jane Gaines and Charlotte Herzog, 229–249. New York: Routledge.

Taylor, Charles. 1989. *Sources of the Self*. Cambridge, MA: Harvard University Press.

Tester, Keith. 2001. *Compassion, Morality and the Media*. Buckingham: Open University Press.

Todorov, Tzvetan. 1973. *The Fantastic: A Structural Approach to a Literary Genre*, trans. R. Howard. Ithaca, NY: Cornell University Press.

Tress, Daryl and Adrienne Fulco. 1995. "Liabilities of the Feminist Use of Personal Narrative: A Study of Sara Ruddick's Story in *Maternal Thinking*." *Public Affairs Quarterly* 9.3: 267–286.

Tulloch, John. 2000. *Watching Television Audiences: Cultural Theories and Methods*. Arnold: London.

Turvey, Malcolm. 1997. "Seeing Theory: On Perception and Emotional Response in Current Film Theory." In *Film Theory and Philosophy*, ed. Murray Smith and Richard Allen, 431–457. Oxford: Clarendon Press.

Tyler, Robin. 2001. "Eminem: Pied Piper of Hate." *The Gay & Lesbian Review Worldwide* 8.3: 12–14.

Van Evra, J. 1990. *Television and Child Development*. Mahwah, NJ: Lawrence Erlbaum and Associates.

Vanhoozer, Kevin. 1991. "Philosophical Antecedents to Ricoeur's Time and Narrative." In *On Paul Ricoeur: Narrative and Interpretation*, ed. David Wood, 34–54. London: Routledge.

Villani, Susan. 2001. "Impact of Media on Children and Adolescents: A 10-Year Review of the Research." *Journal of the American Academy of Child and Adolescent Psychiatry* 40.4: 392–402.

Walker, Janet. 2005. *Trauma Cinema Documenting Incest and the Holocaust*. Berkeley, CA: University of California Press.

Walton, Kendall. 1990. *Mimesis as Make-Believe: On the Foundations of the Representational Arts*. Cambridge, MA.: Harvard University Press.

Walton, Kendall. 2006. "Fearing Fictions." In *Philosophy of Film and Motion Pictures: An Anthology*, ed. Noel Carroll and Jinhee Choi, 234–246. Boston, MA: Blackwell Publishing.

Warner, Marina. 1993. *Cinema and the Realms of Enchantment: British Film Institute Working Papers*, ed. D. Petrie. London: British Film Institute Publishing.

Warner, Marina. 1994. *From the Beast to the Blond*. London: Chatto and Windus.

Weaver, C. Kay and Cynthia Carter, ed. 2006. *Critical Readings: Violence and the Media*. Maidenhead: Open University Press.

Weil, Simone. 1952. *Gravity and Grace*, trans. E. Craufurd. London: Routledge and Kegan Paul.

Weil, Simone. 1956. *The Iliad, or the Poem of Force*, trans. M. McCarthy. Wellingford: Pendle Hill Pamphlet.

Weil, Simone. 1978. *Lectures on Philosophy*, trans. H. Price. Cambridge: Cambridge University Press.

Weisberg, Mark and Jacalyn Duffin. 1995. "Evoking the Moral Imagination: Using Stories to Teach Ethics and Professionalism to Nursing, Medical, and Law Students." *The Journal of Medical Humanities* 16.4: 247–263.

White, Alan. 1990. *The Language of Imagination*. Oxford: Basil Blackwell.

White, Hayden. 1991. "The Metaphysics of Narrativity: Time and Symbol in Ricoeur's Philosophy of History." In *On Paul Ricoeur: Narrative and Interpretation*, ed. David Wood, 140–159. London: Routledge.

Williams, Bernard. 1973. *Problems of the Self*. Cambridge: Cambridge University Press.

Williams, Linda. 1995. "Film Bodies: Gender, Genre and Excess." In *Film Genre Reader 2*, ed. Barry Grant, 140–157. Austin, TX: University of Texas Press.

Witherell, Carol. 1991. "Narrative and the Moral Realm: Tales of Caring and Justice." *Journal of Moral Education* 20.3: 237–241.

Witherell, Carol and Nel Noddings. 1991. *Stories Lives Tell: Narrative and Dialogue in Education*. New York: Teacher's College Press.

Wollheim, Richard. 1987. *Painting as an Art*. London: Thames and Hudson.

Yokota, Fumie and Kimberly Thompson. 2000. "Violence in G-Rated Animated Films." *The Journal of the American Medical Association* 283.20: 2716–2721.

Filmography

8 Mile (2002) directed by Curtis Hanson.

21 Grams (2003) directed by Alejandro González Ińárritu.

American Psycho (2000) directed by Mary Harron.

Amores Perros (2000) directed by Alejandro González Ińárritu.

Arrival of a Train at Ciotat Station (1895) directed by Auguste and Louis Lumiere.

Babel (2006) directed by Alejandro González Ińárritu.

Batman Begins (2005) directed by Christopher Nolan.

Dead Man Walking (1995) directed by Tim Robbins.

Eternal Sunshine of the Spotless Mind (2004) directed by Michel Gondry.

eXistenZ (1999) directed by David Cronenberg.

Irreversible. (2004) directed by Gaspar Noe.

Little Fish (2005) directed by Rowan Woods.

Lost Highway (1997) directed by David Lynch.

Man with a Movie Camera (1929) directed by Dziga Vertov.

Mulholland Drive (2001) directed by David Lynch.

Nil by Mouth (1997) directed by Gary Oldman.

Once Were Warriors (1994) directed by Lee Tamahori.

Pi (1999) directed by Darren Aronofsky.

Scream (1996) directed by Wes Craven.

The Boys (1998) directed by Rowan Woods.

The Cook, The Thief, His Wife and Her Lover (1989) directed by Peter Greenaway.

The Lion King (1994) directed by Roger Allers and Rob Minkoff.

The Iron Giant (1999) directed by Brad Bird.

The Matrix (1999) directed by Andy and Larry Wachowski.

The Piano (1992) directed by Jane Campion.

Triumph of the Will (1935) directed by Leni Riefenstahl.

Index